Creolizing the Nation

Creolizing the Nation

✦

Kris F. Sealey

NORTHWESTERN UNIVERSITY PRESS
EVANSTON, ILLINOIS

Northwestern University Press
www.nupress.northwestern.edu

Printed in the United States of America

10 9 8 7 6 5 4 3 2 1

Library of Congress Cataloging-in-Publication Data

Names: Sealey, Kris, 1978– author.
Title: Creolizing the nation / Kris F Sealey.
Description: Evanston, Illinois : Northwestern University Press, 2020. | Includes
    bibliographical references and index.
Identifiers: LCCN 2020017245 | ISBN 9780810142350 (paperback) |
    ISBN 9780810142367 (cloth) | ISBN 9780810142374 (ebook)
Subjects: LCSH: Cultural fusion—Philosophy. | Cultural fusion—
    Caribbean Area. | Cultural fusion—Latin America. | Nationalism—
    Philosophy. | Decolonization—Philosophy. | Race relations—Philosophy.
Classification: LCC HM1272 .S43 2020 | DDC 303.482—dc23
LC record available at https://lccn.loc.gov/2020017245

In loving memory of Eli Nathan Sealey, our little Superman

(February 2–11, 2019)

And for Ishmael Curtis-Terence, a radiant child

CONTENTS

ACKNOWLEDGMENTS

This book wouldn't have been possible without the intellectual communities that have been part of my world for the last six years or so. The Collegium of Black Women Philosophers provides a vital space for so many of us to engage with the stakes of being black women philosophers. I am grateful to the Collegium friends and colleagues who were gracious with their attention and time as I worked through the big and little weeds of this book. Without a doubt, I am indebted to Kathryn Sophia Belle, not only for eighteen years of friendship and support but also for curating and sustaining the Collegium for all of us.

The conversations that I was lucky to be part of at the gatherings of the Caribbean Philosophical Association provided ground for the questions that ultimately led me to this project. I'm grateful to the leadership of that community—Lewis Gordon, Jane Anna Gordon, Paget Henry, Douglas Ficek, Rosario Torres Guevara, Neil Roberts, Michael Monahan—for continuing to make room for the intellectual work coming out of the Global South and for sustaining the demand to shift the geographies of reason. In particular, my gratitude goes to Mike Monahan, who read drafts of my ideas before they were quite fit for public consumption and who always remained gracious with his feedback. Mike, I appreciate all our conversations (and your impressive efforts to help me find a beer that I can call my own). I am also grateful to Jane Anna Gordon for her formal and informal guidance throughout this project. Her trailblazing work on creolizing philosophy has been profoundly instructive for me.

My home institution, Fairfield University, gave me the time needed to sit quietly with the questions permeating this project, to write (sometimes slowly, sometimes not) the claims it offers, and to be in the intellectual partnerships out of which a book like this grows. Long-standing support from the Humanities Institute made this book possible—my thanks go out to the 2016–17 Humanities Institute Seminar fellows who helped me shape its founding claims. I'm particularly grateful to Provost Christine Siegel who, through the Office of the Provost, was willing to invest in the final stages of this book so I could have time away to write. I'm grateful to Richard Greenwald, dean of the College of Arts and Sciences, for his advocacy of the humanities on our campus, and for valuing my contributions to our intellectual community. And, perhaps more intimately, I am grateful to my colleagues in the Philosophy Department at Fairfield University. Dennis Keenan and Sara Brill have been my strident mentors for the last thirteen years, and this book is a testimony to their friendship and support. Beyond the third floor of Donnarumma Hall, my gratitude also goes to Bryan Ripley Crandall. Knowing that your kind spirit is either right across the way in Canisius, or down the road in Stratford, has been a lifeline.

My editor at Northwestern, Trevor Perri, has been a phone call or an email away during this entire process. My thanks go to him for his faith in this project and for tending to it with such care and vigilance. I've had Trevor's support from the very beginning of writing this book, and he's been an advocate for me when it mattered most.

My sister-circles sustained me as this book figured out what it wanted to say and how it wanted to say it. To the girls—Sonya Huber, Emily Orlando, Anna Lawrence, and Gwen Alphonso—what an amazing powerhouse of brilliance you are! To get to call you my girlfriends, to dine with you, to laugh and cry with you has given me so much inspiration. Truly, I want to be like all of you when I grow up. My brown-skin girls, Myisha Cherry and Axelle Karera, always keep me on my intellectual toes and always give me hope. Your friendship and intellectual comradery has stretched me in ways that I couldn't have anticipated. I love that we get to be black women philosophers together (#mem). Nathifa Greene and I somehow found our way back to a friendship that began a very long time ago, in an old Anglican church in Trinidad. Her genuine friendship and her love for Caribbean philosophy kept me up while writing this book. Likewise, my dear sister from another mother, Lauren Kizi Alleyne, sustains me. Lauren, your poems are able to say things with a poignancy that all the words of this book never will. I appreciate you for being my friend, despite my clunky philosophy ways, and I hope our next respective projects end up being one we do together. I'm also grateful for the community at the Furious Flower Poetry Center at James Madison University. Together with Lauren Alleyne, they nurtured the very early stages of this project with vibrant conversation and engagement

For Robert Bernasconi, whose mark on my intellectual and professional well-being is perhaps too large to put into words, I have unending gratitude. For Linda Alcoff, whose kindness and support (in tough times and in happy times) never ceases to amaze me, I have unending gratitude. For John Drabinski, whose friendship gives me joy and whose careful reading of Glissant always gives me so much to think about, I have unending gratitude. For Joy Gordon—a mentor, a lifelong friend, a human being with a generosity of spirit that far exceeds the imagination—I am grateful not only for the homemade jams but also for the numerous phone calls and dinner conversations that supported me through writing this book. And to Yannik Thiem and Rebecca Kennison, whose friendship over the last two years weaves so many good things into my intellectual life—my thanks.

My Trinidad family continues to love and affirm me in the most powerful ways. This year was perhaps the roughest we've had in a long time, and it made so real the ways in which heart and home are both "here" and "elsewhere" all at the same time. Kyle and Levi, Natalie and Lorraine, Mom and Mama, the pages of this book were written with all of you close to my heart. Knowing that I could use it to make a space in our world for little Eli helped push me through to its end. And for the love and support from this side of the pond, I thank Mom Wooley, Stacy, and Gerry. I appreciate all the ways you've been there for me during the years it took to put this book together.

To save the deepest and the dearest for last, I thank the band of people who live with me and who continue to be the best bunch of humans someone could get to call "family." Justin, Dee, Isaiah, and Ishmael, your excitement about the various stages of this book is what made it worth the while. Each of you has so much to give to this world. I can't wait to celebrate your books and poems and paintings and music with the same joy you've given to me. More than everything, I have to thank David—my partner in crime, comrade in teaching for the revolution, and just plain love of my soul. You are the critic who matters most to me, and everything in this book was written with "I wonder what David will have to say about this?" in my mind. Thank you for giving me the gift of your intellect, for allowing me to talk with you about deep and important things, and for loving me through all of this.

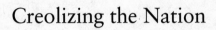

Creolizing the Nation

INTRODUCTION

The seeds of this book were planted in my reading (and ultimately my review) of Mike Monahan's work on the creolizing subject.[1] In that work, Monahan juxtaposes his conception of a creolizing subject against a subject of purity—one for whom "an inner coherence or wholeness . . . is pitted over against an external world (the *object* of her contemplation, knowledge and action)."[2] The creolizing subject, on the other hand, is one who understands experience in terms of ambiguity, openness, and dynamic articulations of borders across which self relates to other. In 2013, Monahan's work inspired me to offer speculations in response to his work, which would (some six years later) culminate in this book. Hence, I'd like to quote my 2013 speculations at length here: "Perhaps the creolizing subject is positioned to radically reconceptualize the workings of borders, and thus generate what would be an antiracist nationalism. Beyond a dualistic logic of purity, borders are not 'all or nothing,' which means that they can be sufficiently dynamic as to condition a phenomenology of permeability. In this regard, the creolizing nationalist would understand the significance of national borders for the ex-colony's pursuit of political and economic autonomy, but would also understand that such borders (and the resulting practices that determine the conditions under which crossing and inclusion is permitted) remain open to perpetual scrutiny."[3]

I've come to formulate this orientation—of ambiguously constituted borders that might be called into question by the efficacy with which they support plural conceptions of freedom—as one that creolizes the nation. That is to say, under the conceptual tools offered by creolization, the ontological formulations of the modern nation-form shift so as to offer conceptions of community, the subject, and relationality that can alternatively ground collective national life. Through creolizing nation-ness in this way, I offer speculative experimentations with the meaning of subjectivity and relationality, experimentations that this book will highlight as already unfolding in the real-time histories of societies that are named "creole." I use Édouard Glissant's reading of these creolizing social imaginaries to argue that, in bringing frames of creolization to bear on nation-ness, we might begin to at least grapple with the possibility of decolonial (more liberatory) determinations of national ontolo-

3

gies and to think generatively about how such ontologies can make room for plural articulations of the human.

To say this otherwise, I use creolization to open up and revisit the presumed finality of coloniality's violence, the terms of which are codified in standard conceptions of the nation. I read these terms—difference-as-allergy, community-as-static, and borders-as-closed—through the lens of creolization in order to trouble the claim that they offer the only possible cornerstones for determining the identity of the subject and the constitution of community. Hence, in creolizing the nation, I have in mind the implications of those everyday disruptive and resistive practices that scholars like Glissant foreground in their analyses of creole societies. At the level of the everyday, these creolizing performances jostle the colonial and neocolonial totalities that make for the impossibility of free black life (or, indeed, that code black life as dispensable). In so doing, these performances generate cracks in the dominant codes out of which other possibilities might emerge.[4]

The possibility of disrupting such a totalizing ontology, I argue, lives in creolization's articulations of alternative ways of subjectivity, relationality, and, ultimately, community. These creolizing practices do not extend their disruptions to the level of state mechanisms. Rather, they undermine the veracity of those mainstream structures from below, producing imaginaries and discursive practices that produce socialities not completely accounted for by that mainstream. Michaeline Crichlow's language of "jostling" appears often in my bringing together creolization and the nation-form, since it provides an apt metaphor for what I find most productive in using creolizing comportments at the level of the everyday as an argument for reorienting our conception of the nation.[5] In the act of jostling, one imagines a level of disruption that doesn't completely *topple* the object being disrupted, but nevertheless forces the object to reckon with the jostling effect (with the *subject* from whom that jostling effect is generated). The claim of my analysis is that, jostled by creolizing comportments, the ontologies that support the mechanics of national formation are no longer *un*affected by creolization's "otherwise."

Hence, from the level of the everyday, practices that are creolizing invite us to think imaginatively about what it might mean to live with and in the nation-form differently, what it might mean to enact Frantz Fanon's "leap," so that invention might enter into national collective existence.[6] So although the overall effect of creolizing the nation is not to undo the matrices of power that stitch together the governmentality of the state, I do want to argue that, through creolization, the organizing coloniality of that power does not have the last word. This book works to demonstrate this, first by offering the conceptions of subject, community, and relationality that Glissant develops out of the frame of creolization; then by bringing these concepts into critical conversation with key intellectual orientations in the Latina feminist tradition; and, finally, by offering Glissant's creolizing poetics as potential discursive support for Fanon's political demand for a decolonial orientation of nation-ness. Across these three sections, I aim to show that, so long as we can imagine (as creolization positions us to) community and relationality in ways not coded for by logics that determine human life as dispensable—even if these imaginative practices happen through networks *below* and not at the level of mainstream political structures—coloniality is robbed of the last word. More significantly, these imaginative practices mean that certain xenophobic constructions of nation-ness do not exhaust what collective national life might be.

For the most part, the adoption of creolization as a mode of theory preserves the originary usage of the term as one that reckons with emergences that result from contact among different cultural and symbolic orientations. There can be the creolization *of* theory, capturing the epistemological frameworks that emerge when radically different modes of knowledge come into relation to generate a new and alternative set of methodologies. There can be the creolization of language, as what explains much of the linguistic modalities in French Caribbean and Spanish Caribbean islands as their inhabitants brought together (out of necessity) European, African, and indigenous tongues in the generation of a singularly new creole mode of speech. To this end, the phenomenon of creolization broadly captures contact and relationality among differences, the trajectory of which does not lead to a reduction of those differences in the name of a higher totality. Rather, creolization is understood specifically as the bringing into relation differences *as such*.

To return to its original context in the Caribbean outposts of colonial empires, contact of this kind could not have happened without the Middle Passage and its ensuing plantation economies. As Glissant tells us (and scholars of creolization are sure to emphasize), this means that the consequences of creolization are grounded in a very particular history. *What* happened to make these creole outposts emerge is constitutive to their lifeworlds being named as creole. This constitutive relationship between the history of creolizing societies and the meaning of creolization (its bearing on the arrangements of life in those societies) will be a key part of this book's analysis. But because these are histories of violent rupture, they position both creolizing identities and social practices of creolization as (somewhat unavoidable) deviations from the single and unbroken lineage narratives that figure at the center of standard accounts of the nation-form. Compositeness and the blurring (or making ambiguous) of borders mark the products of creolization, a process that calls into question the value of pure origins, faithfulness to such origins, and the stasis needed for the authentic replication of origins, in terms of both the identity of the creolizing subject and the community constituted out of creolization. It is on these counts that I argue for using processes of creolization (in particular, their reimagined conceptions of belonging, belonging-with, and the meaning of difference in collective life) to determine a path to alternative conceptions of the nation-form.[7]

Stakes

Stakes are involved in my query, so I am compelled to lay them bare. I return to a single experience that began my ruminations on nationhood, citizenship, and migration. I was hours away from giving birth to my first child, a glorious little boy I call Isaiah. For reasons too weighty to detail, July 3, 2005, found me as an international student in the United States, in between immigration statuses, with no work authorization and no health insurance. The actual process of giving birth via cesarean section was a doped-up blur, save for the distinct memory of my son's first cry. In between morphine drips that silenced the throbs of the fresh incision out of which Isaiah emerged into the world, I opened my eyes to a pretty decent maternity recovery room. In those first moments (minutes, hours, it remains difficult to gauge), I didn't know where my baby was. I only assumed that he was receiving the best neonatal care that the state of Florida could provide.

It turned out that I was right. The gamut of usual tests were run on him, and, with the exception of his bilirubin count, he passed them all with flying colors. Isaiah was diagnosed with jaundice, so what looked like a crossover between an incubator and a miniature tanning bed became a permanent fixture in my comfortable recovery room. He spent hours under the contraption's phototherapy lights. Even though this meant he couldn't be in my arms, I garnered comfort from knowing that this was the medical care he needed, and that no expense was being spared to turn his yellow underglow brown, to transform him into a thriving little human being.

It wasn't until day two, when another crossover entered the room—a social worker who was also an immigration adviser—that the cost of all this state-of-the-art medical care became a question. For my son (I was told), all costs were being covered by Florida's Medicaid program. His U.S. citizenship entitled him to this coverage, which meant that everything, from his emergence through (what was by then) the painful C-incision, to his last heel-prick, was paid for by U.S. tax dollars, the tax dollars of his fellow community members.

And here is where, to my mind, things became weirdly aporetic, in a way that such postcolonial situations—like Isaiah's birth out of an immigrant mother and into the racialized metrics of US citizenship—always are. The C-opening that was performed on my body would not (could not) be covered by Medicaid. The room that I healed in for three days, as I established breastfeeding amid Isaiah's phototherapy treatment, would not (could not) be covered by Medicaid. The rounds of morphine dripping into my body, to dull the pain of the incision through which my little U.S. citizen entered the world, would not (could not) be covered by Medicaid. So in sum, my health and well-being, unavoidably necessary for the health and well-being of the baby citizen, was an obligation outside the boundaries of the community of which that baby citizen was now a part. And, as a matter of financial transactions, this comes as no surprise. But there is also that other matter of the logics of nation-ness and citizenship—how it frames belonging, relationality, ethicality, the possibility of full humanity. Distended by such logics was what was supposed to be a quite natural relationship between mother and child (extension of mother *into* child) but, instead, turned into a most naturalized postcolonial situation, whereby the commitment to stasis in our border constructions strain under the complexities of traveling subjects and their global entanglements. For Isaiah's birth, the C-cut of my incision literally functioned as the border across which his legal entitlements and self-formation became disassembled from mine, *as* it simultaneously conditioned the fundamental grounds of his self-formation. A postcolonial situation indeed—where the nation-form's boundaries between self and other arrange around it the meanings of fecundity, family, and the possibility of community.

This only meant that I got the bill from Coral Springs Medical Center around the time Isaiah turned one month old. The amount reflected all the wonderful care and treatment I received during those three days in my comfortable recovery room. But it also reflected what I can only now see as the liminal point of constitutions of citizenship and belonging, of how the circulation of bodies across a globe jostles the core of such constitutions. If a nation is to take on the charge of providing its citizens with the ingredients for well-being, what comes of that charge when one of those ingredients is the well-being of a citizen's so-called alien parents? What does it mean to prioritize neonatal thriving, when the conditions for that thriving (like, for instance, the health of the infant's mother) surpass the boundaries of obligation determined through the narrative of national belonging? In a similar vein, what does it mean to promise the rights and privileges of citizenship to U.S.-born children while at the same time (at best) remaining indifferent to or (at worst) undermining the family structures needed for those children to turn into wholesome adults?[8]

These questions are not new to mixed-status families, both in the United States and elsewhere. And to be sure, such quagmires find some resolve in immigration policy reforms that point toward fairer and more pragmatic paths to citizenship. My project will not include such policy issues in its analysis, not because they are not vitally important for addressing the crises affecting the millions of human beings who are, for varied reasons, caught in between national borders, and in between how those borders constitute their right to be full human beings. Rather, creolizing the nation seeks to make explicit the ontological frameworks out of which such crises are born in the first place, and to use creolization to develop a different kind of cultural imaginary—one in which contemporary crises like these no longer find traction. To that end, my interests lie in detailing a creolizing ontology of nation-ness, out of which configurations of identity, community, borders, and belonging can take into account the dynamism and ambiguity of postcolonial situations and thus can clear conceptual ground to think differently about difference and relationality. Hence, this book very modestly aims to open up the possibility of another way of understanding nationalism and nation-borders, and, by extension, the very meaning of "minority" communities. Guided by Glissant's deployment of creolization, his intersections with Latina feminists' modes of theorization, and the relationship between Glissant's poetics and Fanon's politics, I detail this other way as one through which difference, sociality, and subjectivity can be understood decolonially. To be sure, this creolizing account of the nation-form would treat the experience of migratory and diasporic peoples *not* as outlier or somehow exceptional conditions, but as central to our everyday negotiations with questions of belonging and community.

Why Work within the Frame of the Nation-Form?

The organizational frame of nation-ness has, for quite some time, been pivotal to how we understand ourselves as subjects in the world and how we have arranged ourselves into politically autonomous and economically viable communities. As such, the transformation of former European colonies into independent and sovereign entities has happened within the organizational frame of nation-ness. This is an important consideration for claims in this book, and as a consequence, I hold that the work of creolizing the nation happens *within* the parameters of nation-ness. So even though the idea of the nation brings its tainted past (one that seems to have acutely reanimated itself in our present political landscape), this book works within (though, *contentiously* within) the parameters of the nation-form.

This is because to do away with the political organization it provides is to think in terms of internationalism, or, perhaps, cosmopolitanism. It is to organize ourselves not in terms of citizens of national spaces but in terms of members of a global village (of sorts). And we *are* that, given the intertwined nature of our planet. However, I am compelled by what decolonial thinkers acknowledge as the need for human liberation struggles to be attuned to the history of global power, shaped by the material and cultural pillage of colonial domination. So even though (as chapter 5's discussion of Fanon's work will show) human liberation has an international dimension, bringing about such a world must be grounded in localized communities, historically situated within a colonial matrix of power. As such, my critical engagement with nationalism happens in terms of the nation, so that my claims avoid the kind of ahistoricity that is blind to the geopolitical urgencies of socially located groups of people. So though nativist modulations of national belonging and allegiance are being revitalized in really problematic ways, for ends that might give at least some of us reasons to recoil from any salvaging exposition of nation-ness, I don't do away with the idea of the nation. Rather, I pursue alternative (and decolonial) encounters with it, at the level of the everyday.

Given how this work is situated, then, I should say why the task I pursue is a creolizing of the nation, and not a nationalizing of creolization. I don't propose that creolized ways of being be operationalized in the institutions (the state bureaucracies) of the nation. That is to say, my claim is not that a creolizing comportment ought to be used to operationalize the economic well-being of a community, or explicitly shape modes of legislative justice, or structure the negotiation of rights in relation to other global players. Rather, *creolizing the nation* seeks to ground these more bureaucratic operations of national life in a creolizing spirit. That is to say, it is a suggestion for creolization to infuse the cultural or quotidian levels of nation-ness, so that alternative problem spaces emerge for determining how such state functions affect the lives of real people. In so doing, creolizing the nation offers alternative ontological ground to condition the possibility of encountering cultural difference, and the dynamism at the core of postcolonial sociality in ways that are conducive to free and full human life. Hence, out of this creolizing spirit I imagine a move away from a national culture that is static, nativist, protectionist, and xenophobic, toward one that acknowledges the emergent nature of its national community and that produces homely spaces absent of "claims to wholeness and finality."⁹ Again, I don't envision this as a move toward cosmopolitanism (or some global internationalism). Local specificity matters, but it also matters that we determine alternative ways to navigate the local specificity of the nation.

For these reasons, the book begins with a stage-setting first part, consisting of chapters 1 and 2. Chapter 1 offers the tropes of purity, unambiguous belonging, access to clearly defined historical pasts, and commitment to a single place or territory as those used by the nation to determine the meaning of subject formation, community, and difference. I establish the ways in which these tropes are grounded in a metaphysical prioritization of the One, which then shapes not only how difference signifies but also how we construct desires for belonging in the context of the nation. My overall goal in chapter 1 is to ultimately trouble these guiding tropes by creolization's framework, so that we might think about contemporary global politics in more liberatory ways. Chapter 2 sets the groundwork for this by showing how, in practices of creolization, lifeworlds in the Americas have not only resisted the totalizing effects of the ordering metaphysics of the One but have also generated conditions of freedom at the level of the everyday. This chapter shows how the spatiality and temporality that order processes of creolization work to disrupt the organizational structures of the nation-form "from below" (as it were), so the task of creolizing the nation offers an account of sociality that more fully captures self-formation and community formation in the context of the nation. To be sure, I do not argue that these creolizing disruptions mark an explicit revolutionary political enterprise. But I do read them as conditioning the kinds of cultural and discursive reorientations that might set the stage for a revolutionary and decolonial political agenda. That is to say, chapter 2 will argue that creolization gives us a frame out of which to theorize those everyday practices of sabotaging mainstream structures and systems of domination. In these practices of sabotage, there is a comportment toward plurality, movement, and ambiguity that undermines the spatiotemporal organizations of the nation-form (outlined in chapter 1).

Part 2 (encompassing chapters 3 and 4) groups together the textual resources for its task of creolizing the nation. I devote chapter 3 to Édouard Glissant's use of creolization to theorize a Caribbean imaginary that centers difference and open-endedness when it comes to an understanding of community. Glissant's work offers an ontology grounded in lived experience, which is to say, an ontology that, as existential, returns us to how truth is encountered in the everyday (in concrete, lived experience), or how it surpasses the reductive mechanisms of the metaphysics of the One. He uses the frame of creolization to make these conceptual moves, and to offer a compelling case for the political and cultural significance of such an existential (creolizing) ontology. It is out of this existential ontology that we get his conceptions of the rhizome and errantry. Chapter 3 will give an account of how these work to support Glissant's reimagined notion of Relation, and (more significantly) how they centralize the role of opacity in that notion of Relation. I show that, with opacity at the center, it is possible to think relationality outside transparency (outside a demand for a full disclosure in the singular subjects being brought into relation). I also show that, with opacity at the center, Glissant's use of creolization is as much about the "All" of the relation's totality as it is about the irreducibility of the local and the singular. This allows him to offer a reading of the Caribbean both as unique in its place in colonial history and as connected and opened up to the totality of the globe. Chapter 3 uses these Glissantian maneuvers to suggest an alternative understanding of what it means to be a nation and of the meaning of collectivities in the national context.

Through creolization's decentering of homogeneity, single territory, and linear time, I argue that we might develop conceptions of subjectivity and community that resist the essentialism and stasis of standard accounts of national identity. The book's fourth chapter turns to scholars of Latina feminism so as to foreground the ways in which their intellectual questions echo those most pivotal in the task of creolizing the nation. In so doing, I attempt to work across what, to my mind, are intellectual traditions—creolization and Latina feminism—that are often, and to our own intellectual detriment, kept apart. Chapter 4 begins from the premise that creolization asks us to reconceptualize the relation between multiplicity and oneness, so that we might, in turn, reconceptualize national community. The chapter takes this to the level of subjectivity and uses the work of María Lugones, Gloria Anzaldúa, and Mariana Ortega to center difference, flux, and ambiguity in the identity of the subject. I also trace the ways in which this account of subjectivity calls for not only different conceptions of belonging, but also a different experience of the social. Like Glissant, these thinkers give us ways to think about difference and coherence, as well as ambiguity and home-making, together. And, in so doing, Glissant meets theorists like Ortega, Lugones, and Anzaldúa across the possibility of thinking community in a relational way, of thinking antiessentialist subjectivity without rendering the identity of the subject moot, and across the possibility of naming historical location without using history for the sake of atavism, nativism, and xenophobic closures.

Part 3 works to flesh out the political implications of these everyday reconstitutions of subject and community. Chapter 5 continues in the vein of significant intersections between creolization and Latina feminism, and develops in more detail the implications of thinking subjectivity otherwise for questions of the social, cultural, and political registers of difference. Like the preceding chapters of this book, chapter 5 avoids a flattened account of history as it brings Glissant's creolization into conversation with Latina feminism across notions of heterogeneity, antiessentialism, impurity, ambiguity. The task of creolizing the nation includes the possibility of determining ontological ground for decolonial conceptions of the subject, of difference, and, ultimately, of the culture and spirit of national community and belonging. My claim is that this requires explicit attendance to the neocolonial implications of colonial history and to the coloniality that shapes the contemporary arrangements of individual lives, communities, and their place in the world. A flattened account of history—through which the openness of antiessentialism and ambiguity's fluidity renders the human ahistorical—would therefore fail on my account of what it means to creolize the nation. Hence, an attendance to the materiality of history grounds the ways in which chapter 5 presents Lugones's conceptions of playfulness, world-travel, and curdling for dialogue with Glissant's account of relationality, opacity, and community without telos. This prepares my analysis to turn to the political work of Frantz Fanon, in thinking about how this antiteleological understanding of community might provide decolonial possibilities for national community and self-formation.

Chapter 6 brings these reimagined conceptions of subjectivity, community, and borders that Glissant's work offers (conceptions foregrounded through his intersections with that of Anzaldúa, Lugones, and Ortega) into explicitly political terrain. I bring Fanon's caution against a regressive form of nationalism into conversation with Glissant's conception of the composite community, in order to offer political ground for imagining the nation as creolizing, as an open community that supports plural modes of the human, and as orienting itself against the stasis of coloniality and toward the dynamic syncretism of a living democracy. In chapter 6, I use Fanon's own call for decolonial conceptions of national culture and identity as grounds for this reading of his work alongside Glissant. In so doing, I also attend to the important differences between Fanon and Glissant (differences that might be captured in Fanon's explicitly political engagements with anticolonialism against Glissant's more

cultural and poetic assessments of coloniality's violence). Despite these differences, however, I do highlight the ways in which Glissant's creolizing conception of community appears in the subtext of a Fanonian account of the
nation, and how both thinkers similarly understand the significance of emergence and alternative productions at the level of the cultural, for imagining
an alternative political future. Hence, my goal in chapter 6 is to read both
critical projects—Fanon's anticolonial revolutionary politics and Glissant's
anticolonial resistant poetics—as opening up new and decolonial conceptual
ground out of colonialism's totalizing historical legacy. From this new ground,
both thinkers develop possibilities for imagining a humanism that is radically
different from the one around which colonial violence organizes itself, and
for thinking the nation in terms that no longer participate in the metaphysical
logics of the One.

In so doing, chapter 6 culminates the work of the preceding chapters, by
posing the following question: Can our conceptions of belonging, of how (and
who) we include in our communities, and how we understand our obligations
and indebtedness to both belonging *and* nonbelonging others attend to the
ambiguities and movements of the many postcolonial situations shaping our
contemporary metropoles? I think about my own experience as an immigrant
who gives birth to a U.S. citizen as an invitation to think through these ambiguities. The story of the New World is a story of moving peoples across borders, and that movement continues to shape what remains with us today, in the
wake of what Sylvia Wynter calls our "1492." In that sense, experiences like
mine—of families whose encounter with the nation complicates conceptions
of single-root belonging and clearly demarcated geographies of home—are
rather constitutive of our moment. Indeed, in the case of Isaiah's birth, we
might read my nonbelonging womb as what conditions a citizenship-project
that must then disavow its very condition so as to sustain itself. (How else
might we read all the investments into Isaiah's thriving that stops short of
investing in the well-being of his mother, precisely at the moment of his birth?
How else might we read a nation-project that acknowledges the rights of the
undocumented child to education, as it sustains practices that place undocumented parents in the shadows of economic and political life?) In a similar
vein, it is out of a posture of nonbelonging that the entanglements of migration (shaped, no doubt, in terms of the originary violence of 1492) condition
the nation-projects of the New World. That is, much like the nonlocation of
my own womb in the conceptual space of Isaiah's birth, the entanglements
of New World movements seem to also condition projects of New World citizenship out of a position of *not quite belonging* to those projects. Yet these
entanglements are not simply there in their absence, but are there *constitutively so*, straining (haunting, even, in that "Middle Passage" kind of way) the
political and cultural logics that continue to disavow them, perhaps so that
these logics might sustain themselves.

In the end, creolizing the nation aims to foreground such considerations, so that an acknowledgment of postcolonial relationalities (like the one between an immigrant's womb and a citizen-child) might clear some ground to ask, Can the political culture of the nation be uncoupled from a logic of rigid purity, and from colonial programs of crisis production, management, and control, without that divestment being the source of the nation's demise? Or, to repeat an earlier question, Can our conceptions of belonging, of how (and who) we include in our communities attend to the ambiguities and movements of the many postcolonial situations shaping our cities, our classrooms, our homes? My hope is to establish that such possibilities exist, if we begin with a properly creolizing conception of "nation." In other words, in creolizing the nation—accounting for creolizing practices at the level of the everyday, through which degrees of freedom are attained by subjects in their determinations of identity, community, and belonging—we arrive at a formulation of nation-ness that can sustain plural conceptions of the human and liberatory, decolonial futures.

Part 1

✦

Setting the Stage

Thinking "Nation" through Creolization

Much can be said of the phenomenon of the modern nation—that iteration of national collective life coming out of the nineteenth and twentieth centuries. However, this book reads, in the modern nation-form's key traits, an account of identity as stably rooted to a geographical and cultural location (indeed, the modern nation understands culture as a phenomenon that *can* be localized). This rootedness gives the nationalized subject access to a sense of belonging and home, which could then be tapped into in the face of historical and societal upheavals, uncertainties that often circulate around questions of who and what legitimately belongs (or doesn't belong) to the national collective. The first chapter of this book traces the ways in which such teleologies of nation-form ground themselves in a metaphysics of the One—a worldview or "imaginary" (to anticipate Glissant's *un*working of this metaphysical orientation) that reduces difference to a failure of representation. That is to say, in both the self-formation and the collectivity that comes out of nation-ness, singularities of culture, epistemological commitments, or lifeworlds acquire legitimacy only insofar as they can be construed as extensions, versions, or copies of a more prior (nationalized) conception of the human. Under this metaphysics, such conceptions carry a stasis (and purity, to return to Mike Monahan's exegesis here); what is conceived as properly or fully human comes out of a narrative that connects to a single past or origin in time and a single place or originating territory. Any ambiguity and movement with respect to such connection points to difference as delegitimately or unjustifiably human. To paraphrase Nelson Maldonado-Torres, differences that fall outside the nation's metaphysically static model of legitimacy are already objects of a "misanthropic skepticism."[1]

In this vein, chapter 1 also treats modern nationalism in terms of its posture against change and ambiguity, against what its mythologies understand as crises to be managed and/or disavowed. We might ask ourselves whether or not there is anything unique to the time of modernity, which might encourage the predominance of such sensibilities. In response, perhaps one would point to the secularization of knowledge productions, and the replacing of divine (transcendent) ordination with the compass of interior reason (both clear markers of the modern age). In other words, one might understand modernity's acute sense of crisis to be a reflection of a more humanized world. It is possible to identify, among the various accounts of modernity's rationality, morality, and its epistemological conceptions of the human's relationship to a nonhuman world, a first premise of humans no longer needing the stars, the gods, or the Transcendent as their orienting cornerstone. Modern humanity *is* its freedom, and as such, modern humans faced the responsibility for their freedom to fail.

Determining such causal relations between modernity and the nation-form will not be a central feature in part 1 of this book. Instead, the task of creolizing the nation is interested in the problem space offered by modern iterations of nationalism, for posing the question of difference. Out of that problem space, this question of difference continues to be shaped within frames of crisis production and management and through the deployment of homogeneity for constructing affects of belonging and community. Because (in our contemporary postcolonial moment) these frames continue to offer us conceptions of relationality that participate in the purity logic outlined by Mike Monahan, they restrict our global imaginary to a colonial Manichaeism of management and border policing, which continues to dispossess and politically disenfranchise both those in the Global South and those black and brown migrants trying to make lives in Europe and the United States. I am interested in bringing this colonial imaginary into critical engagement with conceptions of creolization.

Central to chapter 2 is the claim that creolization gives us an alternative imaginary out of which collective political life might be understood differently. More specifically, I show that, through this imaginary, creolizing practices offer a way to constitute the nation-form for a genuinely *decolonial* conception of human life. At its historical origins, the creole represented a particular mode of citizenship, or a certain way of ascribing to national belonging that pertained to a person of European descent, born in the Caribbean or southern American colonies of the European empires. In chapter 2, I detail the ways in which the history of the European creole often worked to retain

the normativity of whiteness, particularly when it came to questions of pro-
priety in the outposts of empire. However, for the purpose of setting the stage
of this book's overall analysis, chapter 2 points to the ways that, in the eighteenth and nineteenth centuries, the white creole signaled a *creolized* conception of citizenship, a modality of belonging to a national collective that was
something other than what it was *before* the unfolding of the consequences of
colonial conquest. Against a certain original European stock, such creolized
identities were inherently "impure." But more broadly, they show us that
colonial entanglements called for new (creolized) performances of identity,
subjectivity, and of subjects in relationship with each other.

My turn to creolization is toward this end. As a conceptual tool, the
creolizing frame foregrounds the centrality of the emergence of the new, via
movements across borders, and so is able to offer us an enactment of nation-
ness that move beyond a colonial imaginary. Chapter 2's analysis is grounded
in this claim, as it carefully attends to the historical particularities that condition the possibility of everyday articulations of creolizing comportments.
In sum, part 1 prepares us to think through a creolizing conception of the
nation so that attunements to multivocality, to complex experiences of space
and time, and to open-ended significations of the social might be brought to
the metaphysical master codes of standard conceptions of the nation. In so
doing, I argue that the nation-form shows up as something other than what
disavows the ways in which our postcolonial moment is constitutive of difference, ambiguity, and relational movements.

Chapter 1

✦

The Phenomenon of the Nation

> This question of universal community is therefore by definition posed in terms of how we inhabit the Open, how we care for the Open—which is completely different from an approach that would aim first to enclose, to stay within the enclosure of what we call our own kin.
>
> —Achille Mbembe, *Critique of Black Reason*

Foregrounding this question of how we inhabit the Open, this chapter orients the vast and multidisciplinary scholarship on the organizing principle of nation-ness. My goal is to prepare this organizing principle to enter into critical engagement with creolization (as a theoretical concept). Hence, what follows is not exhaustive of all that has been theorized about the nation, nor should it be read in terms of a thorough analysis of the historical meaning and relevance of the nation. Instead, I ask that readers consider this chapter's focus on the temporality central to the nation, the spatial organization that grounds the nation-form, as well as my discussion of the reliance of nation-form on the metaphysics of the One as a preparation (of sorts) for the trace of the theory of creolization that follows in chapter 2. In short, my analysis of how the nation organizes the social, political, and cultural aspects of human life is shaped strictly by my desire to creolize this organizational phenomenon, so what I offer is curtailed to that goal. It is possible that the inclusions (and exclusions) of this chapter becomes intelligible only toward the end of this book.

In what follows, I offer what I hold to be the nation's central determining tropes: purity, unambiguous belonging, access to clearly defined historical pasts, commitment to sacred place, and a relation to the "other" that keeps in place a metaphysics of the One. I want to ultimately trouble these tropes by creolization's framework, so as to open up new ways to think through how contemporary global politics might unfold in alternative and more liberatory ways. Hence, a sampling of the guiding questions for this chapter are as follows: How have these tropes responded to a postcolonial epoch that bears witness to neocolonial power grabs, new manifestations of imperialism, and migrations that strain the ways we have historically organized our national allegiances and alliances? What would an adequate theoretical accounting of such a response look like? To be clear, I do not read into these stakes some historical signal that the end of nation-ness is nigh, or that we are approaching a "borderless world."[1] But I do identify in them a call to which we ought to respond. And that is the call to give an account of the multiple modalities of how national belonging is experienced, the frequent manifestations of transnational solidarities in the name of a better, more just planet, as well as the ways in which cultural productions both attend to *and* travel beyond origins that are national in kind. In short, though we might not (or perhaps never will) approach a borderless world, the world we live in seems to call for significantly different narratives around what it now means to be a "national being."[2] This book argues that creolization offers us a conceptual framework that might be used to respond to this call.

The following organizational scheme will help us parse through this and other pertaining questions. I begin with a section on the question of purity, or orientation in terms of a metaphysics of the One. The second section focuses on the role that single pasts and places (or territories) play in the idea of the nation, or, more specifically, how the commitment to a single past and place allows this idea to respond to our desire for stability in the face of historical contingency. A third section pursues the question of home and belonging. What does this desire for home tell us about ourselves, and what is the significance of the relation between this desire and the experience of national belonging? This third and final section also brings this to bear on the question of difference, or on how the history of the nation-form has both generated a notion of the other and then shaped our orientation toward that "other." To reiterate, the scholarship on the nation is vast and expansive and grows out of numerous disciplinary enclaves. This chapter tries, as best as possible, to account for the major moments in these academic traditions. But without a doubt, my scope is limited. My hope is that readers will see such limitations as a consequence of the specific task at hand, which is to bring into conversation the phenomena of "nation" and the theory of creolization.

The Metaphysics of the One

The scholarly engagements with the idea of the nation can be arranged into two argumentative strains. One strain argues that the organizational structure of nation-ness has roots in the very genesis of human living and thus organically reflects the ways in which we have always organized ourselves in terms of kinship, clan, and ethnic loyalties.[3] The other strain understands the nation as a more modern phenomenon, arising in response to the social and economic urgencies of a world rapidly shaped by colonial conquest and the Industrial Revolution. My analysis in this chapter aligns with the latter of these two strains, given what I hold to be its greater accuracy when it comes to articulating implications of the nation-form for contemporary modes of life. So although the question of whether the nation is a product of or precedes modernity might be an important one, that question will not figure into my project. In other words, my interests in creolizing the nation means that it is of little significance as to when (or where) we locate the "threshold event" across which communities of people went from understanding their collective coherence in the "absence of nation-form" to "deployment of nation-form" for their organizing principle. What *is* significant is that our experience of nation-ness today is undeniably shaped by the experience of colonialism, that it is "entirely circumscribed by the history of colonization and decolonization."[4] Thus, any of our questions about the role of the metaphysics of the One (and how such a metaphysics then shapes the meaning of difference, community, and national belonging) would need to move through a conception of the nation as already shaped by the seminal event of modernity—European colonialism and its aftermath. It matters that *our* experience of nation-ness is ultimately through its modern diffraction. What might have preceded this modern diffraction has little bearing on the operation of the metaphysics of the One within our encounter with nation-ness, nor does it bear on the possibility of thinking the nation through a further diffraction of creolization.

Ricardo Sanín-Restrepo's exposition of decolonizing democracy is grounded in a thorough account of how Plato's conception of the forms results in a prioritizing of the One over the many (over difference).[5] Though my goal is different from his goal of radicalizing Gilles Deleuze's philosophy of immanence so that it can do the political work of decolonizing democracy, his Deleuzian critique of Plato is relevant here. Sanín-Restrepo writes, "Plato inaugurates what Deleuze called the *long history of the error of representation* . . . forming the mythical and incontrovertible tribunal that divides the world between the authentic and the fake as the only way of being *in* and *with* the world."[6] A nation-centric mode of being in and with the world is no exception to this, insofar as nation-ness similarly prioritizes the authenticity of the "original" over what, under this model of the One, signifies as copies whose value measures how successfully it mirrors an "original." Sanín-Restrepo writes, "For Plato, truth corresponds to the supreme idea of the *Model*. Therefore, all things can copy integrally the model, and hence deserve to live, or they can betray the model and constitute mere *simulacra* that must perish."[7] Carried over to the nation-form, this Platonic conception of *national* truth means that the unfolding of the nation in real time is held accountable for reproducing a perfect original model of itself, a model that not only demands near-perfect representation but is also unchanging across time. That is to say, within the nation-form, modes of life that copy a singular and perfect model of life have access to the rights, privileges, and protections of national belonging. Modes of life that diverge from this "model to copy" lineage show up as what must be purged from the nation's space, lest it undermine (at the ontological level) the very being of the nation, and (at the political level) the nation's chances of surviving and reproducing itself-as-model.[8]

To be sure, the structure of Plato's metaphysics stipulates the concrete absence of the model or form: the essence of the model demanding authentic copies of itself is its *transcendence* from the time and place of experience. Sanín-Restrepo describes such models as both "void and impossible," which is to say, impossible to encounter (and consequently, to replicate) insofar as they are void from the space and time of the human. So it is not simply that a single and original model holds the key to what counts as true (worthy of being) and false (worthy of an ontological elimination). More significantly, this ontological power is an empty signifier, calling to be filled in and to signify in a concrete sense. It is out of this call that Sanín-Restrepo identifies the violence inscribed in this metaphysics of the One (the single and transcendent model), since, out of this call, certain concrete "iconic" copies take on the truth-discerning work of the transcendent One. "[Given] the void and impossible place of the model [by definition, it is never *in the world* to be found] the copy erects itself as the model. In the absence of a true model of *courage of man*, etc., what follows is that a particular and finite version begins to fill the void place of the model."[9] By extension, we might also say that, given the absence of a true model of "national being" or nation-form, a finite version of nation-ness fills the void of this absence, to then do the work of eliminating what is encountered as failed copies of this finite version.

The ways in which the nation operates politically, socially, and culturally are intertwined with this metaphysical prioritization of a (pseudo-)transcendent One. It shapes the nature of the nationalist spirit required to sustain the nation-form over time.[10] Indeed, Étienne Balibar notes that societies took on the shape of nations precisely because "that form made it possible (at least for an entire historical period) for struggles between heterogeneous classes to be controlled."[11] Insofar as its historicity is concerned, in other words, the social and political function of the nation (unifying in order to control, and controlling in order to unify) points to an underlying commitment to a metaphysics of the One. In a later section I focus on what is perhaps the most obvious implications of a metaphysics of the One—the meaning and role of difference. For now, permit me to show the ways in which such metaphysical valuations around iconic copies determine the nation-form's primary function of establishing meaning in the face of change, and security in the face of the contingencies of concrete life.

George Mosse reads the appeal of modern nationalism as a quest for community in the midst of the uncertainties of modern life. On this account, the modern nation represented what a people could identify with, in common (language, cultural practices, and traditions), so that such singular national representations could take individuals beyond the particularity of their existence and into a more meaningful collective existence. Balibar describes this relation between the individual and the national community as a consequence of a project toward *producing* the people. Through this project, the community with which each individual will identify is produced and reproduced "through a network of apparatuses and daily practices" that extend from "cradle to grave."[12] In looking ahead, the unfolding of this project (of nation-production) at the level of the everyday will be central to the case I want to make for reimagining nation-ness through the theoretical lens of creolization. Balibar's framing draws our attention to the vital role of the quotidian and the mundane, when it comes to not only sustaining the meaning of the nation but also legitimizing or naturalizing how we encounter that meaning as both inevitable and invariable. My engagement with creolization acknowledges these quotidian practices, as precisely where we learn and potentially *relearn* how to be national beings. But for the moment, my interests lie in drawing attention to the sense in which the feeling of affinity—of experiencing the national community as a community of people who are *like me*—is, to a large degree, a consequence of this dynamic production. Balibar names this project one of "fictive ethnicity," not because it is less than true but precisely because its truth is despite the unnaturalness of the affinity experienced for and within a national community. "No nation possesses an ethnic base naturally, but as social formations are nationalized, the populations included within them . . . are ethnicized—that is, represented in the past or in the future *as if* they formed a natural community, possessing of itself an identity of origins, culture and interests which transcends individuals and social conditions."[13]

Mosse's analysis shows how this fictive ethnicity was of particular importance in an age of mass politics, where the population at large, in all their varying cultural sensibilities, found stakes in the political arena. Because the nation functioned as what would be "transcendent" to those cultural and social differences,[14] and to a large degree *countered* the multiple factions that might arise out of such differences, this nation-transcendence subscribed to a metaphysics of the One. The account that Mosse gives of the role of rhythm in the making of modern national anthems very much underscores this point. "The age of nationalism was also the first age of mass politics, and this fact led to the introduction of rhythm into all ceremonies . . . in order to transform the undisciplined masses into a [single] disciplined crowd. . . . Goethe linked rhythm with the need . . . to find firm ground under [our] feet, to pull a piece of eternity down into [our] lives."[15]

When it comes to the nation-form, we can understand the iconic copy to be that concrete and particular national collective, against which a particular community of people is measured as truth-bearing or not. In other words, the void of the metaphysical One is filled in with a concrete cultural, social, and political formulation of national collective life, whose disciplinary effect is to shape a community of people into an authentic replica of itself. This concrete formulation (the iconic copy) sustains itself over time by either eliminating or reducing any simulacra that threatens its replication as the standard of truth.

The link between an all-encompassing oneness and the eternity of the sublime points to the temporality that comes out of a metaphysics of the One (namely, the temporality that the nation needs to perform all these related functions). Chapter 2's analysis of creolization will make this clearer, but for now, suffice it to say that this particular temporality, insofar as it cauterizes the effect of real historical time, is therefore resistant to signifying differences. That is, the oneness of national community must subscribe to a destiny that, though unfolding *in* time, disavows the dynamism of history, precisely because this dynamism opens onto difference. Hence, the homogeneity of national life grounds itself in the nonmoving, timeless nature of the eternal (or, at the very least, the nostalgic construction of a stable past).[16]

Benedict Anderson's *Imagined Communities* traces the roles of census-making and mapping in the development of nationalism, and it is clear that both processes are motivated by this temporality of the metaphysics of the One. Anderson notes that, ultimately, these practices were all about reducing the multiplicity of a lifeworld into entities that could be identified, categorized, and counted as parts of a unifying whole.[17] "The 'warp' of this thinking [involved in the census and the map] was a totalizing classificatory grid" on which persons and places were located, or, at the very least, made locatable.[18] Through the map, the messy complexity of collective life got serialized, or turned into many representations of a unifying type. Whereas the map transformed (by carving up) spaces into discrete and measurable boxes, the census transformed people into discrete and measurable (or at least observable) kinds. Through both, the nation became a grid through which "[one could] say of anything that it was this, not that; it belonged here, not there."[19] Management and control of the national collective was made possible through such acts of measurement (and, indeed, surveillance), acts that subscribed to a metaphysics of the One that, as Sanín-Restrepo rightly points out, "[serves] as the basis and method for fixing the truth in every sphere . . . [engulfing] politics, law, and all strata of subjectivity."[20] Grounded in this metaphysical orientation that locates truth in the sameness of the One, such surveillance practices assumes that the "*real*" is a single, unified body—the nation. All else is surveyable through and measurable in terms of this singular, national One.

In foregrounding the indebtedness of the nation-form to the metaphysics of the One, we are also able to complicate a reading of nation-ness which holds that nations emerge around preexisting communal affinities (that pertain to kinship and bloodline, cultural ties, or linguistic similarities). What this underlying metaphysics of the One shows is that, even where these preexisting affinities exist, the *continued* experience of homogeneity within the life of the nation cannot be explained solely in terms of a homogeneity that predated its construction; the mapping of lives in terms of its representation of the iconic copy of national being is a project that must be actively pursued in order to be encountered as true. As Balibar writes, "The imaginary singularity of national formation is constructed daily, by moving back from the present into the past."[21] In other words, the production of the myth of homogeneity (ascription to a transcendent model of nation-ness) is dynamic and active in its operation as it is simultaneously static and stable in its apprehension.

Azar Gat locates, at the source of the spirit of nationalism our "innate human preference for [our] kin-culture groups."[22] For the most part, when Gat makes such claims in support of the primordiality of the spirit of nationalism, the language he deploys is in terms of ethnic and not national communities (he writes that "ethnic bonds of affinity, identity and solidarity remained central to state existence and politics throughout history").[23] In this sense, Gat's analysis does not divorce ethnicity from the political. But to what, precisely, does his analysis refer in the notion of ethnicity? He often refers to the "real material and historical connections among communities of people," which signify in terms of a shared understanding of their place in the world, and the way in which that place shapes their way of life.[24] He wants to orient an account of the nation in terms of such shared worldviews, which perhaps results from people living in the same place over the course of several generations. In the end, Gat sources these ethnic bonds "deep within the human psyche" and wants us to understand them as the origination of "all . . . forms of identity, affinity and solidarity," the most important of which are national in kind.[25]

In anticipation of a later section on the question of difference, and on the notions of home and belonging, I argue that accounts like Azar Gat's leave out experiences of either not being at home in a nation, or experiences of *complicated* belonging to a nation. Such experiences persist despite and alongside rigid, closed-off archetypes of who belongs (and who doesn't), including those captured by descriptions like Gat's (of the ethnic affinities that permeate the spirit of nationalism). In other words, any homogeneity in nation-ness is less a consequence of the existing affinities (cultural, linguistic, or otherwise) among persons and more a consequence of what is determined in advance as that iconic copy of nation-ness and belonging (that concrete instance of national identity that fills the impossible void of a transcendent, predating model) that acts as the disciplinary force that gives shape to the nation. This would mean that the so-called primordiality of affinity and shared worldviews (offered by Gat) is always tenuously performing the task of reducing "many" to "one," and always in need of legitimizing narratives that are able to sanction this reduction (lest its claim to primordiality is called into question). The persisting reality of either those who are officially outcasts of their communities, or those who reside in communities tangentially or tenuously, speak to the ways in which assumptions such as Gat's—of shared ethnic affinities that predates the production of national community—hide these homogenizing effects of a more prior commitment to the metaphysics of the One.

Against such analyses, I would argue that communities do not come together across a shared set of similarities that predate their coming together. Rather—and this is precisely what the experience of nonbelonging, or of being in between national borders, tells us—these sets of similarities are, in an important sense, conjured in the atavistic imaginary of a community that *wants* to hark back to a shared, single ethnicity (way of life, mode of being in and with the world) to then justify not only the existence of the nation itself, but also those (present and subsequent) practices of marking those who do and do not belong. It is one thing to make the argument that, among groups of people living together for prolonged periods, there is a collective creation of a single and unifying culture, such that similarities come to exist over time. It is quite another to claim that these similarities are *those across which* these groups come together. In later chapters devoted to tracing the processes of community-making (and nation-making) in the aftermath of colonial violence, it is precisely this claim that I call into question.[26]

From this alternative reading, the affinities one might observe within communities (national and otherwise) do not evidence the absence of otherness or differing sensibilities. Instead, these observed affinities signal the prioritizing of one set of life codes and mores (namely, those signified in the iconic copy of the nation) over another. From Eric Hobsbawm's account of state-sanctioned education in the nationalist program, as well as its role in the implementation of a single national language, it is clear that this is precisely what happens when the nation is faced with cultural sensibilities from multiple backgrounds. I go into further detail about this in the section that follows, which discusses the interplay between the general will of a nationalized people, and the meaning of difference within the national frame. But for the moment, suffice it to say that the spirit of nationalism, as it has been witnessed throughout history, subscribes to a metaphysics of the One, and codes for practices that must engineer this oneness, given the void impossibility of the Model. These practices rest on an allergy toward difference, which often manifests itself in terms of "internal enemies" of the state, or as the immigrant refugees referenced in Gat's analysis.[27] In the distinction between ethnic and civic nationalism, for which he accounts in chapter 6 of *Nations*, Gat acknowledges that civic nationalism is nothing but the result of a singular ethnic sensibility made to perform dominantly (which is to say, made to marginalize and perhaps vilify all other ways of living). His point is to minimize what some scholars read as real differences between nationalisms founded on ethnic or *Volk*-ish similarities, and other more modern types that grow out of the Enlightenment's abstract conceptions of humanity. But I reference it here to suggest that, of the tendencies characteristic of ethnic nationalisms, we might also say that they preside over those "civic" nationalisms as well. In both cases, the commitment to a metaphysics of the One is used to determine what gets marginalized, or made to disappear, in a community's harking to some singular way of being.

Gat himself is critical of such a reading of the nation-form insofar as it fails to capture what, on his account, stands for our *primordial* (read here "natural") affinity for the same. Quite dismissively, he names liberalism as an ideology ill equipped to diagnose the underlying ethnic affinities that, according to his argument, grounds all human communities. He writes, "[It] is not a coincidence that the pioneering modernist theorists were all Jewish *immigrant refugees* [who] experienced changing identities and excruciating questions of self-identity."[28] He frames these immigrant and refugee experiences as the kinds that somehow skew one's conceptual analysis of what the spirit of nationalism *really* is (namely, one with deep and material roots in shared similarities, particularly those that are materially grounded in ethnicity and bloodline).

I find it ironic that Gat claims to ground his position in the material conditions that have marked the development of tribal communities, nations, and, ultimately, nation-states. Scholarship ought not to shy away from these material conditions, he tells us, and I could not agree more. Scholars of the idea of the nation, and of the ways in which this idea shapes our historical and contemporary condition, ought to begin from the concrete, from the actual histories from which this idea emerged onto the human stage. However, it is precisely in so doing that one encounters the historical force of creolization, a force the analysis of which Gat's account is completely bereft. In his essay "Symptomatically Black," Barnor Hesse suggests that "[perhaps] we should . . . consider the West as always already creolized by virtue of its modernity and coloniality."[29] What we should understand by Hesse's claim is that, without framing an analysis of the nation in terms of "a history of contact" across uneven power terrains, and "the subsequent process of indigenization or nativization of European settlers," we do precisely what Gat urges us not to do, and, more importantly, what I claim he himself does—put forth an analysis of nation-ness that fails to reckon with how historical processes of contact filter through the more metaphysical commitment to the One in the nation's constitution of itself as a community of affinity.

I devote chapter 2 to creolization as a theorizing of this history of contact and colonial conquest. But my point in this brief mention of Barnor Hesse's essay is to suggest that Gat's dismissal of those "immigrant experiences" comes from an ahistorical perspective, which privileges the experience of belonging, geographical stability, and national homogeneity without any ground in history. He has done what scholars of creolization warn against, which is to universalize the (often Eurocentric) experience that emerges at the top of the stratified power terrain of which colonialism and European conquest is a legacy. More significantly, and very much in line with the metaphysics of the One, Gat has allowed a specific and concrete experience of nation-ness to speak in the void left by a transcendent model and to bring with it the violence of homogenizing in the name of replicating itself as iconic copy. Furthermore, the way his account addresses the question of difference is invariably shaped by this blind spot that assumes the nonexistence of the historical process of creolization and, as a consequence, naturalizes the metaphysics of oneness on which the idea of the nation rests.

In his essay "The Politics of Literary Postcoloniality," Aijaz Ahmad writes, "[The] traffic among modern cultures is so brisk that one can hardly speak of discrete national cultures that are not fundamentally transformed by that traffic."[30] Movement across national borders generates a dialogue between and among peoples, which, at the very least, calls into question the idea that groups (national, cultural, or otherwise) are self-contained, monolithic entities that can be understood independently of their relationship to each other. To that end, the differences among ways of life would inform the human signature of communities, more so than any (constructed) similarities of which we claim that signature to reflect. To reorient one's idea of the nation in this way would be nothing short of understanding national comradery and fraternity to grow out of "the many," not out of "the one."[31] Can the conceptual contours of the idea of the nation sustain this shift in metaphysical grounding? Is there "nation" if we begin instead with a metaphysics of "the many"?

Such questions shape my analysis in the following section, which gives an account of the linearity of both the time and place of the nation. By this I mean to convey the sense in which nation-ness is committed to an identity that is presented as beginning in a single moment in time (a single past), and growing out of (or at least with respect to) a single place, ground, or territory. Ultimately, this linearity of national time and space is very much hinged to the nation's metaphysical commitment to the One.

Linear National Time and Singular National Ground

Benedict Anderson identifies a prenation mode of temporality through which social collectives organized themselves before national borders gained traction. This sense of time, he claims, was indistinguishable from cosmological time: through the temporality of the nation, "the origins of the world and of men [were thought to be] essentially identical."[32] This conflation marked the birth and trajectory of human history with a layer of the immemorial; our species (whose march, the claim went, is in step with the planets and the stars) had a sense of "always was and always will be" about itself. For Anderson, this played a key role in the burgeoning of the idea of the nation. Namely, nations emerged with an understanding of themselves as entities with antiquity, rooted in a sacred past that was transcendent to the contingencies of its material history. In a similar vein, Balibar describes the nation's conception of the past (*its* past) as a signifier in the present through which "[the] formation of the nation . . . appears as the fulfillment of a 'project' stretching over centuries."[33]

In this sense, communities were able to replace their own accidents of birth with the necessary existence (indeed, necessary being) of the cosmos and of nature. So the role of time in the shaping of the nation, ironically enough, gave the nation a timeless character, thus setting up its contingent existence to signify as absolutely necessary. The unfolding of its national being was a necessary event coded for in a past (a past constituted as such), so what the nation is, in present time, is really what the nation always was (or always meant to be). And as Balibar points out, what this means is that the nation's temporal project requires the constitution of a national destiny. "[The] process of development from which we select aspects [of who we were, are, and always will be] retrospectively, so as to see ourselves as the culmination of that process, was the only one possible, that is, it represented a destiny."[34] Because the nation's linear arc in time is about fulfilling this destiny, there is a vital *moral* imperative to the manifestation of that arc. That is to say, what shows up in contestation of, or in critical relation to, that arc is always already delegitimized, since not only does the nation move in time toward the realization of its destiny, but it *ought* to do precisely this. In other words, "pastness therefore is preeminently a moral phenomenon," which obligates the nation to be and act in accordance with the temporality constituted through its own temporal project and to stand in opposition to forces and practices that are critical of that project.[35]

In Anderson's treatment of the policies employed by colonial regimes, he also underscores this harking back to a bygone past for the purposes of legitimacy and the justification of rule. To be sure, violence was synonymous to colonialism's governing program, and to that end, it was the domination of force that secured the "right" to rule the people of colonized territories. Nevertheless, Anderson tells us, these regimes "attached themselves to antiquity as much as [to] conquest" in order to complete their control of colonized populations.[36] In other words, this recourse to the moral legitimacy garnered in the idea of a destiny transformed colonialism's violence into a justified violence. Hence, if colonial domination was part of the nation's destiny (necessary in its being), then that domination (despite its violence) was legitimate. To claim a mode of being that went back to the time of old, to an immemorial time, was to present the nation as that entity already "lined up in the stars," ordained to be precisely where (and how) it was at that particular moment in human history (even when that historical moment was constituted through inflicting violence on a sovereign people).

As the link between the human and the cosmos became tenuous (as was the case in an epoch centered around the human instead of the divine), the need emerged for national narratives to reinvigorate and rearticulate this temporal transcendence (the eternalness of its being). "[The] search was on," Anderson tells us, "for a new way of linking [tenets of the nation, like fraternity and power] and time meaningfully together."[37] In his work on Western nationalism's relationship to the timelessness of nature, Mosse identifies a similar search in projects of national self-representation. Such temporal orientations made sure to establish the nation as noncontingent, as a necessary emerging without which the very notion of time would be effectively altered. Most apparent in aesthetics pertaining to war and patriotic sacrifice, Mosse observes that, in giving one's life for the sake of the nation, one died that most noble of deaths—a death through which "[the] soldier was part of an unending chain of being that reached beyond death" so as to join with the eternal being of the nation itself.[38] The fallen soldier's sacrifice for the sake of the nation meant that his life was given purpose beyond the contingencies of his own personal meanderings, and as such, he joined the nation's necessary (timeless) being. Mosse points out that often memorials that commemorated fallen soldiers were strategically entangled with natural surroundings (wooded forests and other such natural landscapes), thus offering the eternity of natural law to the being of the nation (represented here in the figure of the fallen soldier). This requirement for a timeless and necessary being also explains why the architecture of civil society, coming out of early modern history, made sure to secure its connection with natural law.[39] This anchoring of the social in the natural served a purpose similar to what Anderson identified in the grounding of national time in cosmological time. They both solved the problem of the legitimacy of national life with the solution of ontological necessity.

Mosse's account of Western nationalism is arranged around the claim that the primary purpose of the nation—at least during the height of modernity—was to inflect human life with a kind of "sturdiness" against the "internal wobble" of the modern age. He writes, "The nation always claimed to provide stability in a restless world. [As such] the nation represented itself through timeless symbols and ancient myths [that] made the time stand still."[40] In this sense, the grounding temporality of national life diametrically opposed the dizzying transformation of modernity's Industrial Revolution. Nature's slow march and timelessness was a reprieve from the speedy progression of science and the mechanization of human life. This is not to say that the nation was opposed to industrial progress. Rather, Mosse's point is that, out of an embrace of this "new" age of exploration, modern humans found themselves swept away, groundless in their own rational enlightenment, and turning to the nation to find reprieve from this angst. The feeling of being part of a community was understood to temper this angst: the nation was called on to provide the sense of community that might mitigate the feelings of existential abandonment that came out of these beginning stages of the industrial revolution. In a section that follows, on the question of difference, I show how this way of responding to angst and change ultimately sets the stage for an allergic orientation toward difference.

But for now, the point is to understand that the time of the nation worked as the anecdote to historical contingency. This work was done through imagery that harked back to the time of nature and, before that, to cosmological time. Both cases resounded with imagery that signified the timeless, or the eternal. In *Imagined Communities*, Anderson devotes a significant aspect of his analysis to a reliance on historical memory, for the sustained lifeworld of the nation, noting the invaluable role of museums, in particular, for this function. To be sure, museums not only played a role in establishing, through historical memory, a sense of the "always has been and always will be" of the nation, but also, most notably, were instruments of display: museums were utilized to make *public and widely accessible* the nation's self-narrative of its deeply rooted past. These public displays of national memory were also part of a larger project of mapping, categorizing, and organizing human life, aspects of which the first section presented as evidence of the nation's underlying metaphysics of the One. Museums and historical monuments mapped the time of the nation to support those legitimizing narratives, which claimed that the nation had a certain right to be, or a certain noncontingent (necessary) existence.

Single National Territory

In *The Age of Empire*, Eric Hobsbawm identifies territorial nationalism as a brand of nationalism that equates political self-determination with an exclusive right to a particular geographical place. He understands this claim to be one that serves a relatively new version of nationalism, emerging around the end of the nineteenth century, a time of multiple changes in the "international situation."[41] Hobsbawm's account does not acknowledge any necessary connection between nation and single place; he would more likely locate the meaning of one's national identity "in the bodies of such men and women as considered themselves to belong to a nationality," rather than in a section of earth to which they claimed ownership rights.[42] But in any event, he finds, in this territorial nationalism, a commitment to the use of a single language that signatures the lifeworld of the nation in question. Hobsbawm writes, "[Linguistic] nationalism had a built-in bias towards [geographical] secession. And, conversely, the call for an independent state territory seemed increasingly inseparable from language."[43] So urgent were these ties between language and land that some nationalist strivings contrived a connection to a defining language, in order to then ground their pursuit for national (and ultimately territorial) autonomy. Hobsbawm reads the Jewish Zionist movement of the late nineteenth century as one such nationalism, insofar as the movement "[identified] the Jewish nation with Hebrew, a language which no Jews had used for ordinary purposes since the days of the Babylonian captivity."[44] He uses this example to underscore how a rootedness to a single place bears intimate connection to the performance of single language, in the idea of nation.

This correlation between rootedness to place or territory and deployment of a linguistic foundation could perhaps be better understood by looking at Balibar's account of the role of language in the nationalization a society. Balibar notes that using a common, national language is one of the two more abstract ways through which a people are produced as such, and continue to produce themselves, in time, as a people (the other, more material way being through the notion of race). What Balibar means by this is that, though the performance of this national language is experienced concretely (in mostly all social interaction, insofar as they include communication in the medium of that national language), it is nonetheless "always possible to appropriate several languages and to turn oneself into a different kind of bearer of discourse."[45] In other words, I do not get to choose what my so-called mother tongue is, but I can freely adopt the national language of a society and establish myself as a legitimate "bearer of discourse" in that adopted national language. It is in this sense that Balibar reminds us that "[one's] 'mother' tongue is not necessarily the language of one's 'real' mother."[46]

As a counterforce to its openness (abstractness), a linguistic foundation to one's nation-ness often calls for strong connections to territory, connections that will operate as the "principle of closure, of exclusion" needed to somewhat undermine the inherent abstraction of the linguistic community.[47] Balibar points to "race" as precisely that principle of closure. For my current purposes (of delineating the relation between nation and rootedness in place), however, I want to stress the role of single territory in the nation's project of developing community around the idea of a single language. What this relationship (between place and language) shows is the constitutive aspect of the nation—that it is faced with the task of *producing* what it will subsequently encounter as its eternal and timeless being. What Hobsbawm refers to as a territorial nationalism is, much like linguistic nationalisms, without any basis in the natural world. Instead, the truth and reality of a territorial nationalism lies in its being part of a narrative that produces a group of people *as though* their belonging to a particular piece of earth were "immanent in the people" themselves.[48] Additionally, Hobsbawm's account is an important consideration alongside analyses like Azar Gat's (discussed in the previous section), which claim that the spirit of nationalism has *always* found itself around ethnically (and, we can add, linguistically) similar groups of people. *The Age of Empire* not only troubles this; it also asks us to consider that the relationship between place, language, and ethnicity is a historically contingent one. In other words, the "place" of place in the idea of the nation responds to the historico-material conditions to which national yearnings respond. The contingency of such conditions generates a need to encounter the territory at the center of the nation's narrative of self-constitution as a necessary aspect of its existence: there is a need for the nation to encounter itself as necessarily rooted in place, so it does.

Étienne Balibar's essay on diasporic citizenship critically engages with this narrative of territorialized national self-constitution. "History," he tells us, "[has] taught us that the origin of the polity . . . lies in a territorial redefinition of belonging that limited, at least symbolically, the powers of *genealogies*, or transgenerational links conserved across migrations and diaspora, together with the name and the kinship relations."[49] Here Balibar seems to regard the role of territory as one that specifically restricts the legitimacy of familial bonds to not only delineate the boundaries of community but also shape the kinds of rights and responsibilities that individuals belonging to those (kin) communities might have had. Alongside this history of the purpose of the nation's bureaucratic arm (namely, the state) of "[eliminating] the function of communities and membership in so-called natural communities," Balibar notes how contemporary patterns of migration call for alternative formulations of the relation between the territory and border (on the one hand) and these bureaucratic capacities of the state to assign and protect the rights of individual citizens.[50] I will not engage here with the conception of a "diasporic citizenship" that he develops to address this political emergence (an emergence that, on his account, potentially changes what it will mean to be a human in the world).[51] However, I do want to note two significant threads that his account foregrounds. The first is the sustained relationship—well into our contemporary age—between nation, the nation-state, and the centrality of single territory in conceptions of national belonging and citizenship. Because of this relationship, Balibar tells us, the ascription and protection of human rights continue to operate through the idea of spatial borders that enclose fixed territories. He rightly identifies this "sovereignty-territory" dyad as a mythical construction with no natural foundation—a construction that "produces the virtual recomposition of a preexisting people, a nomadic community, and a virtual recomposition of the *ethnos* as *demos*, a community of citizens which is its 'own' community."[52]

Second, his account shows that such constructions—people, community, community of belonging—"cannot be taken as an already established notion but consist of an act of permanent creation and re-creation."[53] Hence, much like the nation's time as eternal and linear, the nation's orientation around a single place or territory is a self-understanding that is continuously in production, for the sake of certain social and political ends. What this means is that the relation between nation and place (between national belonging and territorial citizenship) can always be revisited and reformulated—perhaps *not* with a goal of returning to a more prior genealogical conception of community and belonging, but, rather, to seriously consider how place and territory might generate new modes of belonging, so as to support the idea of "citizens *in the world* as it is."[54] To return again to Hobsbawm, the goal would be to consider how place and territory might better respond to our present "international situation."[55]

In short, the relationship between the idea of the nation and territory is very much historically determined. Nationalism, as a means of working through questions of identity and community, emerges when the forces that determine the movement of people call for radically new ways of figuring out the meaning and political implications of human relationships. Out of such shifts, the land shows up as a way to navigate such questions, and one such way is the grounding of the nation-form on the notion of a single territory. To be sure, there have always been reasons to feel a connection with the land, the most powerful of which was an agricultural way of life.[56] But the point is that these kinds of connections (the ones that Azar Gat reads as primordial, and consequently, always part of the spirit of communal living) do not exhaust the potential roles (and meanings) of territory in the idea of the nation. How territory figures into the nation-form seems to have more to do with nation-ness as a response to important *shifts* in the meaning of and exigencies surrounding communal living than with how "things have always been."

Much like linear national time, the commitment to a single territory in the nation's self-constitution responds, in large part, to the need to regard its being as noncontingent. To be sure, such a posture is certainly one that registers in the vein of needing security in the face of threat: it seems that only in the face of threatening forces would the ambiguity (wobbliness) of a contingent existence be untenable. Hence, we might consider rootedness to a single place as what produces the sturdiness needed to stand firm in the face of equal and opposing forces. More than this, the ways in which the idea of destiny unfolds in such narratives means that the nation's existence is a necessary component of something must larger than itself. As my analysis in subsequent chapters unfolds, I will be interested in how such an orientation (in terms of linear, destiny-filling time, and single, necessary place) produces a calcified conception of the nation, which meets with resistance any reimagining of belonging, community, or subjectivity. I offer my account of a creolizing conception of the nation as an alternative to this, so chapter 2 focuses on how the nation's commitment to linear time and single place shifts when its being undergoes creolization. To that end, this chapter's next (third) section prepares us to think through the ways in which the nation's understanding of difference shifts when its being undergoes creolization. But outside such creolizing processes, rootedness to a single place and harking back to a single past secures, for the nation, its participation in the permanence of the eternal. This participation keeps intact a priority (within the nation's narrative) of a metaphysics of the One.

Home, Belonging, and Difference

To return to a point that George Mosse makes in his account of modern nationalism, "Everywhere [in the early twentieth century] men and women wanted to be part of a community, desired integration into the nation as giving new meaning to their individual lives and providing security and shelter."[57] Throughout his exposition, Mosse goes on to identify this quest for community as the defining attraction in the idea of the nation. Indeed, the socioeconomic changes of the modern period greatly undermined this sense of community (and belonging), particularly insofar as the micromigrations into urban centers in search of factory jobs during these beginning stages of the Industrial Age meant that more traditional family units were torn apart. Hence, the nation has certainly been the place to go to, not only for the purpose of feeling at home but also, more importantly, for the purpose of *sharing* that feeling with others. This section visits this relationship between belonging and nation-form, a relationship that also opens up onto the question of difference. The stakes involved in my examination might be captured in the following question: Do we compromise the conditions for the possibility of belonging (of the experience of belonging) when a community is *not* one of like-minded or similarly bodied people? To pose this question differently, must I find, in a community, certain replications of myself before that community can be a place in which I can feel at home?

In her own work, Mariana Ortega addresses this question of home, and the ways in which the notion of home has typically framed the meaning of difference.[58] I introduce this work here because of Ortega's guiding premise, or, perhaps more accurately, her guiding question: What possibilities of belonging exist for subjectivities whose mode of embodiment means that, instead of being at home *in* the world, they exist (concretely) "in between worlds" (interstitially), at the world's edges? This and related questions frame the chapters in part 2 of this book. But I bring attention to it here insofar as it helps orient what this section sets out to accomplish. Namely, this Ortega-inspired question acknowledges that the experience of being at home is neither primordial nor necessary. Ortega's conception of hometactics shows that, to the contrary, the experience of being at home comes out of a creative act (a political act) of *making* a home for oneself. The sociopolitical conditions of my existence can support that creative act, in which case I barely encounter it as an act at all (barely recognize that I exert the energy involved in the act of creating). Or conversely, I make a home for myself *against* the grain of the sociopolitical. Thus, the success of my creative act is perhaps foreclosed by the conditions out of which I act, to the degree that I must work against a systemic inertia. In helping us to orient the question of the relationship between home (or belonging) and the nation in this way, Ortega's account of hometactics denaturalizes this relation. It asks us to understand the nation as a set of material conditions out of which people engage in the project of home-making, a project that produces belonging for some, and nonbelonging or alienation for others. To this end, and most importantly, the question also takes us directly to these material conditions. Precisely what cocktail of structures makes it possible for me to feel at home? What happens to this capacity for home-making when difference is left to signify as such, instead of being reduced under a metaphysics of the One (as is often the case through the frame of nation-ness)?

In their brief exposition in *Who Sings the Nation-State?*, Judith Butler and Gayatri Spivak discuss this relationship between belonging and difference, as one finds it playing out on the public stage of national politics. Some sections of this text are dedicated to decentering the priority of national belonging, for the sake of vibrant political life. But other sections question the ways in which national belonging or, to be faithful to the language of the text, "the public sphere" has historically mandated "cultural familiarity as the basis of shared governance."[59] As intimated in Azar Gat's description of ethnic nationality, finding a sense of home in the nation often means that I experience myself to be part of a homogeneous cultural imaginary. That singular cultural space would then minimize (or perhaps, outright eliminate) the work involved in arriving at consensus when it comes to the logistics of shared governance. Indeed, the general will of a people will be, for the most part, a *single* will of a single machinery—the machinery of a culturally like-minded body politic.[60]

Both Butler and Spivak urge that this cultural familiarity is produced and performed as members of a national public sphere *learn* to articulate and embody (they learn to "sing") the nation-state. We hear, in this, the role of moral education in Rousseau's account of civil society, Hobsbawm's tracing of the emergence of public elementary education toward the end of the nineteenth century, and Balibar's more contemporary analysis of the role of the family-school dyad is the nationalization of a people.[61] Overall, it demonstrates for us a connection that, instead of being natural, is quite *naturalized* between community and belonging, on the one hand, and the minimizing of difference, on the other. To be sure, there is an important sense in which difference is determined as the anti-spoke in the wheel of national belonging. To this end, Butler calls on her readers to "think about the nation-state as a political formation that requires periodic expulsion and dispossession of its national minorities in order to gain a legitimating ground for itself."[62]

Balibar makes a similar point when he notes that "[the] question of whether nationalism is in itself an ideology of domination or exclusion is . . . a pointless one."[63] By this he means to acknowledge that the production of a people as a "nation" is sure to deploy some principle(s) of exclusion, principles that are "the very essence of the nation-form."[64] He does go on to make important distinctions between the nature and material outcomes of such exclusionary principles, acknowledging that they can be "rigid or supply, restrictive or expansive."[65] But Balibar's ultimate point (much like Butler's and Spivak's) is to show that the nation-form works to keep heterogeneity at bay. What this means is that, through its ideological form, the nation "[revitalizes and subordinates differences] to itself in such a way that it is the symbolic difference between 'ourselves' and 'foreigners' which wins out and which is lived as irreducible."[66] Difference is allowed to exist, but never as what is most prior to the formation of the nationalized individual, or to the nationalized collective to which that individual understands herself to belong. Any signification of heterogeneity (moments that are often a consequence of immigration, activist reimagining of cultural institutions, and/or radical demands from subaltern pockets of the nation) calls for purging cycles through which the nation uses its institutional and quotidian discursive tools to foreground the contours of "the people." Heterogeneity that is encountered as being unable to subordinate itself to those contours is vilified in order to be expelled. Differences of this kind (so the narrative goes) diametrically oppose "home" life, since their identities are incompatible with the identity of national belonging.

In this sense, to be part of a community that is national in kind means to be in community with others who are familiar—who are like-minded, hold similar views, and understand the world in similar ways. Again, this is all constructed through a complex network of institutional practices that shape both private and public life. Out of these practices emerge an experience of difference as the very detriment to community. Balibar accounts for how this threatening figure of nonbelonging difference has become a permanent fixture of many contemporary nationalisms, particular in Europe and in North America. As both permanent (needed in order to sustain the politics of security that grounds such nationalisms) and unwanted, this figure points to "the increasing reduction of the category of the . . . 'unwanted stranger,' to the figure of the *enemy*, a social, cultural, religious, and in the end internal political enemy . . . [which then] calls for a politics of national, social and cultural security."[67] The question for us, as I offer a creolizing account of the nation, is how a national people might be produced without this formulation of difference as the unwanted, "enemy" stranger.

Mosse tells us that in the age of popular sovereignty, politics came to be the mouthpiece of the general will of the people. That is to say, popular sovereignty meant that the political was no longer a realm set apart from the everyday lives of everyday folks. Instead, the life of the individual was inflected with the political, as it was with economic, cultural, and social concerns. The general will was understood as the conceptual mechanism through which individuals, now regarded as the collective entity of "the people," expressed this political aspect of their everyday lives. This general will, in turn, "was mediated by the nation"—a constructed notion that transformed a people into a *national* community, an "imagined collective product [whose members] recognize[d] the state as its own."[68] To be sure, the task at hand involved unifying a diverse group of desires, proclivities, and worldviews into a sufficiently single and expressible political volition. More importantly, the age of mass politics (of the politicization of the people) *needed* to be in the business of this process of unification, lest the very possibility of a politics grounded in popular sovereignty become undermined through the tyranny of the many.

Nonetheless, the question remains as to the fate of those nonbelonging differences (those unwanted enemy-strangers) in the institutional and everyday production of the general will. The assumption seems to be that the diverse proclivities that are unified signify as (to borrow Balibar's framing) "primary identities [that] can be considered to be one of the 'legitimate mediations' of the secondary national identity."[69] In other words, it would seem as though, for one to be included in those diverse proclivities that participates in the single political volition of the general will, one's difference cannot be the radical kind that marks the unwanted enemy-stranger. Such differences are categorically excluded (at the outset) from the production of the "people" to which a general will belongs. As Balibar describes it, this figure of difference represents an undoing of the very possibility of nation-forming: "The foreigner whose figure becomes that of an essential stranger, whose dif-

ference becomes intensified, is no longer one with whom . . . you can either
wage war or make peace; he is one with whom peace as such is impossible,
who will remain a threat to be permanently monitored."[70] Balibar offers this
framing to account for the "*migrant* as a racial category," which determines
the shape of present-day European politics. However, as scholars like Sylvia
Wynter and Frantz Fanon have shown, this figure of difference has been the
cornerstone premise of colonial, neocolonial, and postcolonial practices of
antiblack racism for much of the modern period. Indeed, we might say that
Balibar's "migrant as racial category" is but a recent modulation of the ways
in which the figure of the African and African-descended subject has *always*
served as colonialism's needed and unwanted internal threat to the possibility
of politics. In working out a creolizing conception of the nation, my hope
is to imagine an alternative (and, to be sure, decolonial) way of living with
difference in the context of the nation.

But to return to the place of the general will in modern conceptions of
the nation-form, and to the practices out of which it was generated and sustained, Eric Hobsbawm's account of linguistic nationalism sheds some light
on the coming into being of the general will. As mentioned earlier, linguistic
nationalism characterized a historical development in kinds of nationalisms,
occurring between 1870 and 1914, which "made language into the primary
condition of nationality," in ways that language had not served before then.[71]
Hobsbawm identifies the need for this single "national language" to have
emerged out of a new raison d'être for a state-sanctioned, publicly accessible
system of education. He describes this period, from the late nineteenth century to the early twentieth, as one that saw a marked increase in the number
of primary schools and primary school teachers all across Europe and in
the United States. The viability of this public education mandated a common medium of transmission, that is, a common national language in which
individuals (namely, young children) could be taught by the state, so that, as
adults participating in a public, political process (through the mediation of a
general will) they could "sing the state." Hobsbawm's analysis doesn't address
the influence of mass media and the availability of print to circulate political
propaganda and ideology (all of which compounded the effect of educating
a society in mass). Nonetheless, state-sanctioned mass education in a single
language reflects the kind of practices out of which the nation was able to
generate, and act as a mediator of, the general will.

One can argue that as the modern period was characterized by collective self-government and mass politics, it was also tasked with determining
the nature of collective self-government in the face of increasing diversity
in the public sphere. Understanding this presence of difference as a challenge, the nation (during modernity) worked to homogenize that difference
through mechanisms of assimilation (to subordinate difference to a mediating
national identity). This means that, ironically, as access to the political sphere
increased, and more (in kind and in number) people entered, the flatter the

variation in voices became. Difference was *less likely* to signify positively in an era of increased participation in the political; the age of popular sovereignty probably brought the reduction of difference at best, or the outright vilification of difference at worst.

But what can we say of the nation (or some equivalent collective device) before modernity, or during an epoch marked by the absence of mass engagement with the political? From Azar Gat's positions that nationalism is birthed from the modern period (in other words, didn't really exist before modernity), he argues that the political urgencies of the modern period simply sharpened the political efficacy of nationalist sentiments that predated modernity itself. In other words, on Gat's account, though the nation-form is a modern form, it capitalized on sentiments that existed prior to its emergence, so the nation-form and all it includes should be read in terms of something primordial to what it means to be human. He writes, "[Popular] sovereignty [a defining mark of the modern age] greatly enhanced national cohesion [which *predated* that popular sovereignty] and the people's stake in the nation."[72] This is because, according to Gat, a group of people once under the tyranny of imperial rule would desire a national identity through which they could express their general will. In other words, popular sovereignty invariably seeks its own national community as a means of resisting the tyranny of dynastic rule. Gat writes, "[It] is awkward to describe a people's urge for collective freedom [from imperial, dynastic, tyrannical control] as anything other than national."[73] To reiterate, Gat is arguing that the spirit of nationalism is really endemic (primordial, to remain faithful to his language) to human living. As such, the nation is not a contingent consequence of modernity; rather, it only took on particular usage and characteristics during this period, given the centrality of mass politics and popular sovereignty at that time.

Indeed, Gat writes, "[Popular] sovereignty [did not] beget nationalism. . . . It set it free."[74] It is worthy to point out that in the nineteenth century "nation" and "race" were almost interchangeable. In this regard, the German *Volk* or the English people function in ways that are similar to what Gat refers to as those "nationalist sentiments" that predated the emergence of modern nations.[75] That said, I do want to focus on the connection he points to—the link between the rise of "proto"-nationalist sentiments and responses to tyrannical rule—in order to approach, from a more ontological level, the relationship between nationalism and difference. Gat's exposition shows that the modern nation represented not only a solidarity in the name of collective autonomy but also, and perhaps more notably, a solidarity *against* the threat of imperial domination. Nationalism determined itself relative to a recognizable threat; it was reactionary, standing as a necessary next step against oppression, and against domination by an established "other" (namely, the empire). On this account, the reason for being, for the modern nation, is freedom from this threat of oppression. Any sense of collective life or national identity is in the name of such an objective. Mosse's trace of the national anthems that emerged from the early era of modernity reflects this fundamental commitment to being primed for attack, or to being ready to avert the forces that would compromise the integrity of the newfound collective (the people, coming to embrace their own autonomy). "Some reference to war and death in war was part of most national anthems," Mosse tells us, "[and] most volunteers [soldiers who would fight in these wars] had experienced a new kind of community held together by common danger [of being demolished by an external threat] and a common goal [of keeping that threat at bay]."[76]

To be grounded, in this fundamental way, in relation to the threatening "other," the modern nation seems to be derived out of a core allergy toward difference. To return to Gat's claim, it is in a reactionary response to imperial domination that the nation performs as a weapon of war, primarily enacted as a "freedom *from*" (threat, oppression, annihilation), and only secondarily as a "freedom *to*" (live a life where one is the author of one's destiny). On this account, one would imagine that the general will of the people (and ultimately the mediation of this general will in the nation) is formulated specifically in opposition to the enemy (within or beyond the nation's borders). On Gat's analysis, the enemy in question is what opposes collective freedom. Pushed to its extreme, though, this position with respect to a (different) enemy is only a short cry from an overall vilification of difference. That is to say, the formulation "enemy as different" comes into its own extreme (intensified) formulation of "difference *as* the enemy." What is familiar is of us and for us, and is therefore safe and homely. What is unfamiliar is against us, signifies as danger, and threatens our sense of being at home.

In Eric Hobsbawm's analysis of the xenophobic turn in the nationalism of the late 1800s, he connects this vilification of difference with what he identifies as the phenomenon of the "middle strata." He notes that an allergy toward difference was most intense in those sections of society for whom disorientation, disempowerment, and loss was the founding experience of early capitalism. National self-representation was a means through which that existential loss could be mitigated, through an imagined superiority of a bygone way of life, or through a past in which "mediocre" didn't mean that one got lost in the cracks of a capitalist system of value. Hobsbawm writes that "patriotism [in the extreme sense of the word] compensated for social inferiority," and this sentiment of inferiority grew out of a radical restructuring of the world that, at the outset, seemed to undermine what, up to that moment in history, counted as effective ways of constructing individual and communal identity.[77] Why would this be acute in that "middle" strata of society? For Hobsbawm, the answer to this question is mostly economic: "Xenophobia appealed readily to traders, independent craftsmen and some farmers threatened by the progress of the industrial economy."[78] Though this economic explanation bears legitimacy, it does not, to my mind, exhaust all possible ways of reading this location of xenophobia in the middle of the social order. Most notably, Hobsbawm's turn to the economic as a fundamental explanation seems to skirt the heart of the issue, which is a more prior incapacity of that so-called middle strata to navigate existential ambiguity and to live with change without resorting to xenophobic closures. To be sure, early capitalism's changes to a world economy would surely have brought about much angst in sectors of a community materially disenfranchised (by the forces of capitalism itself) to participate in such transformations. But more deeply, such responses to change seem to point to a particular kind of encounter with the ambiguity of human living. Caught in the middle (as it were), such ambiguity would be most apparent for these "traders, craftsmen and farmers." And angst in the face of having to create alternative modes of self-identification would be one way of responding to this ambiguity. But for the questions I am using to engage the phenomenon of the nation with creolization, I note, of this middle strata's response, a resistance to movement, process, and (as noted above) ambiguity. Chapter 2 explores the question of what would happen to this response (of xenophobic closure for the sake of self-identification) if there was no such resistance. In other words, what happens when, through creolization, we encounter another way of relating to ambiguity and movement?

Nevertheless, we see the ways in which the course of modern history has marked difference for the sake of vilification, demonization, and outcasting within the nation-frame. By no stretch of the imagination has this tendency—to make an enemy out of the other—ended with modernity. To the contrary, it continues to characterize how we negotiate national life today. The pinnacle of Nazi Germany's program of National Socialism saw the physical elimination of those who were deemed either unable, or unwilling, to pledge real allegiance to an authentic German ancient sensibility. Prior to this, the vilification of the other resulted in mass sterilization programs across the United States, all in the name of purging the nation of certain "incurable and permanent" internal threats to its moral, cultural, and often biological gene pool. As I mentioned earlier, twenty-first-century racism is nothing but a partaking in this ontological bent toward difference, which marks what is different as a danger to be permanently monitored and to be dealt with through either outright elimination or suppressive containment and suspended life.[79]

Interestingly, Benedict Anderson situates racism in terms of class politics first, and only secondarily in terms of national politics.[80] For him, the source of late nineteenth-century racism is what he names "official nationalism"—the nationalism originating from old (premodern) aristocracies, in response to modernity's delegitimization of their power. To the degree that the investments of this kind of nationalism amounted to retaining political power for the sake of material wealth, the accompanying racist narratives were ultimately class-oriented as well. He writes, "[Racism] dreams of eternal contaminations [and to this one might add, eternal privileges of purity] transmitted from the origins of time through an endless sequence of loathsome copulations: *outside history*."[81] Anderson argues that nationalism was a fundamentally historical project and that therefore, unlike racist identities, the identities and worldviews coming out of the nationalist frame are experienced as historically situated and as subject to the ebbs and flows of historical change. However, in the second section above, I outlined the sense in which the temporality of the nation form also situated the nation's being outside time (and in the sphere of the eternal). Thus, though the nation's being may in fact be historically constituted, it is encountered in a very similar way to more racially oriented identities (and worldviews). Both are *experienced* as being independent of historical context, permanent to the extent of being written in the eternal (as a destiny to be made manifest), and possessing the trait of the "always have been and always will be." Hence, this language of racism that (as Anderson points out) allowed the aristocracies of early modernity to establish the eternal superiority of their material, or earthly power is no different from the language contained in nationalist ideology, which established a similar legitimacy (sacredness, even) to a nationalized collective.

Indeed, Anderson argues that racism, as a form of xenophobia, worked to *undermine* the significance of nationhood, in the sense that it located the essence of personal identity in the timelessness of eternity, or in the permanence of biology. "Jews, the seed of Abraham, [were] forever Jews, no matter what passport they [carried] or what languages they [spoke]."[82] Again, I read this claim to downplay the importance of the roles of the eternal and the sacred in the production of the nation's narrative. Timothy Brennan notes this as well when he quotes Regis Debray's account of the "form" of the nation. "[This form is made out of] a natural organization proper to *homo sapiens*, one *through which life itself is rendered untouchable or sacred. This sacred character constitutes the real national question.*"[83] It is in this sense that I trouble the somewhat easy binary that Anderson sketches, between the national narrative as historical and the racial narrative as eternal. Though the nation is in fact a product of history, its self-representation seems committed to a narrative of *forgetting* its historical contingency. Very much like a racialized conception of identity, a national identity is always in the making, in need of practices that sustain and propel its being into the future precisely because it is radically contingent.

Nevertheless, Anderson does compel us to think through the relationship between nation and race, between nationalist strivings for political autonomy that are squarely grounded in a racialized identity.[84] This is especially pertinent for the nationalist struggles of previously colonized societies for independence from colonial rule. However, it is not that these postcolonial nationalist movements are the *only* nationalist strivings with race at their center, given that European nation-states adopted racialized narratives themselves, in order to sustain their own sense of national identity during their colonizing of Africa, Asia, and the Caribbean. In chapter 6, I devote a sustained analysis to the ways in which Fanon's account of nationalism *both* acknowledges the centrality of race *and* avoids the xenophobic closure of a racially based nationalism. But I note this here to point out that, though such anticolonial nationalisms are clearly oriented *against* domination under colonial rule, it is possible (as Fanon shows us) that what emerges out of these nationalist movements is *decolonial*—built on something other than an internal logic of antidifference, feudalism, and tribalism.

My engagement with Fanon's work in chapter 6 will establish this. More significantly, it is in bringing his work into dialogue with a theory of creolization that chapter 6 is able to make this clear. Meanwhile, chapter 2 traces the theory of creolization in its many iterations and disciplinary frames. I show that, throughout its multifaceted manifestations, creolization clearly prioritizes the importance of movement, dynamism, and engagement among parts whose very being emerges out of that engagement. To say this otherwise, creolization is precisely that process that emphasizes the many instead of the one, movement instead of stability, and difference instead sameness. How would our understanding of the nation change if we thought about its mode of being in terms of creolization, and its encounter with difference as an encounter shaped by practices of creolization?

In moving into the following chapter on the meaning of creolization as a theory and cultural phenomenon, I want to return again to Azar Gat—namely, to his somewhat problematic account of the nations of Latin America. He writes that the nation-building process in this region is far less advanced than in places like the United States, Canada, and the Balkan states, because these Latin American nations comprise multiple ethnic communities, each founded on their own respective ways of life and linguistic practices. As a consequence of this heterogeneity, Gat claims, national cohesion is not as attainable as it could be: the presence of real diversity acts as an impediment to robust nation building, insofar as these multiple cultural proclivities "[compete] over and [challenge] the concept of the nation."[85] What Gat seems to say here is that there is no single national ethnicity for the majority of these Latin American countries, and as a result, "nation-building is an ongoing project" that has to wrestle with these persistently multiple entry points into the meaning and value system of the nation.[86] This, he says, is unlike those more "robust nation states," an example of which is the United States. Instead of multiple ethnic affinities existing side by side, "there exists a very distinct American culture [in the United States] encompassing mores, symbols, social practices, and public knowledge."[87] On this account, differences are made to assimilate into this single American ethic, which assures the success of American national life.

An analysis like Gat's would do well to consider creolization as a formative process when it comes to the emergence of a nation. Gat identifies Latin America as a region similar to other regions of the world—diverse and nonmonolithic. He traces this diversity to a history of immigration, very much like what one finds shaping the development of the United States.[88] But what he seems to underestimate is the pivotal driving force of this diversity and movement in the nation-building process. When it comes to the Latin American situation, it is not that singular ethnic identities compete with and undermine the idea of the nation. Rather, it is that the idea (or, perhaps, the goal) of a single national identity is more or less forced to take seriously the real diversity within these countries.

Hence, what Gat notes as a *problematic* consequence of this ethnic plurality—that it means "nation-building [must be] an ongoing project"—is what my project of creolizing the nation notes as an invaluable (and perhaps unavoidable) *asset* of nation-ness. Gat reads, in this ongoing (open) nature of nation building, a failure on the part of such communities to "get it right," to establish an overarching and single national culture or ethnic bent into which multiple "minority cultures" can melt.[89] Instead, I understand the phenomenon of the Latin American nation, much like the phenomenon of the Caribbean nation, to point to something more positive. That nation building remains an open process indicates what I will name the creolization of the nation-form. Out of this creolizing process, the contours of these nations are made to perpetually respond to the dynamic and heterogeneous forces their respective *living* communities encompass. Chapter 2's account of this process of creolization may highlight the blind spot in analyses like Gat's, which are unable to account for the ways in which creolized communities, throughout history, have not only encountered and lived with difference but have done so while producing a sense of cohesion and community.

Chapter 2

✦

The Time and Place of Creolization

But look at the creole garden, you put all the crops on such *put all crops native to the land* a little lick of land, the avocados, the lemons, the yams, the sugarcane . . . plus thirty or forty other species on this bit of land that doesn't go more than fifty feet up the side of the hill, they protect each other. In the great Circle, everything is in everything else.

—Édouard Glissant, *Traite du Toute-monde*

In 1882, Ernest Renan described the "existence of nations [as] a good thing." He wrote that "[their] existence is the guarantee of liberty, which would be lost if the world had only one law and only one master."[1] In 1882, Renan viewed the existence of the nation as the protector of the kind of heterogeneity that would guard against the forces of totalization, a force he identified as counter to the spirit of reason that would condition the possibility of a thriving humanity. I begin this second chapter with this quote from Renan because of its curious alignment with the phenomenon of creolization. While Renan understands the nationalism of the late nineteenth century to be the guardian of diverse global players, one can certainly make the case that, by 1882, the nation-form's indebtedness to colonial domination and imperial arrangements of global power meant that nations and nation-states had already established themselves as the nemesis of such diversity. (Indeed, as Aimé Césaire notes in *Discourse on Colonialism*, Renan's working conceptions of differences among human beings supported a presumed *hierarchy* of superior and inferior races.[2]) As chapter 1 delineated, the centrality of commitments to purity, tightly bordered spaces of belonging, and narratives of single origins have shaped the political culture of the modern nation into one that prioritizes homogeneous ways of being. Such iterations of the idea of the nation make Renan's point particularly noteworthy to the degree that, even in 1882, it was possible to acknowledge the value of local and multiple lifeworlds, to locate the preservation of such multiplicity in a world of nation-states, and to acknowledge that such multiplicity conditioned the possibility of human liberation.

In this chapter, I hope to establish that the phenomenon of creolization ought to be lauded for similar reasons. Indeed, creolization accounts for the ways in which lifeworlds in the Americas have not only resisted the totalizing effects of the nation-form's homogenizing structures but have also generated everyday experiences of degrees of freedom. So, though I do not suggest that such practices name a revolutionary politics of antiblack, anticolonial liberation, I do argue that creolization gives us a theory to understand the everyday practices with which subjects engage—so as to sabotage—systems of domination in order to move themselves just that much further away from subjection. To borrow from Wynter's rumination on the possibility of undoing colonialism's divide between self and its other, I want to position creolization as a set of practices that align with those of "the jester, the clown and the rogue," which "through a dialectics of rigidification and rupture . . . [generate] carnivalesque inversions . . . of self-justifying discourse."[3] Indeed, as Mimi Sheller reminds us, the Caribbean history out of which the theory of creolization emerges is precisely one of anticolonial and subaltern resistance (of carnivalesque agency) that, at the level of the everyday, bears witness to decolonial productions of new modes of being in the world. She urges scholars to foreground this history—to honor the "responsibilities and solidarities" to the Caribbean subaltern—so that creolization might be appropriately rendered as "a conflictual process of re-homing or re-grounding, rather than simply a playful [sanitized, ahistorical, and apolitical] uprooting or re-mixing of dislocated cultures."[4] What is left out in standard conceptions of the nation-form when we fail to take into account how these creolizing practices effect everyday disruptions of its master codes?

For societies like those of the Caribbean archipelago, historically emerging through creolizing processes, the conservation of cultural and political norms is not an option, insofar as the structures of these norms code for the subhumanity of such communities. As a process that is both resistive and creative, creolization allows these communities to invent mechanisms through which their discursive (and sometimes material) liberation becomes possible at the level of the everyday. "[New] power relations and aesthetic dimensions," Robert Baron and Ana Cara tells us, are the stakes involved in creolizing societies, whose task it is to "[resist the] domination and asymmetrical power relations" that promote the humanity of some at the expense of the humanity of others.[5]

The historical context of creolization often means that an orientation toward difference shapes these inventive modes of free life. In other words, a plurality of lifeworlds, cultural comportments, and ways of being are all characterizing markers of societies that would be named "creole." For this reason, we might understand creolization as a process that, in our contemporary political moment, responds to the worry expressed by Renan in 1882, about the totalitarian grip of "one law and one master." In other words, in presenting an account of how creolization calls for alternative frames of experience in time and space, this chapter establishes how the creole attunement to multivocality facilitates conditions for resisting the spatiotemporal organization of the nation-form. My orienting question is as follows: How does the temporal ordering of creole products of culture and social practice, as well as their complex connections to territoriality, point to an honoring of difference, an open-ended signification of both humanness and human society, and, perhaps most importantly, an alternative understanding of what it means to be a nation?

To be clear, the account given of creolization in this chapter is explicitly shaped by the proposal to creolize the nation. So though there are many ways to outline the creolizing process, my account is grounded in the stakes outlined in chapter 1, concerning the founding allergy toward difference at the core of the idea of the nation. Hence, I should preface what follows by first recognizing two manifestations of the ideology of nationalism, both differently positioned with respect to the history of colonialism and the building up of Empire. That is, I openly acknowledge that colonialism has shaped the movement of human history, perhaps more substantially than any other global institution has. To acknowledge this is to see the error in clumping the European nationalism of the eighteenth century to the late nineteenth together with the nationalisms of people of the global majority during the 1940s through the 1990s, which emerged through their anticolonial struggles for political and economic sovereignty. Colonialism matters. Therefore, *how* one is situated with respect to the colonial project matters for the signification and historical meaning of one's nationalism. Timothy Brennan brings this point to bear when he writes, "The terms of nationalism have from the European perspective apparently reversed. Not freedom from tyranny, but the embodiment of tyranny. The question is: how much is this new perspective a result of owning rather than suffering an empire?"[6] To ask this otherwise, does one's position on the receiving end of the bayonet of colonialism and empire inform the meaning of one's nationalism? And if so, might the move that unequivocally marks nationalism as a political expression of tyranny be a hasty one, calling for the nuance of historical context? Like Brennan, I engage with the idea of the nation through the historical movement of empire, so as to attend to that nuance. Others, most notably Fanon, have taken up this question as well and argue that the nationalist positions for African ex-colonies (for instance) take on a significance that ought to be gauged independently of a reading of European nationalism.[7]

It is against this historical backdrop that I bring the idea of the nation into an explicit engagement with creolization. More specifically, my question is this: What might creolization have to offer, as we attempt to imagine alterative iterations of the phenomenon of the nation? In what ways should conceptions of the nation be accountable to those liminal moments and sites out of which creolizing practices produce alternative modes of identity and

belonging? I ask these questions along with Michaeline Crichlow's interroga-
tions: "Which citizenship, what memories, what subjectivity, what "space,"
"place," "mode of dwelling," or "homing" is being articulated . . . in [the
creolizing] liminal site?"[8] In attending to what I argue are the *constitutive*
liminalities of nation-ness, might foregrounding the process of creolization
change a nation's commitment to a narrative of a single origin in time? Such
narratives are either about returning to a mythologized past that disavows
its empirical contingency, or about re-enlivening it so as to author a collective
destiny. Indeed, Brennan argues that it is precisely a desire for control that
gives meaning to a culture's self-narration of an absolute beginning in time.
"A point of origin [in the sense of an Ark story] is fixed . . . [and this] zero
point or starting point is what allows ritual repetition, the ritualization of
memory, celebration, commemoration," all of which are ways to travel back,
across time, in a gesture that grasps the reins of destiny.[9] In other words, a
narrative like the story of the Ark gives us a single moment out of which we
might derive agency in the face of the fated irreversibility of time.

To this end, to give an account of one's collective identity in terms that do
not resort to single moments in time, and, correspondingly, to single spaces
in place, is to reopen these existential questions. Is it possible to negotiate
national identity and belonging in ways that do *not* locate legitimacy in some
founding territory, purity, and single origin? In chapter 3, I will offer Édouard
Glissant's work as a way of taking up creolization in order to grapple with
similar questions. Perhaps in anticipation of this we might turn to Eric Prieto's reading of Glissant in order to heed to his reminder of the significance of
cultural contact in the shape and unfolding of postcolonial globalization. In
foregrounding contact, the contemporary meaning of national identity and
belonging is faced with the task of "understanding . . . our own place even as
[we situate our place] within the larger global context."[10] The goal here "is
to reconcile the local and the global, to gain this totalizing perspective but
without losing track of the particulars."[11] Creolization offers the nation a
frame for articulating such reconciliations.

To return to the question with which the last chapter ends, is it possible
to navigate the collective that is the nation in ways that are hospitable to
difference, to different accounts of origination, and to diverse ways of being
human? These are the stakes that ground this chapter's trace of the process of
creolization. My goal is to position this process as one that might reimagine
the "problem space" in which the questions of collective identity and relational living circulate, so as to ask them in ways that open us up to possibilities for liberatory living.[12] This chapter will show that creolization happens
precisely when human living must begin as a resistance to domination. In that
resistance, the process births "new power relations and aesthetic dimensions
[that facilitate] new ways of being in the world," precisely because, without
these new ways, liberatory modes of human living remain impossible.[13]

Creolization as Cultural Entanglements

Central to practices that are named "creole" is the fluidity of entanglements among fragments, the existence of which defy any claim to authenticity, or faithfulness to some original moment or place. To say this differently, creole entanglements precisely do not participate in a metaphysics of the One, of the single and unchanging iconic copy that Ricardo Sanín-Restrepo critiques.[14] Rather, connections with the original are across iterative *differences*, instead of copied similarities. Of this rejection of a metaphysics of the One, creole is both "a movement away from origin [that includes] the difficulty of reconstructing a path back to [the past]" and, as a consequence, "the generation of new modes of dwelling with difference."[15] The cultural artifacts that emerge out of such practices are not new in terms of creation ex nihilo; rather, they are new in terms of the emergent, entangled patterns among pieces of predating forms, iterations of which both retain resemblance and resist simple replication.

Richard Price's essay on creolization traces the different assessments of using creolization to theorize cultural life in the New World. One such assessment is the somewhat critical reading of creolization, which claims that "the slave trade and subsequent transfer of New World plantations was not . . . quite as randomizing a process as posited by those who argue that Africans had to *start from scratch*."[16] In other words, such critiques of creolization read, in the first premise of entanglement among cultural fragments, the intimation that, because creolization centers inauthenticity and decenters the priority of origins (of both place and time), the process lays claim to creation ex nihilo (i.e., starting from scratch). However, what Price's piece allows us to see is the fine distinction—on which rests much of my account of the nation properly creolized—between (a) retaining a relationship to the past in which one is determined *by* that past, and (b) retaining a relationship to the past in which one is not free *from* but, rather, free *in* that relationship to create iterative temporalities. Hence, the methodological first premise of creolization (both as a theorizing of New World blackness and as a theorizing of nation-ness in the wake of New World, postcolonial contact) is the idea of being free in one's relation to a past (to history) without being ahistorical. To that end, creolization reads the transmission of African cultures and lifeworlds into New World settings in terms of (or across) disjuncture and not linear continuities, thus undoing the foundational significance of the single and unchanging iconic copy on which the metaphysics of the One rests.[17]

Stuart Hall uses the trope of translation to account for this disjunctive temporality and historical ambiguity, writing that translation "always bears the traces of the original, but in such a way that the original is impossible to restore."[18] To this end, the "new" in creolizing newness is about beginning again (not the same as "starting from scratch") from a "number of ethnic

paradigms and informed by the present crisis [of New World plantation life],"
which historically took place in slave communities in the Caribbean and in
the Americas.[19] It should also be noted that given the history of the Middle
Passage and the slave plantation, which foregrounds processes of creole emergence, this impossible restoration of pasts is conceptualized not as a failure
but as the founding historical circumstance out of which needed and new
ways of collective life and identity formation arose.[20] In other words, this
history of impossible return conditions the possibility of how creolizing practices generate moments of "the otherwise" that rupture the terrain of power.
Hence, when Hall names the iterative emergence of creole entanglements
"translation," he means to capture the ways in which the spatial and temporal movements of cultural creolization traffic in complicated relationships
between past and future, as well as between same and different. I am interested in how such complex spatiotemporalities effect the nature of communal
identity within the context of the nation.

In their essay "In Praise of Creoleness," Jean Bernabé, Patrick Chamoiseau,
Raphaël Confiant, and Mohamed B. Taleb Khyar celebrate this syncretic process as not only the source of Caribbean identity but also the promise of a
lived Caribbean sovereignty in the wake of colonial occupation.[21] In a later
section of this chapter, I focus on the implications of how creolization has
been taken up as an explicitly political identity in the Caribbean. But for now,
I want to highlight the tensions alluded to this celebratory essay, between
creoleness in its potential for supporting an essentialist conception of identity
(on the one hand) and creolization as a mode of permanent *im*permanence,
perpetual becoming, and, ultimately, the *impossibility* of identity-as-closed-
off to difference (the other).[22] According to these creolist scholars, to understand themselves as Caribbean is to both "plunge into [their] singularity"
and to "reach out for what [they are]."[23] They argue that, in the plunge,
one dismantles the alienation of a colonial culture, through which a version
of oneself is curated only to be encountered as strange. This "old fatality of
exteriority" meant that, instead of finding oneself anchored in the intimacy
of one's inner subjectivity, one finds a self *for* the imperial gaze, whose speech
is for an imperial ear because its language is the language of the imperial
metropole. In place of this borrowed (and, as a consequence, alienating) identity, Caribbean creoleness calls for a reappropriation of that inner space of
subjective life and for self-narratives that actively resist the oppressive reach
of the colonizer's legacy.

That is the plunge. However, the authenticity that it produces (so that it
can then be found) ought not to constitute Caribbean identity as a closed-off
encampment. According to the authors of this "Praise" essay, this discovery
of *inner* authenticity is simultaneously a discovery of the ways in which the
external world is implicated *in* the intimacy of the self. This underscores
what Crichlow names "the bricolage that is modernity's space," such that "an
Atlantic world space . . . [folds] back into Africa but yet [goes] well beyond

that continent."[24] Given this entanglement, creoleness must be (and is, according to Bernabé and others) an open principle, or a sustained being-in-relation with the diversity of cultures out of which Caribbean history is constituted, and through which the Caribbean basin is really a modern phenomenon.[25] Créolité (at least at this level of theoretical exploration) is not predicated on one's tightly bordered separation from what one "is not." Crichlow rightly points to the limits in creolization processes to "proffer an (absolute) 'outside' to those [like Caribbean subjects] entangled in this incipient modernity after being caught up in the violent vortex of its formation."[26] We are called to understand creole being as a creole becoming—always in moving, communicative relation with the diversity of the world. For this reason, Bernabé, Chamoiseau, Confiant, and Khyar describe this "double move" (the plunge into interiority that is also an opening of identity) as one that "survive[s] in Diversity." As such, the creole identity they celebrate bypasses identity constructions that are founded in some totalitarian fear of the vitality of difference and differentiation.[27] Indeed, the "diversality" of creoleness is presented in this essay as a corrective and contrasting trope to the universality that flattens difference for the sake of homogeneity.[28]

Hence, creolization is the process out of which emerges "de-essentialized cultures" and "beautiful inauthenticities."[29] In reading Kamau Brathwaite's assessment of creolization alongside the poetic and musical oeuvre of Wayde Compton, Heather Smyth further develops this "double movement" metaphor. Her account is particularly important for the question of the need for (or possibility of) an oppositional politics that might emerge from a cultural identity grounded in the diversality of creolization. The Caribbean archipelago stands as an archetypal location for the production of creole cultures insofar as they are also the location for brutal dislocations and loss throughout its history. This history of violence (of the slave trade and of a plantation economy) serves as the grounding conditions for the syncretisms and translations that shape creole Caribbean identity. Hence, one would imagine that a consciousness of this history would produce social and political commitments that were attuned to the legacies of that history; the historical specificity of communities such as those in the Caribbean would be wary of an erasure (or revisionist retelling) of the memory of colonial domination, given the role of such memory in creolizing productions of new social and cultural possibilities. How might such historical grounding persist in the midst of a creolizing process that works against absolute significations of place and time? Would a "de-essentialized" creolizing identity foreclose the possibility of an oppositional identity politics that might resist the legacies of colonialism?

What I offer in the analysis of part 2 of this book, by way of bringing creolization into dialogue with the work of Latina feminist traditions, takes these questions head on. But for now, I want to return to how Smyth's work treats the artistic form of turntabling, since her account offers some metaphors for addressing how we might approach the complexity of this relationship between dynamic de-essentialization (on the one hand) and the politically necessary attendance to history (on the other). In the art of turntabling, the DJ manipulates recorded music in order to reorder its sound and thematic. Smyth borrows from Juliana Snapper's descriptions of this performance, in which she writes, "Turntable techniques situate recorded musical performances in ways that consistently disrupt the forward motion of the record and the process of sound playback. . . . The overarching enveloping narrative is displaced and issued instead in fragmented contradictory folds."[30] Smyth names such products "wrong," or creative "misduplications"—terms that point tellingly to the ways in which processes of creolization shape their cultural landscapes, *and* to a rejection of what Plato's metaphysics offers as criteria for truth and being.[31] The music productions of the turntable are, themselves, copies without models (to borrow from Ricardo Sanín-Restrop's analysis) insofar as they articulate a mode of being that centers the somewhat paradoxical simultaneity of their radical difference *and* relation to what came before them. In a similar vein, processes of creolization give rise to social and cultural landscapes in which differences emerge in chaotic disassemblages of geological lines to authentic originals, all the while retaining traces of relations to those originals. "Origin" signifies not as what must be kept sacred and intact but as what must undergo the bricolage of modernity's adaptive life. To this end, creolization asks us to think politics, culture, and social existence as both grounded in *and* unencumbered by "impositions of geography, of geographical location; the *nation-state* and local identity."[32]

Smyth argues that because "turntablists toy with memory [and authentic origins]" in this sonic way, they also end up "[pulling] the rug out from under racial definitions while paradoxically reinforcing subnational [and, for our purposes, historically situated] communities."[33] Such formulations are important for the creolizing implications of questions of identity (of the possibility of a productive creole identity politics). In my culminating chapter on Fanon's critique of a narrow nationalism, I give an account of how he understands the role of identity politics in dynamic anticolonial struggles toward productive articulations of sovereignty. But for now, I point out that Smyth's metaphor of the turntablist "pulling the rug under racial definitions" approximates Fanon's critical assessments of a narrow or "ultra"-nationalism. In both cases, history matters without legitimizing rigid determinations of one's relationship to the world. We can also bring the turntablist's sonic maneuvering of identity constructions into conversation with Paul Gilroy's development of his critical planetary humanism, in which he imagines the possibility of human community no longer tethered to the identifications supplied by early modern raciology, all the while understanding that a robust acknowledgment of that history is precisely the path that conditions such a planetary humanism.[34] What might it mean to take this creative reworking of memory and narrative, across sound, to its broader cultural implications, namely, to the boundary constructions that support distinctions between identity and difference? Can one trouble the rigidity of racial definitions (and their founding historicity), so that when creolization occurs—cultural movement, redefinition, and creative misduplications—there is retained the relationship to history needed for robust resistive political work against hegemonic expressions of imperialism? Indeed, these are the questions raised by John Drabinski's treatment of Glissant's deployment of creolization. Can we read, in creolization's jostling of rigid borders (so that, as I discuss in a later section, they signify as permeable and moving boundaries), the possibility of "a postcolonial articulation of place" that is as much decolonial in its engagement with history as it is postcolonial?[35]

Smyth also echoes the descriptions that Bernabé and others give in their praise of creolization's capacity for developing a richer, less alienating experience of Caribbean identity. She foregrounds how their essay situates creoleness as the modality through which one will "scrutinize the chaos of this new humanity that we are, to *understand* what the Caribbean is." To recall, this scrutiny is simultaneously a "plunge into [Caribbean] singularity" so as to derive an understanding of Caribbean cultural identity and the historical location that gives it meaning, *and* a "[reaching] out for what we are," as a consequence of what that identity entails.[36] This plunge-and-outreach seems to capture how turntablism (in Smyth's description) shapes historically situated communities (the plunge into identity) in ways that toy with racial definitions that, as a consequence of a certain rendering of that history, risk calcifications that run counter to the creative translations and syncretism that potentially open up onto new (and decolonial) ways of being in the world.

It is also in this vein that Crichlow reads, in creolization processes, their capacities for generating new modalities and subject orientations amid the web of modern, global power. To think about creolization in this way—as a generative process of "cultural struggle and transformation"—is to locate within these processes what Crichlow calls a "liminal dialectics" that unfolds in the spaces within communities and that persists despite forces of homogenization.[37] Crichlow writes that, within these liminal spaces, the "future meets with [the] past" for time to occur, for becoming to occur, so that obscure futures take on meaning and point toward the options for newness in the world. In this formulation, Crichlow reminds us of how creolization ought to be understood—as a set of practices that are both attuned to local urgencies *and* call for inventive responses to those urgencies. In its tenacity for "dreaming in blasphemies," creolization also points beyond the confines of the "here" and the "now."[38]

The definition of creoleness presented by Bernabé and others is as follows: "the *interactional or transactional aggregate* of Caribbean, European, African, Asian, and Levantine cultural elements, united on the same yoke of history."[39] This description tells us that out of (and despite) this yoking onto a place and a history, the whatness of Caribbean culture lies in the communicative play among the cultural identities in question. Insofar as the "what" of Caribbean-ness emerges in this movement of communication and interaction among these cultural pieces (all of which are already translated "misduplications" of an irretrievable original), identity happens as, and *in* motion. As John Drabinski rightly notes, insofar as this Caribbean identity centers itself in creolization, "principles of relation and influence" are at the center.[40] There is no assumption of purity, no expectation for authenticity. In a similar sense, Hall asks his readers to understand identity in terms of its impossibility, and Crichlow grounds her exploration of creolization in a notion of "identity as something profoundly incoherent."[41] Such conceptions of identity (as impossible, as incoherent) stand in sharp contrast to certain essentialist or naturalist conceptions because they view identity as a process, "a process never completed—always 'in process.'"[42] Through this account, Hall orients identity not in terms of the "what" of identification but, rather, in terms of the "how." As a never-complete process—precisely because of the centrality of relation—the creolizing syncretism that occurs upon the "common yoke of a Caribbean history will always be subject to the 'play' of *difference*. It [identification-as-process] obeys the logic of more-than-one. And . . . as a process that operates across difference, [it is] the production of 'frontier effects.' It requires what is left outside."[43] To this end, any identity-based politics that grows out of this creolizing way of understanding the boundaries between "same" and "other" will avoid the problematic of a strictly walled-in community in disavowal of its indebtedness to plural modes of engagement with the world. In other words, Hall's identity-as-impossibility, much like the turntablist's commitment to the messy fragmentation of memory and sonic narration, avoids the pitfalls of the plunge into history divorced from the outreach of Relation.[44]

Heather Smyth's work also recalls Wayde Compton's account of having his prerecorded poems played through the turntablist's fragmenting and reassembling. "My pre-recorded voice and poem is broken and re-broken, arranged and re-arranged, combined and re-combined with a shifting repertoire of other sources. . . . The poem is not inside me, waiting to be expressed. It is in our crate, waiting for us to position it."[45] In a similar vein, identity birthed through cultural creolization accomplishes a similar breaking and rebreaking, arranging and rearranging of cultural units. Attempts to "suture" (or close off) the frontiers of interplay among such units is bound either to prematurely leave some vital piece out of the "how" of identity or to have already included (in the identification-as-process) the alterity it tries to disavow.[46] *How* the cultural fragments in question move with each other says more about their cultural identity than what is prepackaged into the individual pieces themselves does.[47] Hence, in Hall's assessment that "identities are constructed through, not outside, difference," we hear affirmations of the conceptual "diversality" deployed by Bernabé and his coauthors to express the creole open complex of a Caribbean identity.[48] At the same time, this open process is not without ground, or without connection to place. This moving relationship among different cultural fragments is ultimately "located within social habituses," as Crichlow notes, "but not determined by them."[49]

A History of Creolization in the Caribbean Context

The first instances of creole communities were not lauded for their creative misduplications or for their inventive relationships to social power. Rather, these communities were seen as affronts to social and rational order, insofar as they decentered the principles that chapter 1 of this work detailed as central to the nation-form. Roger D. Abrahams urges us to remember this, particularly in light of the postmodern tendencies of contemporary scholarship that celebrate the creative vibrancy and decentered conceptions of identity intimated in creole phenomena. He writes, "Deep anxieties about disorder and dread of contagion saturate the texts written by observers [of the Creole cultures that were first observed in the seventeenth centuries]. Terms such as 'dunghill,' 'cesspool,' and 'shit-heap' resonate through the early descriptions of those outposts of empire."[50] In the language of Sanín-Restrepo, these cultures signified as those simulacra void of truth and being. Out of a frame that determined such ontological truth in terms of Oneness, loyalty to origin, and the purity of one's relationship to that origin, these early accounts of creole peoples presented their creolizing comportments in terms of human community gone dangerously wrong.

As Sheller's genealogy of the history of creolization points out, the notion of a creole identity both is historically rooted in a Caribbean context *and* has traveled beyond this context to name more diasporic (and perhaps transnational) iterations of postcolonial subjectivity.[51] Nevertheless, all scholarly accounts describe creolization as a commitment to the local informed by the brutality and racial terror of historical processes like the Middle Passage and plantation economy, and as one that persists despite the ways in which such historical brutality complicates one's relationship to "place of origin." But from such accounts, there is also a way to conceptualize creolization as a diasporic phenomenon that speaks to the experience of movements away from homeland and family roots.[52] However, regardless of how one's reading of creolization is situated with respect to the local and the global, creolization is ultimately a creative phenomenon, describing the generative practices of communities who must begin from the memory of radical separation (from a homeland or original territory). In this regard, Crichlow rightly situates creolization along three axes: "creolization generalized, creolization historicized, and creolization dynamized."[53] What she means by this is that, though the concept is grounded in the sociocultural and imaginative specificity of the Caribbean, creolization as "a process that [transcends] an emphasis on its originary places, populations, and spaces" also takes us beyond the local.[54] This gesturing beyond ultimately points to the creative practices—emancipatory in their not being strictly *determined* by the local—that emerge in response to having to be fully local to a place, while negotiating the memory of being from "elsewhere." In this sense, it is difficult to imagine a postcolonial accounting of community, belonging, and, ultimately, nation-ness that does not seriously engage with the phenomenon of creolization.

In short, "[the] term 'creole' is itself unstable" and very much relies on the political itineraries that it serves.[55] This is visible in the history of the phenomenon of the Caribbean creole, which is quite layered. Sometimes the term retains the original sense: that to be creole is to be the white European, estranged from the metropole. At other times, to be creole is to be infiltrated with African culture, African blood, or, more broadly, with what might be considered African ways of being in the world. But no matter which way one is named a product of creolization, one is always no longer "pure" and no longer in a position to legitimately claim a single culture or lifeworld as the causative principle of one's way of being in the world. Most originally, the term "creole" described white French West Indians (*békés*), who were "white [persons] of pure race born in the Antilles."[56] Percy Hintzen notes that, for such "white creoles," their creole status meant that, despite their obvious European blood or lineage, they were more organically connected to the Caribbean islands in which they lived (the place they called "home") than to the European metropole. The "creole" in "white creole" meant that the cultural ways of the islands accounted for who that European was, more so than the culture of the European metropole of her ancestors. In other words, the political and cultural commitments of the white creole was to be found in the Caribbean, which meant that those commitments were already in relation with (under the influence of) the plurality of fragmented identities of a Caribbean place. Even in its original designation, the white creole was already impure, already Africanized, if not with respect to bloodline, then most certainly with respect to culture and comportment.

In tracing this history, Stuart Hall reminds us that, as "creole" referred to "white Europeans born in the colonies . . . who had lived so long in the colonial setting, that they acquired many 'native' characteristics," the term also named the black slave who had acquired the everyday competencies of living in the colony.[57] The creole slave was the slave who was "seasoned" to the abject conditions of plantation life and therefore offered a more attractive and less difficult work tool for the slave master's economic agenda. Hall writes, "The distinction in any 18th-century plantation document . . . between 'Africans' and 'creoles' [assessed] how . . . acclimatized [the slaves were] to the harsh circumstances and rituals of plantation life."[58] Conversely, to *not* be creole indicated that a program of seasoning was needed—an often brutal program of conversion through which the slave became normalized to the necropolitics of the plantation. Hence, in this original usage, "creole" in no way designated a critical stance against the brutality of plantation slavery;

rather, it named a comportment that kept the plantation system unproblematized and even sustained its legitimacy.

Indeed, the historical use of creolization facilitated the racial capitalism out of which the economies of the New World grew. Hintzen makes this clear in his account of the early implications of the "creole nationalism" found in the discourse of the Caribbean region.[59] The white creole residents, who acquired a critical residing mass on the Caribbean islands during the eighteenth and nineteenth centuries, used their creoleness to pose questions that pertained to legitimate belonging and, most importantly, legitimate land ownership on the islands. Pegged against the European white (of the metropole), the *creole* white—as a consequence of being there for so long, and perhaps also as a consequence of being able to trace generational lineages in the Caribbean—had access to more cultural capital in the region. As such, when it came property ownership, the creole white used his status as a basis to argue for his stronger rights to own land and other such resources, relative to his white metropolitan counterpart. This meant that, in the struggle for national sovereignty (in other words, freedom from rule by the monarchs of Europe), the *békés* of the French Antilles enjoyed an elevated political, cultural, and national status. "Creole nationalism came to be associated with a free European peasantry that had prior claims to the territory [which were] linked to a history of land ownership."[60]

These historical foundations of creolization are significant to the extent that they present the creole, and the resulting notion of creole nationalism, as an "in-house fight" between local and metropolitan (white) Europeans. More importantly, this in-house fight retained the racial hierarchy that oiled the machine of the plantation economy and that completely excluded those of African descent from the category of rights-bearing (and landowning) personhood. Hence, its history shows that creolization amounted to very little by way of undoing or problematizing the colonial violence of plantation life. To the contrary, this history of creole nationalist identity shows that creole culture originally worked to *support* a climate of white supremacy: as some scholars of Caribbean creolization point out, to the degree that it was situated along a spectrum between two (European and African) poles, créolité worked to retain the racial hierarchies inherited from a colonial plantation society. This spectral creolization works to reimplement colonial or European racial gradations and, as a consequence, the economic exploitation of non-European-descended peoples. Hintzen writes, "The creole at the European end of the spectrum is always tainted by contact with the 'uncivilized' that has emerged historically as a creation of the European discursive imagination. At the African end, the creole is saved by whiteness from a past rendered 'savage' in the panoptic gaze of the conquering European."[61] On such accounts, creolization does not speak to a critical reimagining of a politics and culture of purity. Rather, it works to enact that discourse, reinforcing the privileges of white purity and the hierarchy between Europe and its (African) other.[62] Such critical accounts of its history establish Caribbean creolization as nothing other than a politics of purity in creole "drag."

Hintzen joins other scholars who identify the creole "European–African" spectrum as alienating at best, or outright violent at worst.[63] This alienation is particularly true for the descendants of East Indian indentured laborers who replaced African slave labor on many Caribbean plantations, beginning in 1838. These Indo-Caribbean communities have a unique relationship to the process of creolization, most notably because, for them, repatriation to the "mother land" of India was, for a long time, part of the discourse that shaped their experience of migration to the Caribbean. Hence, Indo-Caribbean indigeneity was markedly different from Afro-Caribbean indigeneity and was ultimately not part of the Afro-European creole narrative. For this reason, Indo-Caribbean scholars are critical of Caribbean creole culture for its *in*hospitality to their experience (in particular), and ultimately to questions of different orientations to the meaning of Caribbean identity and belonging. They point out that creole nationalism retained binaries for the sake of domination and control and held on to hierarchies that foreclosed the possibility of liberation from colonialism's social order. As Crichlow puts it, "The [creole] political project of nation building, and the rationalities of decolonization, which bestowed full citizenship on all, belied palpable exclusions."[64]

Indeed, from such readings, other than the white creole identity of the *béké*, nothing was really creolized. To the extent that creole nationalism continues to subscribe to "notions of European civilization and African savagery," those categories remain standards of purity against which systems of valuation operate. The absolutely civilized human being is purely white, and the absolutely savage human being is purely African. All else in between acquires a coding in terms of these fixed and, more importantly, *separate and unmixed* binaries. To be sure, empirical mixing has happened in the Caribbean context, which is to say that historically, there has been a hemorrhaging across cultural, ethnic, racial, and linguistic lines. But such phenomena can be, and often are, coexistent with discursive frames that valorize not only the pure but also, more importantly, whiteness. Indeed, the claim central to those critical of Caribbean creole identity is that such empirical mixing has done little to replace these discursive frames of purity and Eurocentricity.[65]

In other words, the effects of certain concrete manifestations of creole discourse are marginalizing insofar as they remain Eurocentric and xenophobic to Europe's other. (Indeed, what can even *count* as Europe's other is specifically circumscribed to Africa and its descendants, leaving out identities like those of the Indo-Caribbean community.) To that end, some nationalisms that claim to be creole undermine projects that aim to disrupt the discursive and material violence of coloniality; also, more actively, these nationalisms have promoted neocolonial systems of oppression and exclusion. However, this seems to have very little to do with creolization (as a discursive force in favor of relation, impurity, and cultural entanglement), and more to do with this Eurocentric strand of creolization (which, one can argue, is not yet really creolization at all). Jane Anna Gordon addresses this in the concluding sections of her book, which offers prospects of creolizing a disciplinary field like political theory.[66] She acknowledges the critical position that many Caribbean scholars of East Indian descent take with respect to creole discourse in the Caribbean. "It has been suggested that these projects [of codifying a national culture of plurality and creoleness] imitated without inverting aspects of colonial societies" and, as such, reinscribed Eurocentric hierarchies at the expense of communities that were never part of the "Africa–Europe" creole spectrum.[67] However, Gordon notes that creolization cannot be what it purports to be (namely, a practice that honors the diversity of political and cultural life) if it is not, at the outset, committed to being always open and never complete. Recall, here, Hall's conception of identity (at the level of the subjective and the cultural) as "impossible." Hence, about concerns like those born out of the experiences of the Indo-Caribbean diasporic community, Gordon suggests that "what is . . . being challenged or rejected [by those concerns] is not the *process of creolization* as much as the way in which its discourses and practices were effectively monopolized and hijacked by a creole elite that set themselves up as idealized [that is to say, static] hybrid exemplifications and gate-keepers in order to interrupt the *ongoing living process* of creolization."[68] That is to say, a creolization that favors stasis, closure, and pure categories (even if those categories are birthed from hybridizing preexisting racial and ethnic categories) has become an antithesis of itself.

We might imagine a creolizing process outside this antithesis: we might ask how the narratives of temporal origin and territorial anchorage that determine the political culture of standard accounts of the nation might themselves be "broken and re-broken, arranged and re-arranged" through the everyday gestures shaped by that creolizing process. We can imagine creolization as a set of practices that points to "the formation of new spatialities and temporalities" beyond the nation-state, and beyond what can be accounted for by calcified national borders.[69] This is not to say that creolization is about denationalization, or that it asks us to replace the national with the global (Glissant's use of creolization to develop a third way between the extremes of generalization and particularism is helpful in this regard). Rather, by keeping creolization within the national frame, we can attend to the way in which local power determines local subject formation. Nevertheless, within (or alongside) these nation-oriented spaces and times are certain "frontier zones or borderlands within the nation."[70] These are what Michaeline Crichlow refers to as "regulatory fractures," liminal spaces and temporalities within the mainstream dominant structures, out of which new performative practices emerge. These performative practices "do not appear to violate existing regulatory frameworks, [but] cannot be said to comply with them either."[71] In this regard, it is possible to imagine creolization as a theoretical accounting for the possibility of new and decolonial articulations of national community *and* national identity. At the very least, it offers an account of how "migrations became the catalyst for fracturing such homogenizing models of national belonging" and thus calls into question those assimilationist or integrationist narratives of the nation-form as somehow absorbing—without *always already* being constitutive of—these creolizing "regulatory fractures."[72]

Alongside this is the question of whether such repurposed, creolizing encounters with time and place render the kind of coherence produced in national communities, or whether such coherence is rendered impossible as a consequence. In this chapter, I hope to make a case for the former. Accordingly, I propose that the creolizing community—for whom time is not linear and place is relational in its signification—does not necessarily need to be "subnational," "anti-national," or nonnational, as scholars such as Paul Gilroy would purport.[73] The following two sections show, instead, that these reimagined conceptions of lineage and geography that we get out of creolization not only result in alternative experiences of *national* identity, belonging, and cultural expression but also generate nonallergic orientations toward difference within the nation-form.

The Role of Origin in Creolizing Spaces

In *Créolité and the Process of Creolization*, Stuart Hall's adoption of translation as the model through which the moving patterns of creole production ought to be conceptualized comes with the warning that "[indeed], 'translation' is suspicious of the language of the return to origins and originary roots as a narrative of culture."[74] That is, the trope of translation calls into question the expectations for and assumption of some cultural "unmoved mover," whose stasis somehow inspires the flux of its copies (the legitimacy of which measures their degree of faithfulness to this core, unchanging origin). Abiding by the metaphysics of the One that was discussed in the preceding chapter, this model of a culturally homogeneous core is what certain rigidly bordered nationalisms would situate as "the first" and most temporally original and thus firmly orienting national time as linear and progressive: linear because, from this model, cultural shifts happen in only one direction (from a past authenticity to future reproductions of that authentic past); and progressive because this model also proposes that, so long as this faithfulness of the future to the past is secured, culture accomplishes better versions of itself over time.

In place of this, creolization asks that cultural production be understood in terms of nonlinear and entangled processes of translation. The temporal relationship between cultural units (indeed, the identity of the units themselves) are much like the turntablist's sonic assemblages, through which she "toys with memory," or, more specifically, with the *linear* time of memory. Of this difference between the linearity of "nation time" and the more entangled temporality of "creole" time," we might turn to Crichlow's account of how creolization expresses "a liminal politics of the nation, [how it describes] the vector that unsettles the spaces [and time] of the nation [as] the 'distracting presence of another temporality that disturbs the contemporaneity of the national present,' disturbs by recalling the trace of a history that is out of time with the nation's historical narrative."[75] As I discussed earlier in this chapter, through her temporal reworking, the turntablist calls into question the possibility of locating the origin of the sonic narrative, since her manipulations entangle "original" and "copies" in ways that undermine the very meaning of these categories. In the words of John Szwed, "[While] it may be possible to identify the history and sources of individual components [of the creolized artifact], when put into use new combinations and totalities come into being that have no apparent specific relationship to their historical sources."[76]

Hence, creolization issues a turning back to history but avoids using history for essentialist purposes. Instead, the process unlocks new ways of framing the future that are for the sake of concrete and present exigencies in communities whose history produces these exigencies. Edward Kamau Brathwaite's description of Caribbean identity (its unity) as "submarine" is a poignant metaphor through which we might understand a creolizing encounter with time, origin, and beginning.[77] In naming the source or grounding of such unity as submarine, Brathwaite conveys the sense in which, to the extent there are Caribbean roots to be named, they are roots with depth and dynamism. As submarine, the meaning of Caribbean identity moves as the ocean does, and in that movement, Caribbean-ness undergoes what we would imagine to be the experience of roots that are deeply submerged in the ocean—they becomes entangled with that which is other, and they partly decompose so as to *give to* that which is other. The ocean, in Brathwaite's metaphor, is in this sense a medium for both dissolution (such that things divest from their original form) and retention (things remain with themselves—atoms remain in the water column forever).[78] Hence, Brathwaite calls his readers to find, in the meaning of Caribbean identity, the depth of history right alongside the change and exchange of the cultural contact. That contact constantly transforms Caribbeanness into iterative versions of itself as it retains the historical depth of the submarine. Submarine roots, in other words, are as anchoring and unifying as they are fluid and moving.

So the drowned origins of a Caribbean history allow for new temporalities to emerge through creolization's cultural and social geneses. The complex (nonlinear) organization of temporality at the center of these geneses also ultimately "[raises] questions about the appropriateness of such concepts as 'descent' [and] 'origins'" when it comes to the newness of the creole product.[79] We are reminded here of Lisa Guenther's reading of Orlando Patterson's conception of natal alienation in the sociocultural structures of plantation life.[80] In Guenther's account, kinship shelter was the means through which one accessed a heritage. Because part of the brutality of chattel labor was the denial of such shelter (through the natal alienation of the slave mother from her children), slave communities invented their own kin structures. The violence of the plantation economy meant that these invented kin structures did not follow lines of descent or bloodline. But as a consequence, they were also neither determined by nor tethered to descent or bloodline. Through these inventive kin relations, heritage was not simply a preservation of one's history, but a more complex and emergent process of *creating* the narrative of a history for the sake of forging a future in which one might find the possibility of human dignity. In the end, producing essentialist constructions of collective identity was *not* the purpose of returning traces of the past in these creative productions of kinship shelter.

Walter Mignolo reminds us that coloniality depends on a particular construction of time as both linear and progressive. As such, creolization's disruption of such a temporal ordering can be read for its transgressive aspects as well. Mignolo writes (quoting Diana Hugh), "[Modernity/coloniality] established modern Europe as the present by creating the 'otherness of the past and the past of the other.' . . . It has served as the justification of the ideology of progress and, in the twentieth century, of development and underdevelopment."[81] Coloniality's presiding organization of the globe in terms of racial hierarchy simultaneously locates these hierarchical differences in hierarchical time phases. *Humanitas*, or European man, participates in a future-oriented march of culture, morality, and political sovereignty, while *Anthropos*, or the colonized and colonizable wretched of the earth, remained frozen in cultural, moral, and (non)political primitiveness. Colonial time meant that what was outside Europe remained in a permanent time-lag *behind* Europe as well, so that progress became a measure of how far from this primitive past Europe's *humanitas* could situate itself. Ultimately, colonial time established Europe's geography as the site of the future fulfillment of what was truly human (or truly valuable to being human).

In more fascist uptakes of colonial temporality (and of colonialism's politics of absolute difference and racial hierarchy), the future was about a "vision of a radically new beginning which [often] follows a period of destruction or perceived dissolution."[82] Though on first glance this seems to be a valorization of the past that stands at odds with the colonial rendering of the past as "degraded/primitive otherness," the fascist commitment to "beginning again" does retain the temporal hierarchy that Mignolo outlines. Insofar as the call to begin again is really about restoring some lost or destroyed cultural purity, which was (or so the claim goes) infected by the presence of a racialized other who signifies in terms of temporal underdevelopment, the fascist commitment to starting over comes down to rescuing the trajectory of the future from the weight of antiprogress (the very dead weight of and in time), embodied in the *Anthropos*. It is on this purging of the future's "other" that the future is able to deliver on the colonially constituted promise of progress.

In her turn to Homi Bhabha, Crichlow reminds us of the need for another organizational frame with which to not only theorize modern spaces and global contact but also, more significantly, theorize the possibility of new and decolonial engagements with the nation-form. She writes, "Bhabha argues that what is 'politically crucial' is the need to think beyond the narratives of originary and initial subjectivities and to focus on the moments or processes that are produced in the articulation of cultural differences. These 'in-between' spaces [within the nation-form] provide the terrain for elaborating strategies of selfhood—singular or communal—that initiate new signs of identity, and innovative sites of collaboration, and contestation, in the act of defining the idea of [national] society."[83] In other words, creolizing processes approach the relationship between the past and future in a radically alternative way, so they point toward "innovative" engagements with modern power out of which newness might emerge. For one, artifacts of creolizing sensibilities (culture, linguistic expressions and inflections, religious practices) do recall the past; thus, the past is not a marker for antiprogression, underdevelopment, or the absence of human culture. But second, the past is recalled precisely for the sake of opening it up onto syncretic future iterations that situate themselves beyond the significations of strict descent, or faithfulness to origins. In other words, the past is maintained, coevally, *not* in order to absolutize it and thus provide some essentializing ground for authentic futures. Rather, the door is left open for past customs to undergo generative translations in everyday gestures. Out of creolizing practices, cultural forms register as "improvisations that embody the new and old in new situations."[84] In those improvisional and translated iterations, past and future circle into a complex web of present life. The future does not signify for the sake of its capacity to remain authentic to a past origin, and the past does not signify in terms of essential roots to be preserved. Temporal modes interlace with each other, such that each presents as a trace of itself already within the translational movement of the creole relationship. In this sense, we might say that a creolizing temporality replaces linear time with something (to anticipate my discussion of Glissant in chapter 3) rhizoming and lattice-like.

To reiterate, the historical specificity out of which such creolizing temporalities emerge is one of rupture and dislocation. It is in this sense that John Drabinski describes a theory of creolization (and Glissant's particular adoption of this theory in his work) as a mode of thinking after the trauma of the Middle Passage. "Forced migration (the Middle Passage) and enslavement (the plantation) radically alter all senses of relation to the past, and so too any senses of the future. This experience demands explorations on its own terms."[85] With the trauma of historical rupture at its center, creolization demands a temporality that replaces the linear time of the traditional nation-form with something else. Hence, this temporal latticework, consisting of translations and inventive interpretations, is necessitated by the fact—in the Caribbean context—of historical rupture. This context of historical rupture means that there is no intact, preserved-in-its-original-form account of a past to which creolizing societies might turn. As a consequence, theirs is not a lifeworld organized around narratives of pure beginnings; the ruptures in question are too radical for such narratives to apply. One might be inclined to suggest that those homages to African origins (of which there are many in cultures across the Caribbean archipelago) say otherwise. But, to return to my earlier account, such retentions of past forms are already by way of syncretism. That is to say, the past is always made anew in its present and refashioned form for the future, and in that refashioning, has already become inflected with forms that are "other" to it and that transform it into a relational plurality all its own. Hence, in all, the temporal organization underlying creolizing processes is invariably resistant to strict temporal boundaries, temporal purities, and the temporal linearity that might allow a community to anchor its sense of self into a homogeneous cultural center.[86]

Bhabha's analysis of cultural difference raises this question of homogeneous cultural cores, for the purpose of identity construction in the postcolonial age. However, his work is of use to us as we develop the time of creolizing community formations. In particular, his conception of ambivalence as it pertains to the relationship between cultural "sameness" and "otherness" is something that, when applied to how processes of creolization entangle past and future, offers a helpful conceptual framework to the project of creolizing the nation. Bhabha writes that, for modes of identity that are born out of experiences of migration and diasporic belonging, identity ought to be understood as a movement between "an interstitial space of identification."[87] This means that, through these modes of living and navigating political, social, and cultural spaces, identity is produced in the order of a doubling/splitting, or as a multiplicity within the interiority of the same. *How* that identity is experienced is between the spaces of those split "terms." This is different from an account of alienation, or of finding oneself in a relation of dis-resemblance to oneself. The doubling and splitting coming out of Bhabha's account make for identity terms that border each other proximally, which is to say that one is in the other in a way that is neither fusion nor schizophrenia. Bhabha will go on to name these identity constructions of postcolonial migrations "minority identities," citing them as loci of movement and becoming, all of which happens in the "in-between," that proximal space of difference.[88]

Hall's conception of identity-as-impossibility is recalled here; the only difference is that Bhabha's development seems informed by contemporary migratory patterns between regions of the global majority and the metropoles of Europe (and perhaps the United States as well). Hall, on the other hand, offers his account of the impossible closure of identification processes to make sense of societies (primarily throughout the Caribbean region) that are marked by creolization. Nevertheless, when Bhabha urges his reader to note the importance of "[acknowledging] the ambivalence within any site of identification," he seems to gesture toward Hall's claim that "identities [in the midst and aftermath of global colonialism] are constructed through, not outside, difference."[89] Outside the field of difference, the subject named by Bhabha's minority identity shows up as the simulacra—as an incidental deviation of subvalue alongside a stably homogeneous (and therefore inherently valuable) cultural core. In other words, assumptions of a center of identity (individual or communal) that is *not* produced through difference is a first premise in those arguments for discursive (or material) programs of purging that have often come out of nationalist and imperialist identity constructions. On the other hand, acknowledging such difference-independent fantasies as a dis-avowal of the "ambivalence within any site of identification" would serve as a first premise of an account of community as "multivalent and ambivalent networks," in which distinctions between "majority and minority" culture, as well as past and future ways of being, become productively blurred.[90]

We might bring this to bear on the question of creole temporality, and propose that creolization—in its proximal relationship to ambivalence, split-ting, and doubling—asks us to replace the time of purity with the time of proximity—a creole time. This temporal entanglement complicates one's relation to a time of origin, as well as the relationship between (collective) memory and recollection. This complication is similar to what, in Bhabha's minority identity, signifies in the ambivalent interlacing of identity and differ-ence, and is positioned in clear contrast to the "proper relations between past and future" found at the heart of certain xenophobic and closed-off articu-lations of nationalist collectivity.[91] Particularly from Paul Gilroy's discussion of diaspora communities, it is evident that the temporality shaping creolizing processes resonates with the ways in which diaspora formations trouble the nationalist articulation of linear time. Both ways of being in community (dias-poric and creolizing) produce tension in this linear temporality, so it is impor-tant to make clear how a project to creolize the nation might be both similar to and different from the structures of a diasporic experience of nation. In tracing this relationship, I will focus on the ways in which the experience of collective time are determined by diasporic and creole communities, respec-tively. I should also point out that in this trace there are also implications for the experience of collective place.

How might the notion of diaspora be different from a society born out of creolization? As Gilroy himself points out, the experience of diaspora pertains to a rift between "location of residence and location of belonging."[92] What this means is that my affiliation with a collective (across racialized experi-ence, cultural comportment, language, or religion) is not limited to—and, more importantly, complicates and renders existentially incomplete—the "here" of my abode. In her own work, Sheller cites Gilroy's project as one shaped by political stakes of "[freeing] the theory of creolization from its nationalist connotations by applying it to the diasporic experience" of black lifeworlds.[93] Hence, on Gilroy's account, those who understand them-selves to belong to a Caribbean diaspora locate a vital piece of the narra-tive of their belonging beyond the place and space in which they carry out their concrete, everyday lives. This is because diaspora belonging, and the comportments of community it grounds, combine the "here" and the "there" in a way that crisscross patterns of migration, flight, and exile, and even certain contemporary instances of forced transplantation.[94] My reading of creolization squarely locates the implications of the process (the translations, cultural syncretisms, the identity formations that happen *in* difference) in the local, or the "here." In other words, though there is important conceptual dialogue between creolizing practices and diasporic societies, emphasis on the intimacy and everydayness of the local is key in my proposal to creolize the nation. Simply put, my proposal uncovers the consequences of the complexities that shape those "locations of residence," when that location must become indigenous to those communities for whom historical rupture from (actual or imagined) homelands compels them to generate inventive modes of living within the confines of where they physically are. To underscore this significance of the local, we might borrow Ana Cara and Robert Baron's warning against conflating creolizing processes with processes of transnationalism. They write, "[Creolized societies] were not becoming transnational; they were creating forms by which to live, even while they were being cruelly tested physically and mentally" by the *local* structures of adversity.[95] We might even say that, through creolization, we encounter the meaning of the local and concrete implications of diasporic entanglements, implications that are full of inventive capacities for making life new and anew.

Nonetheless, despite this difference, there are similarities through which we can better understand how creole temporality reimagines an experience of collective time in ways that are more conducive to free life at the level of the concrete. Both notions of diaspora and creolizing communities work to "[reject] the popular image of natural nations," which ground themselves on a movement of time that goes from past origin to a morally, culturally, and politically progressive future.[96] Both present a more complex relationship between "then" and "now," which (as discussed earlier) also reveal a complex relationship between "same" and "different."[97] And last, both diaspora and creolization "[disturb] the suggestion that political and cultural identity might be understood via the analogy of indistinguishable peas lodged in the protective pods of closed kinship."[98] Hence, like creolization, diaspora living testifies to the inadequacy of conceiving identity as fixed, of conceiving cultural cores as homogeneous and unchanging, and, most importantly, of locating difference outside the making and unfolding of identity.

It should be noted that, in Gilroy's analysis of diasporic life, he presents diaspora as "outer-national," and sometimes even as "*anti*-national" in its transcultural aspects.[99] Given the ways that diaspora and creolization similarly trouble the temporal constitution of the nation, would an account of diaspora as beyond (behind, or other than) the nation-form undermine the possibility of creolizing the nation? In other words, *can* the nation be creolized, if, like the diasporic, the outcomes of creolization must necessarily gesture toward what the nation is not?

Diaspora is where we find the "fragile stability" of chaotic nodes of identity constructions and emergent relations.[100] And as we have already seen, all of this complicates my relation to moments of origin, inserts ambiguity into my sense of belonging in relation to my place of residence, and calls for fluid entanglements between identity and difference. Is it possible to locate such complications (which Gilroy describes as "non-national" and "anti-national") *within* the space and time of the nation? Might the "non-" and the "anti-" of Gilroy's framing convey too dichotomous a picture of the relationship between the nation and its "other," or between dominant cultural forms and its "other" (to return to Bhabha's account of minority identities)? To think beyond this dichotomy calls for a sense of chaotic and moving borders, porous and yielding in their sectioning off of "identity" and "difference," such that we truly are able to account for what Gilroy himself describes as the diasporic "sameness within differentiation and differentiation within sameness."[101] This more complex organization would allow for a more complex picture of the creolizing relationality between same and other (in general), and ultimately between national and (what Gilroy names) "anti-national" articulations of community.

To that end, the task of creolizing the nation prioritizes this need to complicate our understanding of what national community *is*, so that we can conceptualize the "anti-national" as precisely what must always be part of the nation's space (territory) and time (the story of its origins). In so doing, we encounter the nationalist's territorial and temporal imaginaries of rigidity and stability as always coming "too late," as it were, in response to the dynamic and moving stability of what the nation actually is. In other words, the nation itself can *be as* iterations of itself—it can be its "impossible identity"—if those diasporic articulations, or those creolizing forces are understood as constitutive disruptions of the nation.[102]

The Role of Place in Creolizing Spaces

The temporal negotiations marking the inventiveness of creolizing practices also call our attention to the ways in which a creolizing experience includes alternative navigations of the space (geography) of the nation. In this section, I aim to make clear how these alternative navigations might be used to complicate the nation-form's conception of place or territory. To return to their essay in praise of creoleness, Bernabé and his coauthors account for the creolizing entanglement throughout the Caribbean archipelago as what is "united on the same soil by the yoke of history."[103] This articulation seems to bridge, in telling and significant ways, the temporal and spatial comportments of creole practices (on the one hand) and that of nation-ness (on the other). Chapter 1 of this work showed the ways in which soil (places of beginning, or anchorage) is at the heart of national identity. We also saw that the closed unity of the nation was deeply invested in this narrative of an original soil, and in a national memorialization of such original soil. Are we to hear, in Bernabé's descriptions of a creole "unity on the same soil," similar nationalist narratives of territoriality? Or is it that, in grounding creole societies in a "diversality" instead of a universality, Bernabé and others seek to reimagine the significance of a soil-specific unity? To be sure, included in the spirit of creolizing lifeworlds is the intimacy of one's relation to the local, and perhaps to the *soil* of the local. In other words, the "here" of the creolizing process is key, since, as the historical context has shown, processes of creolization are really about a community becoming indigenized to their immediate, every-day environment.[104] To be sure, this indigeneity is both forced and neces-sary, which is to say that it emerges out of the brutality of historical rupture constitutive of European colonialism. Nonetheless, creoleness directs us to the intimate places where the creolized collective finds itself. The soil—its geography, foliage, aesthetic, and the like—matter at this intimate level of cultural negotiation and world-making. Hence, it is all the more necessary to determine how the signification of local place, in the context of creolization, fares in comparison to the role of place in the context of nationalism.[105]

Hall writes that créolité "has always been about cultural, social, and lin-guistic *mixing* rather than about racial *purity*."[106] In other words, the process of creolization places the emphasis on the moving syncretisms that happens within the confines of the local (on the soil that localizes the creolizing pro-cess), rather than on any possible legitimating capacities of that soil. Hence, there is an attunement to place—to the local and everyday gestures that transgress the hegemonies that make such inventions necessary—that does not have any authenticating function (does not differentiate authentic from inauthentic belonging). In the absence of such differentiation (gatekeeping, really), this attunement to place signifies as something other than the nation-alist narrative of original soil. These narratives are born out of desires to dis-avow those "minority differences" within national political culture, and their authenticating functions either presuppose or seek to bring into existence the kind of static collective identity that is problematized in the moving cultural syncretism that Hall references. So though geography, soil, and becoming indigenous to soil are part of the creolizing story, all three aspects are for the sake of a de-essentializing conception of collective identity and culture, and for a de-essentialized signification of place. To return again to Drabinski's for-mulation: out of creolization, we find the possibility of both "an anticolonial defense of place [and] a postcolonial articulation of place."[107]

In his account of creole languages, or, rather, the creolizing process through which such linguistic adaptations emerge, Szwed captures the radical nature of these adaptations. "[Linguistic] creolization involves the merging and dissolving of language images, the ambiguous play of language forms and meanings, of forms and styles, *all decentered* with no clear sense of which language is primary or foregrounded, all maintained . . . with no apparent fixed boundaries . . . or of nonshared syntaxes."[108] What Szwed notes of these linguistic phenomena mirrors social and cultural artifacts of creolization as well, so we see that, as a process, creolization contests structures of place that presuppose the stasis of being, as well as those static borders that condition the possibility of rigid and permanent divisions within being. Processes of becoming replace being, and porous event horizons replace borders.[109] We saw, in the preceding section on creole time, how such alternatively under-stood temporal boundaries allow creole practices to maintain tradition in its futurity, or "new" cultural comportments alongside the preservation of old ones. How do similarly reimagined spatial boundaries facilitate creolizing conceptions of place, and shape the implications of belonging to that place?

To better understand such implications, we might turn to Edward Casey's work on edges, in which he offers a reading of borders as impenetrable, and boundaries as porous and malleable.[110] Casey notes that, unlike bor-ders (in their impenetrability), it is the boundary that is "often [an] integral [member] of entire life-worlds, cultural as well as natural," since impene-trable borders act as "artificial intrusions into [these lifeworlds]."[111] On this account, a boundary's "fit" into a lifeworld is a consequence of its being able to facilitate motion, or the dynamism of systems, practices, and phenomena pertaining to that lifeworld. This would mean that the boundary ought to be understood not only as a region of relation and movement but also as a perpetual adjustment of itself, or as a becoming-other-to-itself so as to make such movement possible. On the other hand, the border functions as rigid and unchanging. It is invariably foreign to the spaces that bear its location, since its stasis is diametrically opposed to the living dynamism of those spaces and therefore disruptive of the moving processes of which those spaces consist. In his account of the political operation of La Frontera, Casey notes that, in almost all of their senses, borders have an "underside" through which they come to act in the capacity of porous boundaries. In other words, within the lifeworlds they occupy, the impenetrable border almost always manifests in terms of its own failure to remain perfectly impenetrable. Of that particular border wall, Casey writes, "However fiercely defended or surveyed it may be, the border wall at La Frontera cannot stanch altogether the flow of land animals and humans."[112] Hence, in the midst of its functioning as a border, this wall at the violently constituted edges of Mexico and the United States is also a boundaried locus of porosity, facilitating transactions of the human and nonhuman kind. Casey uses this political phenomenon to postulate that, in the end, borders "are *built to be breached* . . . [bringing] about their own demise as if by a subtle form of self-destruction."[113]

This conception of the border and its "double" (the border in terms of its becoming-other-to-itself) is pertinent to the rich metaphors within creolist literature, as scholars grapple with the structural challenges to language and imagery that creolizing practices produce. To be sure, these metaphors have temporal resonance, but I focus here on how they call for a reworking of the ways in which we assume things to be arranged in the space of place. More specifically, they are metaphors that work through how subjects themselves force space to remap itself as they use creolizing practices to make place for themselves. This figures prominently in Crichlow's account of creolizing processes—the ways in which, via creolization, spaces constituted in terms of matrices of modern power are "appropriated" for uses not determined by that power, and *by* subjects not legitimized by that power. She writes that, alongside state-sanctioned configurations of space and presence, resisting subjects are always in the process of "homing" themselves through the "tributaries of creolization."[114] In this account, Crichlow shows that space itself (how it comes to signify) is transformed through this homing process, which is to say that the spatiality of the nation is *determined* not only by structures of power and modern governmentality but also by the results of "[postcolonial subjects] *wrestling* with the conditions for expressing place and moving one's place-in-time."[115] It is through this wrestling by subjects at the level of everyday that the border becomes its double, and space becomes immanently other to itself.

Of course, this all happens against (under) the constraints of modern power. To underscore this important point, Crichlow calls her readers' attention to the slave art form of limbo. "[The] spatiotemporal dimension of the process of creolization calls forth the limboing strategy of 'making place' which is the basis for subjects negotiating their differences across the spaces [under the bar] of hegemony and its silences of nonidentity. Limbo symbolizes here . . . the liminal process of transformation by negotiating space through chains of power; of making space where there is little or none, and transforming constraint into *degrees* of freedom."[116] Through this metaphor, Crichlow calls us to not only think creolization in terms of embodied, everyday practices that are in contesting relationships to power, but to also think about the effects of those "chains of power" on embodied subjects as never quite as totalizing as they intend to be (or to say this differently, as a totality out of which an affirmation can still emerge out of a space of negation). "Limbo is thus deeply symbolic of the liminal process of change being articulated in the practices of creolization," through which new and emergent relations to power reconstitute the enactment and meaning of national space.[117]

These new modalities that emerge out of processes of creolization evidence a conception of place that is not unitary and total unto itself but, rather, constitutive of "tributaries" and liminal sites. Much like my proposal for how we might more productively read the anti- and nonnational to be internal movements of the nation's discursive and cultural architecture, "creolizing place" offers a conception of place that is transient and contesting within and onto itself. Ultimately, metaphors like "amalgam," "spectrum," and "kaleidoscope" (to name a few) are often employed to convey this sense of movement and multiplicity in creolizing encounters with space. In creole societies, "two or more formerly discrete cultures [are conjoined] in a new setting to create a social order in which heterogeneous styles, structures, and contexts are differentially preserved while becoming wholly constituted in and adapted to new circumstances, with new and multi-faceted meanings."[118] Robert Baron traces the use of these metaphors, noting that the very methodology of "exploration-through-metaphor" points to the "lexical gap" encountered in attempts to precisely define what creolization *is*.[119] I would further add that this gap in language rests on a more fundamental ontological gap, which points to the kinds of poetics and politics "otherwise" grounded in creolizing practices.

The metaphor of the prism is used to convey the ways in which the discrete components of the creole artifact are only ambiguously distinct from each. Much like the relational web among "distinct" colors in a refracted beam of light, the ancestral pieces of the creole product "mix in a spectrum" that is neither linear nor stable. Baron writes, "[A] prismatic conceptualization of creolization . . . offers an alternative to a linear approach to the interaction of cultures [since] the colors refracted through a prism mix in a spectrum . . . that is not fixed, rigid or predictable."[120] In this imagery, the idea of a plurality organized in terms of discretely bordered units is replaced with a spectrality within which the beginning of one unit ambiguously blends into the end of another. We can imagine this prismatic metaphor deploying Edward Casey's understanding of the porous and self-differentiating boundary to capture the spectral blending among its units.[121] Additionally, because the creole artifact is always incomplete, always open to entering into relations with other products (open, in other words, to emerging as a different kind of entity), metaphors of oscillation are paired to that of the prism to capture creole outcomes as "interactional and transactional [aggregates]" or "emergent rather than fixed entities."[122] The oscillation metaphor conveys a necessary unpredictability of the variations involved in the creolizing process.

In a similar vein, metaphors of coalescing ("[coming] together, so as to form one [without] necessarily [entailing] the loss of identity of individual components"), and telescoping (where "one thing fits or slides into another, as in the tubes of a telescope") all grapple to illustrate the alternative organizations of place and borders called for by processes of creolization.[123] More importantly, these metaphors struggle with the new (fluid, emergent, non-dichotomous) ways in which creolization arranges "same" with respect to "other." If edges are round and borders are really porous boundaries, then that which is "other" is already part of the same, liminally and perhaps also disruptively so. On this account, culture is an open-ended negotiation with what is both here and elsewhere, with what is both territorially grounded and "yet to come." Hence, though the creole experience of place is one connected to soil, it is also one of movement and constant negotiation within the local-ness of that soil. This invites a reimagining of "the symbolic organization of space, place, and political community," which in turn generates the possibility of thinking about national community otherwise.[124]

Creolizing spaces are most known for their cultural plurality. Indeed, the process emerges when the cultures coming into contact are foreign both to each other and to the space in which they find themselves. The process is about diverse lifeworlds and ways of being finding themselves in an unavoidable web of relationality, too far removed from their respective homelands to facilitate return, and too closely interconnected with a new place to avoid an inevitable home-making. It is precisely this "home-making" that happens as creolizing societies determine the codes through which coexistence happens. It is also important to recognize the resistance to colonial conflict and violence that serves as the backdrop of these creative home-making practices. Failing to do so would amount to "the appropriation of creolization as a universal signifier of border-transcending cultural confluence and a tame term for multicultural mixture [divorced from questions of power, resistance, and survival]."[125] In other words, the alternative spatiotemporal orderings of community life and alternative modes of living with difference that emerge in creolization are not simply about generating new lifeworlds; rather, they are about the grounding of that newness in an oppositional, everyday politics that survives alongside and despite those master codes of violence.

Out of these resistive and grassroots practices, subjects make a place for themselves. In the words of Rex Nettleford, these practices represent a "two-pronged phenomenon of decolonization and creolization. . . . [They represent] the awesome processes actualized in simultaneous acts of negating and affirming, demolishing and constructing, rejecting and reshaping" circuits of colonial power.[126] In addition, despite the perpetual motion involved in the construction of identity as decentered (as ongoing process, or as "profoundly incoherent"), and despite the moving boundaries that simultaneously separate and entangle self and other (old and new), creole life is not merely one of uncanny malaise or disruption. Ambivalence, in this creole context, does not generate existential dissonance. To the contrary, these dynamic cultural adjustments serve as "hearth" conditions for the communities in question. In other words, there is every sense in which creolizing spaces are homely spaces, consisting of indigenized peoples who enact the kind of investment that one might expect from a community in relation to what (and where) they consider home.

This has important implications for the "nation" question. In particular, it opens onto the question of finding the kind of collective coherence within creolizing societies, which might mirror the coherence of the nation without replicating its stasis and xenophobia. At the heart of this question is whether or not "nation" (as an acknowledgeable social whole) can remain subsequent to creolizing it. In the chapters comprising parts 2 and 3 of this book, I bring the concept of creolization into engagement with the work of key thinkers in the Latina feminist tradition, using their conceptualizations of identity, community, and belonging to pursue such questions. In preparation for this engagement, however, chapter 3 offers Édouard Glissant's use of creolization to establish such a possibility—the possibility of thinking community as both creolizing and coherent, as both "*chaos monde* and *toute monde.*"[127] That is to say, Glissant's notion of the composite community—and the rhizome model that he uses to ground this notion—deploys creolization in a way that suggests that, indeed, as alternatively imagined, "nation" can persist *as creolizing*.

Part 2

can we sustain the current definition of "nation" if it were to be creolized?

Part 2

✦

Living Ambiguously

Intersections between Creolization and Latina Feminisms

In proposing to decenter homogeneity, single territory, and linear time in conceptions of the nation-form, I am ultimately in search of ways of being a self, and of being in community with others, which resists the closure, essentialism, and stasis in standard accounts of national identity. Chapters 3 and 4 bring the work coming out of the Latina feminist tradition into conversation with Édouard Glissant's use of creolization because, on my reading, both bodies of scholarship pursue questions that echo those most central to the task of creolizing the nation. Additionally, in offering creolization for engagement with Latina feminist formulations, this part works across intellectual traditions that are often, and to our *own* intellectual detriment, kept apart. In attempting a corrective to this, this section develops a dialogue between Glissant and the work of thinkers like Gloria Anzaldúa, María Lugones, and Mariana Ortega (to name a few). In her reading of Anzaldúa's work, Ortega notes a tension in Anzaldúa's attempts to give an account of her lived experience that "includes both multiplicity and a sense of oneness."[1] There are clear echoes here of the ontological stakes at the foundation of processes of creolization, which point to an important (though, as the literature exists, absent) dialogue between a thinker like Anzaldúa (for instance) and a creolist like Glissant.[2] Chapter 3 shows that in Glissant's account of the rhizome, there is a central theme of how "many" can reside in "one"—many as and in one—as "neither fusion nor confusion" (or, in the context of community, neither reductive assimilation nor an incommensurable identity politics). In their expositions of navigating U.S. neocolonial domination, scholars working in the Latina feminist tradition have developed existential and deeply political analytics that innovatively grapple with similar complexities. This is particularly true in frameworks used to capture the experience of belonging ambiguously and the sense of community formation that is both grounded in history and open to the transformations that might provide plural conceptions of the human.

To be sure, the Latina feminist work on which chapter 4 focuses is invested in a kind of resistance that is more explicitly political relative to the cultural and discursive subversions I foreground in chapter 3's treatment of Glissant. Later—in chapter 6, where I bring Glissant into conversation with Frantz Fanon's explicitly political project—I say more about how this project of creolizing the nation understands the intersection between the political and the cultural/discursive. However, in as early as chapter 3's account of his analysis of the Caribbean, I lay the groundwork for the claim that Glissant's new imaginary and poetics includes very explicit causative implications for radical political change. Even when scholars like Anzaldúa, Lugones, and Ortega trace the conditions for the possibility of a coalitional politics of resistance, there is also a sensitivity to the poetic, imaginative, and even spiritual; practices (in the particular case of Anzaldúa's work) that imbue the political with meaning. For instance, Anzaldúa describes her understanding of the new mestiza consciousness to be "participating in the creation of yet another culture, a new story to explain the world and our participation in it."[3] It is clear that the intimate negotiations involved in creolizing practices are also about articulating this "new story" that will then ground new modes of everyday participation in the world. That is to say, the stakes of this new story have political resonance as well. Colonial dehumanization happens in and out of every crevice of human experience. As such, poetic creations of new realities—cultural-discursive inventiveness, new ways of imagining ourselves (or of insisting *on* ourselves)—will invariably shape the possibility of political resistance (resistance to the totality of colonial violence). Resistance would have to be found in the recesses of intimate spaces, quotidian spaces that infiltrate at the level of private sensibilities and personal proclivities. We might resist through the patterns of our breath, and in so doing, articulate another moment of usurping power.

Creolizing the nation thinks through resistance (and through the nature of the dominations to be resisted) in these terms. What, in concrete instances of creolizing engagements with the social world, resists the old and imagines new determinations of social coherence, cultural identity, and human relationality? The following two chapters show how Glissant's conception of creolization intersect with certain politico-existential stakes in what Anzaldúa develops in her mestiza consciousness and nepantla, or what Lugones articulates through her conception of world-traveling, plural selfhood, and street-walker tactical strategies. I also offer for consideration how we might take the idea of creolizing the nation into conversation with Ortega's account of multiplicitous selves engaging in hometactics. In short, I am interested in possibilities of engagement between (a) Glissant as a scholar who works in the register of creolization in order to name the kinds of antiessentialist and fluid modes of being, and being-with, and (b) scholars grounded in a Latina feminist tradition that pursues the meaning of existing in the aftermath of neo-imperialist oppression, cultural erasure, and material theft. Both areas work with possibilities of belonging, cultural complexity, and identity formation in the aftermath of colonial rupture. For both modes of theorization, fragmentation matters, contradiction matters, and one's ambiguous relationship to colonial hegemonic formations matters.

At the same time, it is important to account for the significant divergences between these two intellectual orientations. For one, these divergences will matter to the extent that they point to important difference(s) between two modes of displacement, and perhaps also to the political implications of these two modes. One such mode—framing Glissant's creolist conceptions—captures the experience of being displaced in a geographical location that is birthplace. This experience is of the subject whose native-ness to a place is grounded in multiple generations but is nonetheless one of displacement in that place, as a consequence of the colonial arrangements of power, subject constitution, and economy that persist in the afterlife of colonial occupation and settlement. The other mode—framing more contemporary migratory patterns constitutive of postcoloniality—speaks to either finding oneself in a location *other than* one's birthplace, or in a location other than the birthplace of one's recent ancestry (parents, grandparents). To be sure, this mode of displacement emerges through colonial and neo-imperial settler logics. But, unlike creole experiences of forced indigeneity and belonging ambiguously, this latter experience is imbued with world-relations constituted by neocolonial globalization, national border constructions, and liberal conceptions of citizenship that generate possibilities of citizenship in the margins. The displacements that frame Latina feminist conceptions foreground liminalities of subject constitutions and community formations that emerge in a neocolonial era invisibly shaped through the creolizing practices of colonialism and empire.

Chapters 3 and 4 will attend to such differences as they note the rich possibilities in bringing into dialogue these two ways of grappling with home, belonging, and conceptions of self. More importantly, bringing the two camps into conversation would only augment what I aim to do—gather a poetics that might disrupt and reframe the everyday practices of nation-ness. This section only begins such a dialogue between creolization and Latina feminist thought; the breadth of theories and scholars included is by no means exhaustive of who (and what) ought to be part of such an engagement. However, it starts this dialogue in response to a curious absence of one.

Chapter 3

✦

On Glissant's Creolization

Our science is detour and coming-and-going.
—Édouard Glissant, *Tout-Monde*

In both *Caribbean Discourse* (1991) and *Poetics of Relation* (1990), Édouard Glissant presents an analysis of Caribbean history anew, and offers a reading of the geography particular to that region as one that gestures toward a radically different ontology (toward a thinking of "being" otherwise). I devote this chapter to Glissant's theory of a Caribbean imaginary for two reasons. First, the methodology he employs situates his ontological positions in lived experience. To that end, the ontology he develops is one that is existential, returning philosophy's grand narratives to how truth is encountered in concrete experience (or to how truth is lived). And second, his work offers the most compelling case for the political and cultural significance of creolization: it is out of Glissant's theorizing of the Caribbean that the concept of creolization is used to think critically (and differently) about identity, difference, and about how we wrestle with that pre-Socratic problem of the One versus the Many.

In the essay "Reversion and Diversion," Glissant opens as follows: "There is a difference between transplanting (by exile or dispersion) of a people who continue to survive elsewhere and the transfer (by the slave trade) of a population to another place where they change into something different, into a new set of possibilities. It is in this [latter] metamorphosis that we must try to detect one of the best kept secrets of creolization."[1] In this vein, Glissant's project of remaining faithful to the concreteness of the Caribbean's past arrives at creolization as the frame and methodology out of which that region might be theorized. Throughout his novels and theoretical essays, this itinerary holds strong—framing, within the conceptual grid of creolization, the emergence of newness in the place of the Caribbean, and thinking through how this emergence is conditioned by the historical trauma of the Middle Passage and its attending violences. That is to say, creolization, for Glissant, is as much about the generation of new cultural forms and relations as it is about the history of rupture that produces the conditions for such creolizing practices. His work, then, acknowledges the significance of the place of the Caribbean (that particular locality and relation to history) as he brings the implications of that place into a more global conversation.

Hence, much of Glissant's approach to creolization is anchored in the transatlantic trading of Africans into chattel slavery. Out of this history of intergenerational horror, and the drowning of persons and memory (what John Drabinski describes as the catastrophic trauma of losing even the *privilege* of loss), one would imagine an aftermath of a radical absence of life.[2] Instead one finds a resilient humanity with cultural depth and social vibrancy, and all of this (one should not dismiss) on the grounds of resistance. This is the event about which creolization theorizes, the event (as Drabinski puts it) of beginning again. On this archipelago, Glissant explains this "new set of possibilities" by turning to the process of creolization, since, on his account, creolization offers a set of ontological resources to explain what it means for emergence to signify, or how what is radically new emerges out of ruptures of a total violence. He identifies life on the slave plantation as uniquely positioned for the manifestation of this kind of creolizing emergence. This is because, at the most intimate levels of life on the plantation, the slave encountered the institutionalization of her silence and nonhumanity. That is to say, to be a slave in this space meant that one had to determine possibilities for life out of entire systems built *only* to rationalize or systematize one's social (and often physical) death. Yet on the plantation there was not only life; there were also (out of necessity) new and reimagined ways of living as human. For Glissant, only through a theory that can account for the unexpected and unprecedented are we able to grapple with this aspect (perhaps the most meaningful aspect) of plantation life.

There are several tropes from which Glissant theorizes the heart of the creolization process. But in all of them, he questions the priority of Being as stable and unchanging; thus, in this regard his work is somewhat indebted to Gilles Deleuze's ontology of becoming and immanence. In his thorough synopsis (which significantly shapes my own understanding of Glissant), Clevis Headley demonstrates the depth of this indebtedness to Deleuze while highlighting the important ways in which "Glissant does not engage in some passive mimicry, but rather strategically uses [Deleuze's] own writings to exemplify his poetics of Relation."[3] I read Glissant this way as well. So though I intermittently underscore connections between Deleuze and Glissant's ontology of becoming, the reading offered in this chapter treats Glissant's work as it should be treated—on its own terms, and in terms of stakes that are unique to his philosophical commitments to developing a theoretical frame out of which a Caribbean political imaginary might be both singularly understood and globally situated.[4]

In his reading, Headley underscores Glissant's commitment to a creolization of being, to a reorientation that replaces "being as transcendent, stable and One" to "being as the process of becoming"—fluid, dynamic, and multiple. Like many scholars of Glissant (Celia Britton, Eric Prieto, and Michael

Wiedorn, to name a few), Headley sees in this reorientation not so much an alternative ontology as a returning of ontology to existence. "The notion of the creolizing of being," Headley writes, "[proposes] thinking being as existence, as *resistance*."[5] When we think being from the perspective of transcendence, the ontological question approaches being as stable and identical to itself. Such assumptions are at the expense of dynamic processes—the processes of becoming—that are immanent to all that is. For the purpose of foregrounding the stakes that are unique to Glissant's ontology of becoming, it is important to understand why this return to dynamic immanence is also (as Headley describes it) a retrieval of being as *resistance*. In other words, it is significant to Glissant's reading of the Caribbean's relation to the world that creolizing practices generate possibilities that are against the grain of what is coded for in the metaphysical "One" of being. Without this possibility of resistance, any process of becoming remains but an unfolding of what is already determined (predetermined) in the transcendental laws of Being. In reorienting ontology toward those traces of existence, it becomes possible to foreground the ways in which what is *above* existence (those transcendent laws of Being) does not exhaust all that is. Or, rather, "all that is" becomes fractured, opened up to possibility, becoming, and becoming-otherwise.

So in naming Glissant's existential ontology as a theory that retrieves resistance from being, Headley calls attention to how, under Glissant's treatment of creolization, events at the level of the everyday determine modalities not yet coded for in the totality of being and (more significantly) in the being of power. In this way, to frame resistance in terms of existence is to not only frame a space for emergence but also understand existence in relation to those metrics of power that determines emergence as impossibility.[6] Glissant's reading of creolization reorients being so as to provide a notion of ontology that might account for this resistance and thereby account for the possibility of that which is radically new, or for Difference as such. As Michael Wiedorn writes, "Glissant sought to elicit radical change in the world, whether in large-scale political institutions or in human beings' most basic ways of interacting with one another in their daily lives."[7] Glissant turns to the Caribbean in order to develop this theory of emergence because, for him, the history of the region (and the sociality shaped by that history) offers the Caribbean as precisely this site of futuricity (of emergence, and of newness).[8] Becoming is only truly becoming when it is the emergence of radical Difference, and for Glissant, creolization in the context of the Caribbean offer us a means through which this sense of becoming might be theorized.

Hence, an ontology that is existential is not only a questioning of Being's stasis but also, more importantly, a questioning of the assumption that newness, or beginning again, is impossible. With his focus on the Caribbean archipelago, Glissant directs our attention to the everyday to find such new beginnings, or what Drabinski rightly describes as beginning creatively out of the absolute violence of the archipelago's history.[9] There are no inscriptions that predate these possibilities, since they emerge out of the immanent "now" of existing; beginning again through processes of creolization is not anterior to the immanent concrete conditions that call for us to determine the meaning and contours of our everyday living. To the contrary, creolization frames our subjective encounter with "what there is," as, indeed, a spontaneous invention.[10]

The centrality of the plantation in Glissant's work is key here, since it is on the plantation that the totality of historical violence bears witness to the contestation of creative emergence. It is both on the plantation and within the confines of plantation economy that relations to the world emerge, which condition the possibility of life precisely when such possibilities were supposed to have been foreclosed. In the words of Omise'eke Natasha Tinsley, it is within this plantation economy that we find existing subjects "[making connections] in ways that commodified flesh was never supposed to."[11] Existence is resistance, in the context of this history. And in turn, creolization offers an account of the existential that not only directs us beyond ontology (qua static Being) but also troubles the lines that might delineate clear separation between the ontological and the political. That is to say, creolization frames ontology as already coded by power and domination (as never politically neutral). So existence as resistance would be existence against such domination. It would be concrete life against the grain of hegemonic totality, the metrics of which work to flatten the immanence of that concrete life. Instead of ontology being about a universal truth of "what is," the undulation of immanence transforms ontology with the singularities of "*perspectives* on what there is."[12] As such, Glissant's existential ontology comes out of a negotiation with *how* being is lived through, and with how it unfolds in the moving processes that produce difference—possibilities of beginning again.

In laying out the ways in which Glissant's notions of Relation, *chaos-monde* and *tout-monde*, rhizome, and errantry realize this project of the creolization of being, my hope is to provide support for the claim that creolization can move us toward thinking the nation otherwise. In *Caribbean Discourse* Glissant writes, of the Martinican intellectual returning to the island from the French metropole, "To be unable therefore to manage to live in one's country, that is where the hurt is deepest."[13] Packed into this sentiment is the in-between-ness, or perhaps even nowhere-ness, of the immigrant, independent of those legal categories (citizen, noncitizen, legal resident, visiting alien) ascribed to her position. Glissant seems to write this from a place of transience, in which one's sense of belonging is long gone, but not yet (or even never to be) replaced by another experience of home. This migrating and returning subject about which he writes is at home neither in the metropole nor back on the island of her birth. But at the same time, this in-between-ness is also not quite an experience of homelessness either. Instead, the account locates a particular meaning of "home" (of the experience of home), which is unique to the concrete (immanent) life of the migrating Caribbean subject.

Out of such experiences, there is a meaning of home that moves us both beyond and outside the (somewhat simple) binary of "home/homelessness," or of "belonging/nonbelonging."[14] Here I read Glissant's point to be similar to what scholars like Ortega, Mimi Sheller, and others articulate, which is that we constitute and come to "home" in multiple ways, and that these constitutions are in turn shaped by how, as subjects, we move within the arrangements of colonial power.[15] Through the experience of the creole subject—the subject for whom questions of origin and belonging are always complex—these negotiations of "home" are new and inventive, always contingent on the exigencies of her history, and of the ways in which that history shapes her encounter with place. More significantly, and relevant to the "nation" question, such constitutions of home and belonging seem to call for an ontology that is able to wrestle with such complexities. Glissant moves us toward this ontology through creolization, so that being might become attuned to these singular experiences of the reality of home, of belonging to the nation, and of national community.

These, then, are the framing questions of what follows: What yields when we creolize our ideas of the nation, of its constitution, and of our comportments toward that constitution? More specifically, how might this alternative (creolizing) signification of "nation" change the marriages between "nation" and single territory, between purity and citizenship, and between static borders and community? Glissant's account of the process of creolization seems to open these questions anew, with much potential for framing national life in terms that might support the diverse and the singular.

Totality and Relation

For Glissant, onto-thinking happens when the endgame of thought is totality, the reduction of uncertainty for the sake of understanding, and epistemological safety. He likens this to the driving motivations of Western scientific inquiry, since, as an enterprise, Western science aims to present a neatly packaged world, which can then be put to use for the sake of (what that enterprise constitutes as) human thriving. Hence, onto-thinking is oriented around a telos of management and control, and it assumes, as the object of its thinking, a world that *can* be managed and controlled in this way. Given this telos, all finds its place in a taxonomy of definitions, and fits into a mapping of Being out of which the metaphysics of the One (discussed in chapter 1's trace of the nation-form) might gain epistemological and political traction. Through this ontological mapping, truth and nontruth (sense and non-sense or anti-sense) are shaped by the theoretical boundaries of Western science and subsequently structure our more everyday relations to the world.

In a 2015 *StarTalk* interview with former president Bill Clinton, astrophysicist Neil deGrasse Tyson describes scientific inquiry in a way that not only maps onto Glissant's assessment of onto-thinking but also makes clear why such modes of thought would be opposed to a creolization of being.[16] Tyson outlines two basic driving motivations for Western science. Presented with two objects, the scientist either tries to understand how they are alike, despite their being two, or tries to foreground their difference, to the extent that they are two. Tyson claims (and President Clinton agrees) that the majority of scientific breakthroughs (the "success stories" of modern science) have been of the former kind, since it is through the scientific project of charting similarities that we have been able to organize our world in terms of unifying principles. Such unifying principles generate, for us, a world that is manageable, meaningful, and, most importantly, primed for the purpose of scientific *and* political "progress." What is significant in this formulation are Tyson and Clinton's assumptions about how difference—its place, the implications of its presence for knowledge-production—ought to signify in such scientific projects. Difference is left out of the organizational frame of science but, as a result, already constitutes that frame through its absence. In a similar vein, Homi Bhabha's "minority identities" of cultural difference are left out of the nation-form's negotiations of postcolonialism's movement and flux, but they also constitute that nation-form by its proximal absences. In this regard, the onto-thinking of Western science is unable to conceptualize Stuart Hall's notion of identity (cited in chapter 2) as already "constructed through, [and] not outside, difference."[17]

In *Poetics of Relation*, it is precisely to this end that Glissant is critical of the movement of onto-thinking.[18] Equipped only with unifying principles, onto-thinking fails us when we are called to encounter the other on her own terms, particularly at the level of the "everyday."[19] Driven by the urge to unify (in order then define), onto-thinking operates on the fundamental assumption that Being is fixed and that what counts as knowledge of Being is similarly unchanging (or eternal). Difference has a place in this model only at the expense of its reduction, which is to say, no longer as difference in itself. As an alternative to a thinking that can only reduce difference, Glissant offers the model of errant thought (or errant thinking). He likens the errant thinker to the poets banished from the *Republic*, insofar as "Plato . . . understood the power of . . . those who [think through] obscurity. . . . [Plato] distrusted the fathomless word."[20] Errant thinking is in the business of producing knowledge that does not totalize for the sake of understanding but, rather, acknowledges the irreducible difference that emerges through the complexity of becoming and movement. The "fathomless word" that Glissant references signifies a limitation for the errant thinker. But to the degree that his goal is not to conquer in the name of knowing, such limitation only furthers the understanding aimed at in thinking errantly—understanding difference as such. "Errant, he challenges and discards the universal—this generalizing edict that summarized the world as something obvious and transparent. . . . He plunges into the opacities of that part of the world to which he has access . . . [The] thinking of errantry conceives of totality but willingly renounces any claims to sum it up or to possess it."[21] The important question for Glissant is also our question: What are the implications of thinking errantly (or, at the very least, of *not* thinking onto-logically) for community?

To reiterate, Glissant's interests in theorizing the Caribbean archipelago ultimately reflects his interest in the contact among cultures that takes place in that region, as a consequence of the mass transplantation of people from across the globe. Whether we understand their emergence as a result of the transatlantic slave trade, the mobilization of Europeans in search of material wealth promised through the colonial theft of "new" worlds, or the more contemporary migration of modern subjects in pursuit of opportunity and capital, communities in the Caribbean and Latin American regions were never the culturally homogeneous spaces of a romanticized antiquity. For Glissant, this means that the contact out of which these regions grew and continue to develop make their everyday cultural comportments particularly primed for thinking through errantly. What this means is that, as it is constituted in the region's history of contact, forced indigeneity, and migratory movements between a (colonially structured) periphery and center, relationality subscribes to something other than the metaphysics of the One, as it gathers pluralities (of cultures, of histories, of geographies) in a way that avoids both assimilation and the incommensurability of a stubborn identity politics.

This other way of relationality Glissant names "Relation," and he theorizes it in terms of a *poetics*, which is to say, in terms of an imaginary the centrality of which is world-relation. Eric Prieto outlines what, out of this conception of Relation, functions as the difference between *chaos monde* and *toute monde*, stressing the sense in which Glissant's poetics points to a totality that maps onto the former and not the latter. Chaos monde is (as the phrase suggests) chaotic, exhausted by the immediacy and pure immanence of the singular in a way that is disconnected from how that singularity is informed by its implications in what lies beyond, or "outside." As such, it is less a totality than it is the impossibility of totality. On the other hand, Prieto writes, toute monde "can be drawn out of this chaos, [as] a unifying perspective, a totalizing vision," which although totalizing does not reproduce the onto-thinking of Western science.[22] *How* this totality is not the totalizing unification of onto-thinking captures the heart of Glissant's work, and explains why, for him, the dynamism of creolization is conceptually productive.

Through creolization, we are able to conceptualize differences in plurality, sustained as singular differences *as* they are in relationship with each other. Glissant uses the geography of the Caribbean to capture this paradox, noting, in the Caribbean's archipelagic constitution, a totality of islands in which each land mass signifies as singularly essential. In other words, within the totality of this archipelago, no one island can be lost, dismissed, or disavowed without at the same time changing the meaning of the totality as a whole. In *La cohée du Lamentin*, Glissant tells us that, in relating to the world in this archipelagic way (what he often refers to as "archipelagic thinking"), one knows that "even the most minuscule of components [of the totality is] irreplaceable," there as part of the totality, but singularly so, protected from the reductionism of an onto-thought (of a metaphysics of the One).[23] Hence, with the geography of the archipelago as his reference, Glissant aims to sketch out a position in which the uniqueness of the local (its singularity, its radical difference) stands cotemporaneously with that "larger puzzle" that is the totality of the global, in which both the "here" of the local and the "elsewhere" of the global is encountered together, with neither taking precedent over the other.[24] Prieto notes the ways this conception of Relation sets Glissant apart from other postcolonial theorists of the Caribbean and has caused him to "[fall] out of favor with critics of a militant or nationalist bent."[25] That is, relative to orientations of Caribbean theory, politics, and literature that focus on what might be read as the region's cultural and epistemological exceptionalism, Glissant's position that "all is Relation" reads as what one would expect it to, under the totalizing projects of Western science and metaphysics—as a disavowal of what is unique to the Caribbean for the sake of its place in the larger project of globalization. To put it differently, Glissant's "all is Relation" is read by some as a forsaking of the many for the sake of the One.

However, alongside this critique there is Glissant's most vital call—to think the "all" of totality differently, to encounter it through an alternative (and perhaps decolonial) poetics and imaginary, bypassing the stalemate of either "protecting the singular" or "assimilating into the One." This bypassing is made possible by the conception of opacity at the center of his poetics of Relation. Herein lies the paradox of how we are to think the "all" of Relation differently—the relationality of Relation is not grounded in an accessibility or transparency of singular differences but, rather, in their *inaccessibility* to the totalizing reach of knowledge. That is to say, Glissant's poetics of Relation is about bringing into relation what will retain its opaqueness, what will *resist* reductionist totalization *through* its opaqueness as it gathers into the "all" of Relation. The stalemate, "protecting the singular" versus "assimilating into the One" is then circumvented in this formulation of an other-than-transparent totality. As Michael Wiedorn puts it, "Archipelagic thought . . . constitutes a challenge to one of the foundational characteristics of Western reason: the fetishization of clarity."[26] Instead of subscribing to this characteristic, Glissant's "all is Relation" asks us to think totality not as a transparent system, but in terms of opacity and ambiguity.[27]

Hence, if onto-thinking moves toward universality, then errant thinking moves toward a gathering of singularities that does not universalize (does not sum up what is gathered). To recall, this is because the errant thinker (likened by Glissant to the banished poet in *The Republic*) is able to encounter and be in relationship with the "fathomless word" in its singularity. What Glissant conveys here is the sense in which errantry names the capacity to relate to the world as an always-dynamic process of becoming and, as such, knows the world void of any expectation that it will be systematic and transparent. To the contrary, errant thinking is prepared to know the world in its ambiguity, as a moving totality of opaque singularities that are linked together despite (alongside) their resistance to reduction. Onto-thinking can only know another totality, one given over to it as already reduced in this way and consequently available to be systematized. Errant thinking thinks the ambiguity of Relation, through which a more archipelagic totality gathers the "here" and "elsewhere" together, to be thought—errantly—together.[28]

It is in this sense that Glissant offers errantry as a modality through which the creolizing products of contact among cultures can be encountered. As creolizing, these products are not static fixtures that might fit into a nonmoving frame; rather, they are dynamically producing singular iterations of themselves. In this regard, there is a perpetual emerging of newness, and only through errant thinking can these new singularities be encountered as such. The kind of composite community produced in the relationality of Relation is unstable, ever-changing, and "a product that in turn produces."[29] It is in errant thinking that one finds the capacity for (indeed, the desire to) understand this mode of totality (of community, of "world," of "*toute monde*") in Relation. Grounded in the logic of becoming and movement, such communities do not close in on themselves, despite their internal coherence. Rather, they remain open to the uncertainty of processes that produce, quite genuinely, that which is new (or perhaps unprecedented).[30] Most significantly, in the historical context of these creolizing communities, they remain open to newly emerging capacities for relating-in-resistance to power and for sabotaging power's calculus in a way that allows for varying degrees of freedom.

In this sense, Glissant's reading of the Caribbean through the frame of creolization—and more specifically through a frame of Relation—allows for two truths to emerge. First, it theorizes an idea of totality that allows for the singularity of differences to signify (the "here" of the local is as meaningful as the "elsewhere" of the global). And second, it brings this frame to the question of power by offering a conception of the totality of power as already punctuated by what remains opaque to its calculus. These opaque punctuations denote those everyday articulations of subjects as they generate conditions for their humanity, which escape the totalizing reach of that power. But at the same time, these liminal folds of escape are also *constitutive* of power: the "all" of power is in terms of Relation—those intimate regions of everyday, creolizing sabotage are in relation to power, aspects of that power, and represent power's opaque constitutions. This account requires a creolizing frame because it points to an understanding of totality that is dynamic, nonessentializing, and ambiguous. The universal is once and for all, so when communities of diverse cultures or sensibilities are universalized, they stand in resistance to the becoming of newness, are rigidly closed off to change. A community in Relation, on the other hand, is amenable to change, since it *is* the dynamism of becoming. With its unifying principles, onto-thinking cannot know Relation in its resistance to unification (it is, indeed, never just "one"). But errantry, with its poetic imaginary, is able to know the ways in which Relation resists the self-referential totality of Being.

Far from static (and therefore capturable by some unifying principle of the onto-thinker), cultural contact at the foundation of communities in Relation is moving, producing new sensibilities that themselves are perpetually becoming other than themselves. Only the errant thinker can position herself in a knowing relationship with such unpredictability. This is because errantry is a mode of knowing that does not (cannot) predict or decide "in advance."[31] In tracing Glissant's creolization of being, Clevis Headley returns to Deleuze in order to capture what it might mean to think in terms of Relation—"to think the real without essence of substrate, and to replace an essentially static account of the real with a dynamic, and specifically *morphogenetic* one."[32] Hence, to return to our earlier question about how errantry might engage our conceptions of community, it is only as errant that thought can think through the idea of a community in Relation; only to errant thought is a community hospitable to difference intelligible.

One has to wonder—how is this not a description of a radically chaotic collusion of singularities? And if so, in what sense can such chaos offer semblance of anything communal? Does this model of a community in Relation get us into diametrical opposition with the xenophobia of nationalism (discussed in chapter 1), only to destroy the very conditions for community? Deleuze and Félix Guattari's account of chaos might be helpful here: "Chaos is defined not so much by its disorder as by the infinite speed with which every form taking shape in it vanishes. It is a void that is not a nothingness but a *virtual*, containing all possible particles and drawing out all possible forms, which spring up only to disappear immediately. . . . Chaos is an infinite speed of birth and disappearance."[33] From this, we see that the relationality of Relation does not foreclose the possibility of community. Rather, such relationality calls for an alternative sense of coherence, one that honors the generative processes of birthing new "particles" (new ways of being human, new ways of resisting the coloniality of power, new modes of encountering the world). Indeed, this alternative sense of coherence accounts for the ways in which, as dynamic, the community in Relation becomes "other" to itself without undermining its existence as a community.

Glissant reads, in Deleuze's conception of the chaos of becoming, an approximation of the process of creolization that, for him, describes the meaning of Caribbean identity and community. "What took place in the Caribbean [the rupturing of history and memory, and the subsequent obligation to begin again, out of that fragmentation of history], which could be summed up in the word *creolization*, approximates the idea of Relation for us as nearly as possible. It is not merely an encounter . . . but a new and original dimension allowing each person to be there and elsewhere, rooted and open, lost in the mountains and free beneath the sea, in harmony and in errantry."[34]

Here Deleuze's account of chaos is given inventive cultural signification in Glissant's conception of creolization. As chaotic (in this Deleuzian sense), the community in Relation, moving through this creolizing process, carries us into a space of real diversity, a space in which community does not come at the cost of totalizing homogeneity and relationality does not happen at the cost of a reductive transparency. To this end, the chaos of the process of creolization is not "without sense."[35] Rather, it is normed differently, its sense grounded in the singularity and dynamism of immanence. Because of this different norming, Glissant uses the term *le chaos-monde* to replace the notion of "universe." Like Eric Prieto's work, Betsy Wing's translation of *Poetics of Relation* leaves the term untranslated because, according to her, attempts to translate would mean that "the implications of ordered chaos implicit in chaos theory would slip away, leaving [only] the banality of world disorder."[36] What the term *le chaos-monde* underscores is the fluidity endemic to real diversity, and it provides a model for understanding how that diversity can be gathered (how it might cohere) without being universalized, or come together without having to undergo the genocide (metaphorical or otherwise) of homogenizing difference.

Hence we can read, in Glissant's deployment of the totality constitutive of Relation, a third option for the nation-form. Alongside the incommensurability of identity politics, and the silencing oneness of nationalism, his work invites us to think through (errantly, to be sure) the possibility of the nation as creolized, as always in the process of making itself anew through the "ordered chaos" of being in Relation. "[Neither] fusion [n]or confusion," *le chaos-monde* captures the process of creolization, in which a community of diverse cultures and linguistic sensibilities are subject neither to "ravenous integration" nor to "muddled nothingness."[37]

Rhizomes, Not Roots

This third option calls for a radical reimagining of how we experience ourselves, in our subjectivity. If I am to be part of this community in Relation, how, then, am I constituted in my capacity as a subject, or even as a citizen? *Le chaos-monde* calls for a reorientation that understands subjectivity as "a product that itself produces," as, itself, a generative immanence in dynamic relation not only to others but also to itself. Thus, instead of understanding subjectivity as a phenomenon identical to itself, rooted and unchanging, the subject instead references a dynamic gathering of differences (of a plurality of "here's" and "elsewhere's"), simultaneously in relation to other similarly constituted subjects.

To think of the process of creolization at the level of the subject, we must think about the self as both here and elsewhere, both herself and "other" to herself. In the idea of the *écho-monde*, Glissant resorts to metaphors of sound (namely, the echo) to capture this kind of othering. By the time the echo is a phenomenon with which one can reckon, it has lost its loyalty to the original sound. It is no longer, in any real sense, rooted in that point of origin, and has become "other" in relation to that origin. Despite becoming other, though, it is still *in relation* to the originating sound: we encounter the echo as part of, or constitutively implicated in, this birthing (original) sound. Glissant's reconstitution of subjectivity is with this model in mind, as he describes the self as a perpetual differing, or differentiation, diffracting and returning as always other than itself. Headley reminds us that "[Glissant's] ontology is concerned with questions of agency and subjectivity, of the coming into consciousness of persons existing in conditions of non-being."[38] This reiterates my earlier point that creolization's capacity to theorize the emergence of newness is historically grounded, informed by the *need* to invent conditions of being human out of power grids that foreclose such conditions. Headley reminds us that, in this creolizing context, the subject herself is also this capacity for inventive emergence—necessarily so, given that she must not only resist power but also, more radically, invent herself as the kind of agential subject capable of such resistance.

What is the ontological status of the subject's "beginning to be," when it is predated only by conditions for the possibility of its *not* beginning to be? In a similar vein, we might also ask: How do Caribbean communities begin to be, in the aftermath of catastrophe? How does life (in all its hopeful vibrancy) emerge out of conditions that seem to determine only the absence of life, or the absence of life's capacity to generate more of itself? To begin with these questions is to see that the ontological implications of creolization are, for Glissant, inseparable from its existential and political significance. In following his reading of the metaphor of the echo, we see how creolization, at the level of the subject, explains the possibility of beginning out of nothing, or perhaps, as John Drabinski rightly says, out of *less* than nothing. In describing the uniqueness of the trauma of the Middle Passage informing Caribbean history, Drabinski writes, "Indeed, loss itself is stolen in the Middle Passage. . . . [There] are no bodies—decaying or ashen—in the shackles. Only the shackles—gone green [on the Atlantic ocean's floor]—remain."[39] Beginning to be, then, must happen in that "less than loss." In taking these beginning conditions into account, we see the urgency in which the Caribbean context is charged with the task of coming to the possibility of subjectivity, community, and humanity in radically inventive ways. That wake-less wake of the violence of the Middle Passage means that the subject's beginning is already a beginning without a ground, without a tethering in any ground (Drabinski reminds us that there is no Middle Passage wreckage out of which we might find a ground, since all has been drowned). It is on this absence that the creolizing subject will participate in the logic of the rhizome.

The echo originates from a source, but this source stands as a beginning that is unable to fully explain the being of the echo. Subjects and communities that must begin again, in the "less than zero" of the Middle Passage's wake, are similarly positioned with an ontological status that is necessarily other than the logic of their (absent) origin.[40] To be sure, this is not to say that the creolizing subject emerges ahistorically; on the contrary, this subject's need to invent itself is precisely informed by a history of rupture and catastrophic violence. The beginning out of which this subject must constitute herself is not so much the absence of a ground as it is the presence of a "tortured" ground, to paraphrase John Drabinski.[41] It is as a consequence of this tortured ground—constituted by absence, the fragments of history, by nothing that might provide viable ground for beginning—that Glissant asks us to understand subjectivity (emerging in and through creolizing processes) *not* as a substantive and unchanging essence, but as "a capacity for variation—yes, a variable."[42] So why does Glissant turn to the rhizome in place of the root? John Drabinski's assessment is apt here: "Roots set and fail to take up in what is less than the remainder [the "less than" of the tortured ground of a Caribbean history]. . . . So, the rhizoming subject must be born unrooted in order to maintain any hope of creating on and in a tortured geography."[43] Hence, Glissant's turn to the metaphor of the rhizome is meant not to dismiss history but to theorize the kind of (rhizoming) subject that would need to emerge in response to the historical specificity of the Caribbean. Ultimately, then, this subject's capacity for variation and relationality—the "here" and "elsewhere" of the rhizome subject—is only out of that Caribbean locality.

Glissant comes to the notion of the rhizome by way of Deleuze and uses it to reimagine the identity of the subject in this way. Unlike the plant that sets roots into vertical depth, the plant that grows through rhizomes exhibits what looks like a multiplication of itself, across a wide range of ground. Growth through rhizomes allows the plant to spread, but in truth and fact, there is no original "it" that spreads. Rather, out of this one emerges a multiplicity of entities, all of which then *also* expand in a similar rhizomatic way. Like the echo's relationship to (its) sound, the rhizomatic offshoot exists in a relation of disresembling dependency to the "first one there." Across time and space, rhizomatic growth generates real multiplicity, unanchored to any one place, with no real beholden-ness to the "originating" source of its life. (Again, in the context of the history in question, this is insofar as the question of ground, source, and origin is troubled from the start.) In this sense, the plant that has rhizomed itself is both "here and elsewhere," perpetually other to itself.

For diasporic communities whose contemporary global status is a consequence of the transatlantic slave trade, "the site of history [is] characterized by ruptures . . . that began with a brutal dislocation."[44] Hence, the metaphor of the root (single origin, fixed in place and time) simply does not capture how one comes to live in and with that history. Glissant's work is an acknowledgment that any conception of community—and, more pertinent to the driving question of this book, any conception of nation—coming out of these experiences would have to be uncoupled from the metaphor of the root. Such conceptions of community would call for an archipelagic thinking that is able to think the rhizomatic movement of the creolizing subject, as well as the constitutive relationality of a rhizoming totality.[45] Glissant writes, "The root is unique, a stock taking all upon itself and killing all around it. In opposition to this [is] the rhizome, an enmeshed root system . . . with no predatory rootstock taking over permanently. The notion of the rhizome maintains, therefore, the idea of rootedness but challenges that of a totalitarian root."[46] On this account, the being of the root is at the expense of all that is other to it. Instead the being of the rhizome is its very relationality to what is other. Hence, root-thinking, when brought to bear on the idea of the nation, aligns with the (onto-)thinking of Being in terms of unifying principles, totalizing homogeneity, and universalizing multiplicity. To put it otherwise, root-thinking forecloses the possibility of encountering difference as such. Rhizomatic thinking, on the other hand, reconfigures the individual subject as a "capacity for variation" and thus as an aptitude to "give on and with" other subjectivities. To this end, to conceive of community as rhizomatic and not as rooted is to also conceive of the possibility of encountering the other in her opacity, as a subject with whom I "give on and with" in a non-totalizing cohesion. This communicative encounter among subjects is archipelagic insofar as, across opacity, singularity resists assimilation as "giving on and with" unfolds.

So the role of opacity in Glissant's formulation calls for rhizoming instead of rooting models of subjectivity and community.[47] The plant life supported by root systems grows while mandating the assimilation of other (plant) life around it; singularities are swallowed up in the totalitarian nature of that root system. For Glissant, this is precisely the antimetaphor of Relation, a system whose relationality makes possible a gathering that is neither "fusion nor confusion." In replacing the "root" narrative with one centered on the rhizome, Glissant articulates the possibility of forging together communities without the dependence on a singular source of origin, in both time and in place. Hence, through the metaphor of the rhizome, we might uncouple the phenomenon of the nation from a narrative of historical origin and also allow for a conception of nation-form without recourse to a nativist conception of territory. Rhizomatic networks spread across space and place, such that there is no one piece of earth, more than another, that determines the plant's foundational reason for being. Likewise, when the nation is formulated without claim to an (original) ground—because that ground is tortured in the sense of the Caribbean's history of the loss of loss—there is conceptual possibility for national, collective life to account for itself independently of the atavistic narrative that typically legitimizes much of modern nationalism.[48] The metaphor of the rhizome (in its depiction of creolizing identities and communities in Relation) then opens up new possibilities for negotiating the meaning of belonging and home in ways that not only foreground a hospitality to difference but also move beyond the static boundaries that condition colonial divisions of the human.[49]

With this breaking away from the legitimizing force of territory, there is also the breaking away from the narrative of bloodline, or filiation, as the mechanism across which one makes sense of the bonds of national belonging. In chapter 1, I discuss the impetus for xenophobia (or, to construe it more broadly, allergic relations to the other) in the kinds of nationalisms founded in ancient kinship and blood ties. Glissant reads such narratives to be of root-grounded national sensibilities that negotiate the existence of community in terms of origin in time (harking back to a single historical moment of birth) and place (naming some founding territory as its necessary geography of emergence). For communities that must begin with a history of rupture or fragmented time, as well as from the placeless-ness that is a consequence of geographical dislocation, the priority of filiation is both impossible and absent. As such, the contours of community—and by extension, of national community—is conceived of otherwise, invented on the grounds of an impossible (yet necessary) beginning. In this generative process of making community, the founding absence is not made whole; there is no once-and-for-all resolution that is promised in this inventive process. Rather, the absence of filiation (the palpable presence of what was drowned) carries through the rhizomatic production of community, giving it the double meaning of both catastrophic loss and inventive possibility, of trauma and the promise constituted in that trauma. Drabinski describes this Caribbean condition as a "[beginning] there, where the ball and chain go green, birthing to the shores where the DeathAbyss unroots, yet glitters still in its bitterness."[50] In this glittering bitterness, we read the sense in which Glissant's theorizing of the Caribbean through the frame of creolization foregrounds the possibility of (1) beginning again, through and despite total violence; (2) community as dynamic and errant, through and despite its coherence; and (3) a kind of relationality (Relation) structured through and despite the opacity of singular difference.

In the model offered by filiation, the lineage between father and son acts as a unifying principle.[51] This principle legitimates modes of belonging to the national community that can be subsumed under their participation in bloodline: what counts as the legitimate future of the nation is precisely defined by its linear connection to the past. Of this patrilineal chain, Glissant writes, "[The historically linear] community precedes any thought of the individual, whose foremost dimension is as a link in the chain of filiation."[52] In this we hear a relationality that is diametrically opposed to the rhizomatic structure of Relation. There is no archipelagic gathering, through which the singularity of the subject makes herself opaquely present. Instead, filial relationality subsumes such singularities, renders them meaningful only in their instrumental support of the linear time of filiation. Reduced to instrumentality, the singularity of difference amounts to those failed copies without models (those failed simulacra) under the metaphysics of the One.

We might liken these reductive lines of filiation to what, in Sara Ahmed's account, gets interrupted by the queer orientations taken up by subjects who are "offline" or relate to the world of objects in a "not right" way.[53] In other words, much like Ahmed's analysis of how new lines of orientations emerge through the presence of queer bodies, the rhizomatic lines of Glissant's Relation begin in a kind of failure—a failure to be in the world as properly belonging in that world, a failure to rightly take root in the tortured ground of that world's territorial space. Ahmed writes, "[Other] things remain possible . . . when one's starting point is a starting point of failure. . . . When bodies take up spaces that they were not intended to inhabit, something other than the reproduction of the facts of the matter happens."[54] In the context of creolizing spaces, this "something other" would be those new (creole) lines of social life, lines of community and kinship that emerge in the wake of destroyed filial lines, so as to displace the reproduction of plantation (and neocolonial) violence. In other words, in the absence of conventional genealogies, the possibility of beginning again emerges and, with that possibility, new modalities of relation through which singularities can signify in themselves.

Ahmed's work also notes the importance of the *sharing* of orientations when it comes to the production and perpetuation of communities in general, and of national communities in particular. In other words, a particular " 'we' emerges as an effect of a shared direction toward some object."[55] She details the ways in which such shared, collective orientations both shape and are shaped by the cultural and phenomenological lines of social life. But what her analysis brings to bear is the question of how such shared orientations figure in the rhizomatic constitutions of Glissant's community. Ahmed's analysis prompts us to ask: What does it mean for the "we" of a creolizing collective (a creolizing nation, even) to rest on a shared orientation toward objects in the world? Given what Glissant details in the errant movement of the rhizome, in what sense *can* the community in Relation participate in a set of shared orientations? Could coherence for such a community in Relation happen without a shared orientation? And if so, how would its coherence (its "we") be understood?

The role of repetition in the production of a collective "we" is helpful here and is particularly significant to how, on Glissant's account, notions of errantry and rhizome allow him to theorize totality differently. Ahmed reminds her readers that when it comes to the collective "we," it is not only a matter of shared orientations but also, more importantly, the *repetition* of those shared orientations: "It is through the repetition of a shared direction that collectives are made."[56] When—as with the weblike and mangroved relationality of the rhizome—the direction is not linear, there are noteworthy implications for the possibility of repetition (for the capacity to repeat directional lines of orientation). This is because the mangrove lines of rhizomatic relationality are errant. They participate in the logic of detour precisely because linear filiation is ruptured beyond the possibility of restoration. In this regard, when it happens, repetition amounts to repeating the *impossibility* of repetition. In other words, lines of orientation multiplying through the errant nature of the rhizome are repeating its foreclosed possibility. It is in this sense that it would be difficult to name the directionality of the creolizing community in Relation (the creolizing nation) in terms of *lines per se*, given that (as Ahmed notes), lines emerge through the repeated movement of bodies in a particular direction. The mangrove zigzags—it doesn't offer historied lines as such. All there is, is detour, beginning again, in relation to spectral absences, in relation to the present loss of loss. In this creolizing context, therefore, we might think in terms of routes instead of lines, routes that are more conducive to a generative openness to orient differently and invent newly the necessary conditions for social life. Thus, about the kind of collective that emerges out of such impossible repetitions, there is perhaps a rhythm in detour and errantry nonetheless, in and about the impossibility—out of which a collective "we" in Relation emerges and (rhizomatically) offers itself to a future.[57] The technologies of rhythm (its musicality, its poetry, its nontotalizing systematicity) seems to better capture how creolizing orientations respond to tortured ground (ground as the impossibility of rooting) through experimentations with homing, with social liberation and with an alternative (nonfilial) "we." Through this experimentation, lines show up as open routes to be disassembled and detoured. Likewise, the objects they offer for proximity show up as "to be jostled," to tremble under the trace of a future (toward which yet another detour points) of another way of being human.

Hence, it is in terms of rhizomed routes that participate in the rhythm of detour that the "we" of a creolizing community might be conceived. Out of the contact shaped through the creolizing process, emergences arise that are radically new (necessarily other than some linear continuation of filiation). That is to say, the ontological status of the creolizing emergent object calls for more than the sum of its constitutive parts.[58] Creolized entities (themselves existing always in their capacity for variation, or for creolizing) constitute a radical break with what came before; it is in this sense that creolization offers Glissant a path to understanding the possibility of beginning out of nonbeing, of beginning after the totalizing violence of colonial catastrophe. Hence, in place of a linear chain, the creolizing community calls for an expansive (and moving) relational web. Rhizoming identities and the subsequent relationality of Relation move through what he calls "expanse and extension." Opaque nodes and obscure twists mark the relationships across history and place, "joining . . . without conjoining, that is, without merging."[59] This is insofar as the unpredictable contact among individuals (loci of singular difference) shapes (and reshapes) the emergence of the creolizing community. Under a rubric of temporal lines, these breaks in the chain of filial connections are but tragic accidents, or illegitimate moments of bastardy in need of repairing, insofar as they threaten the very life of the community. "If legitimacy [as temporal linearity] is ruptured, the chain of filiation is no longer meaningful, and the community wanders the world, no longer able to lay claim to any primordial necessity."[60] No longer able to establish its necessary existence, the community ungrounded in a linear historical past (no longer connected to some rooted originary moment of birth) is, quite literally, an ontological accident. But here is what Glissant says about accidents: "Accident . . . is the consummate vice (the virus) of any self-enclosed system, such as the computer."[61] To the degree that the creolizing community is diametric to a self-enclosed system, its poetic logic (its poetics of Relation) understands the expansive web of nonlinear temporality not as illegitimate accidents but as both a consequence of and constitutive to the dynamic gathering of individuals who "give on and with" together. Community, from the perspective of this poetics, rejects the logic of filiation and, along with it, the violence linked to that logic, which codes for "the absolute exclusion of the other."[62] To this end, creolization, "safeguards the particular" and thus orchestrates the kind of totality that "guarantees the energy of Diversity."[63]

At this juncture, we return to our driving question: Can this reimagined conception of community also offer a reimagined conception of the nation? In his essay on the role of opacity in Glissant's idea of totality-as-Relation, H. Adlai Murdoch reminds us that, for Glissant, "[there] is no detour when the nation has been possible. . . . Detour is the ultimate recourse of a population whose domination by an Other has been hidden; the principle of domination, which is not evident in the country itself, must be sought elsewhere."[64] Here Murdoch captures Glissant's own reflections on the existential mood of his home island, Martinique. However, these reflections are also very much applicable to postcolonial nations in general, which, despite their independence, are nevertheless caught in a hegemonic gridlock of neocolonial domination. Out of this deferral of (real) national sovereignty, the movement of detour takes hold to create community in the absence of that possibility of a national sense of cohesion and sovereignty. What Murdoch points out is that, for Glissant, the relationality of Relation (detour, errantry, rhizome) exists when "nation" does not. The former attests to a failed emergence of the latter, and, conversely, the possibility of the nation signals the end of community in (detouring) Relation.

However, my overall argument is that "nation," as it is used here, is precisely what is open to reconceptualizing by way of creolization. In other words, the impetus of my overall claims would reformulate Glissant's assessment of the relationship between nation and errantry and offer that Relation is nonexistent when the nation represents a community forged out of the unifying principles of filiation and metaphysical Oneness. Detour cannot coexist with conceptions of the nation that deploys static determinations of belonging and nonbelonging. This conception of the nation is built on principles of temporal linearity, or on a history of filial ties that trace back to a single origin. More importantly, out of such principles subjectivity signifies (and is even performed) as fixed and radically exclusive of that which is other. Hence, in Glissant's naming of the nation in terms of its failure to facilitate detour, errantry, and Relation, we might read the presupposition that the nation in question is still colonial and therefore built in terms of a telos of management and control. On this reading, a project of bringing creolization to bear on the possibility of an alternative formation of national life is not *derailed* by Glissant's somewhat dismal assessment of the nation's diametrical opposition to the possibility of detour. Rather, this assessment foregrounds what, to my mind, is the very question at the heart of Glissant's analysis of creolization—how must we rethink the phenomenon of the nation, so that detour *can* live?

It is on this point that I identify his account of creolization to call for engagement with the phenomenon of the nation that we find in the work of Frantz Fanon. Given Fanon's account of "the nation without nationalism," there is potential for rich engagement between his decolonial politics and Glissant's idea of a dynamic community in Relation (potential to think nation and detour together, and perhaps even coconstitutively). In his exposition of this idea of the nation without nationalism, Grant Farred reads Fanon's work as a call for the postcolonial nation to be "nationalist but not ultra-nationalist."[65] We read this in Fanon's own acknowledgment for the need for a revolutionary, anticolonial violence (on the part of the colonized) that, in reclaiming a right to human dignity, must also be *de*colonial. That is to say, the violence that Fanon identifies as necessary to a successful anticolonial struggle must also necessarily give way to a decolonial agenda that refrains from replicating the xenophobic practices of othering and static closures characteristic of colonialism. To bring such conceptions into conversation with Glissant's account of creolization is to connect Glissant's notions of Relation and errantry with Fanon's approach toward the postcolonial nation as built on open-endedness instead of closure, and on a reverence for the alterity of the other human being. The "new species of man," put forth in *The Wretched of the Earth* as the goal toward which all anticolonial revolutionary violence must advance, is revolutionary precisely through its refusal of the colonial stasis of which Fanon is so critical. For Fanon, in replacing the colonial mapping of human beings with this new species of man, decolonization must be about building something other than colonialism's rigid (nonchanging) conception of the human, and something other than its rigid conception of the nation-form. We can certainly liken this to Glissant's rhizomatic conception of community (through which diversity is safeguarded) and to Relation's rejection of singular legitimizing narratives that reproduce the homogeny of (colonial) unifying principles.

I develop these synergies between Glissant and Fanon in the sixth (and culminating) chapter of this book. There I bring these two thinkers together across a reimagined conception of the nation that is not at the *expense* of detour but, rather, built out of Relation and rhizomatic articulations of community, belonging, and national life. Before this, though, chapter 4 turns to certain key concepts developed by Latina feminist scholars, which support such a reimagined account of community. These scholars—Gloria Anzaldúa, María Lugones, and Mariana Ortega (to name but a few)—offer conceptual frameworks that foreground difference, flux, and ambiguity in their development of an experience of the social. As such, their work gives us conceptual resources that are aligned with those we find in Glissant to think about subjectivities in relation in ways that avoid thinking about difference and coherence as necessarily oppositional. These Latina feminists give us ways to think the chaotic of communal life (Glissant's *chaos-monde*) as grounded, as what Glissant describes as a "moored whirling," which captures both the "All is Relation" and the nonstasis (of that Relation) that is a consequence of the opacity of the singularities being gathered.[66]

To this end, the objective of part 2 (chapters 3 and 4) is to highlight what I identify to be important convergences between Glissant's theoretical frames and a Latina feminist intellectual tradition, convergences that move us toward thinking (1) the possibility of community in a relational way; (2) antiessentialist subjectivity without rendering the identity of the subject moot; and (3) the significance of history and material location without using history for the sake of atavism and xenophobic closures. I believe that by bringing these two modes of theorizing into conversation with each other, we get the necessary tools for assembling alternative and more decolonial conceptions of the nation-form and national community. That is to say, Glissant's articulations alongside the conceptions I trace in chapter 4 will bring into sharper focus both the possibility of and stakes in creolizing the nation. Hence, the reading I offer of Anzaldúa, Lugones, and Ortega aligns their fundamental driving questions with Glissant's: How can we think through the production and proliferation of community, of being in the world *with* each other, in a way that is no longer tethered to colonial arrangements of lifeworlds as hierarchically ordered?

Chapter 4

✦

Subjectivity Otherwise

In his expositions of the coloniality of being, Nelson Maldonado-Torres reveals, under the skepticism that grounds Descartes's conception of *ego cogito*, a more fundamental *colonial* skepticism, a skepticism that he captures in the term *ego conquiro*.[1] Much like the Cartesian ego cogito, the ego conquiro needs to establish the certainty of its existence. But beyond what the ego cogito pursues, the ego conquiro must establish a certainty of its value—of its existence bearing proper human value. The ego conquiro grounds this certainty in the "*misanthropic* skepticism" of the humanity of racialized peoples. In other words, the conquering ego (ego conquiro) knows itself to have certain value insofar as the value of a racialized other is called into question.[2] This is similar to the way in which Descartes's cogito grounds the certainty of its existence in its doubting of the existence of an external world. Under that Cartesian formulation, my existence is predicated on the contentious (and degraded because uncertain) existence of difference (that which is other, whether the external world or the external other). Maldonado-Torres shows that, on the colonial scene, the absolute difference of the racialized other is similarly encountered as a threat to certainty. The subject that emerges out of this frame is one for whom the certainty of immanent life is grounded in the suspended value of a radically other, whose exteriority is both beyond the realm of certainty, and threatening as a consequence.

Hence, thinking subjectivity otherwise would mean thinking about the subject's relation to difference beyond the ego cogito and ego conquiro. This subject would not only stand in an alternative orientation toward difference but would also *be* in the world differently (in a way that might condition the possibility of this alternative encounter with difference).[3] Both creolist and Latina feminist scholars have taken up this task of envisioning subjectivity otherwise. Theirs is a search for a conception of the subject that (a) is relational, (b) avoids essentialism, (c) is grounded *not* in the fear of the power of the other, and (d) conditions the possibility of a coalitional politics.[4] As Ortega describes it, at stake is the question of whether or not we can think of the identity of the subject as "an affective, ethical, existential ground for solidarity."[5] It is important to note that at the heart of this reorientation is a move from the question of *what* the subject is, to *why* (for what purpose) this subject is "subject." This latter question points us in the direction of the political and asks us to think about the role of the subject in its encounter with difference.[6] For instance, Ortega develops the notion of the multiplicitous self, which ultimately addresses this question of why the subject is who she is. She begins in a Heideggerian register, pushing the notion of "being-in-the-world" into critical conversation with the liminality and border living that shape experiences like hers, of being Latina in North America. From that existential position of being in between, Heidegger's being-*in*-the-world becomes "being-in-between-worlds," which is to say that (1) the subject resides in multiple worlds (and not just one world), and (2) the identity of the subject is multiplicitous in a way that allows for that kind of liminal existence. Already, this gives us an encounter with difference that is unlike what one finds with a closed-off ego conquiro, whose nonchanging stability rests on preventing the invasion of that which is other to itself. Ortega's being-in-between-worlds involves movement, fluidity, and transition, and it points to a subject who is able to understand herself as unified despite her multiplicitousness. In other words, her sense of self as unified is not bought with the price of a homogeneity of immanence (of the ejection of difference).

María Lugones also takes up a nonstatic, nonhomogeneous account of the subject in her work on liminality. Her descriptions of subjectivity are quite similar to Ortega's multiplicitous self, as one that contains "possibilities of anti-structural understandings of selves."[7] To account for this possibility, Lugones uses the notion of ontological plurality, which does much of the same work as Ortega's understanding of a multiplicity of worlds. Both begin with an understanding of "world" as a discursive space out of which meaning is made. According to Lugones, there is always more than one such space in an experience of the social, such that the liminal subject would be one who world-travels among and across such multiple spaces. For Ortega as well, sociality is multiple, and the subject is in movement between and among these multiple discursive spaces. Out of Lugones's conceptions of ontological plurality, world-traveling, and social heterogeneity, an antistructural self emerges "without an underlying 'I,'" which is to say that the identity of the subject—like the identity of the ontological—is plural.[8] On Lugones's account, the subject navigates across and between worlds, holding on to the various selves that find comportment in each world. In that sense, there is no "real self" that is ever betrayed in the movement of world-traveling. Rather, it is a question of which identity the subject will foreground in her encounter with a particular world.[9]

In a later section, I discuss how Lugones accounts for the coherence of such a subject. But before that, we should note that, for her, this ontological plurality (along with a plurality of selfhood) is able to explain how there can be resistance in the midst of what seems like a totalizing oppression.[10]

Because Lugones's ontological plurality conceptualizes multiple worlds, she is able to explain how marginalized subjects can access something sufficiently otherwise than the logics that bring about their oppression. In other words, resistance against oppression might require me to profoundly delink from *this* (discursive) world, insofar as my oppression is coded for—in a most totalizing way—by this world. The possibilities that *this* world provides, no matter the permutations, will ultimately reproduce my oppression. But because world-traveling allows me to enact an alternative self, in an alternative world, I have avenues available to me via which to resist, despite this totality.[11] This possibility of finding alternative avenues of resistance and liberation, in the face of what on the surface appears to be a totalizing oppression, is significant in my use of creolization to rethink the idea of the nation. That is why this chapter traces connections between theories of creolization and the theories developed by Latina feminists like Lugones and Ortega.

Of Lugones's account of ontological plurality, Ortega writes, "[Her] onto-logical pluralism is necessary so that oppressed people can have the open-endedness or the ability to know themselves in different realities in which they can be and act differently than the alternatives offered in those worlds in which they are oppressed and marginalized."[12] For Ortega, however, there still remains the question of coherence. In what sense can I encounter an experience as mine if, as Lugones claims, there is no unitary "I" beneath this structure of plurality? Lugones turns to memory in order to account for the sense in which this plural self can still have experiences of the world that are given over as hers. In her descriptions of world-traveling, the plural subject enters and exits multiple worlds across a "shift from being one person to being a different person."[13] The memory of this shift, which exists alongside the shift itself, allows for a kind of coherence (or, at the very least, guards against a complete *incoherence*, through which it becomes impossible to name an experience as "mine"). Lugones writes, "Those of us who are 'world'-travelers have the distinct experience of being different in different 'worlds' and of having the capacity to remember other 'worlds' and ourselves in them . . . of having memory of oneself as different without quite having the sense of there being any underlying 'I.'"[14]

Ortega is critical of this problem of coherence, and for that reason calls into question the need to couple ontological plurality with a plurality of selves. In other words, Ortega's conception is precisely a *multiplicitous* self, and not one of *multiple selves*, because she finds it both dangerous and unnecessary to ascribe to multiplicity in a way that would undermine the coherence needed to navigate between worlds.[15] At the same time, Ortega warns against a *false* sense of coherence that sacrifices the existential truth of multiplicity. In the fourth section of this chapter, I show how Ortega's account of hometactics grows out of efforts to attend to this tension—between the ambiguity of lim-inal existence, and the existential need to belong (both to oneself and to make a home in the world).[16] She finds resonance with her own efforts to grapple

with this tension in Anzaldúa's articulation of the new *mestiza*: "[The] inter-
esting question is how the experience of contradiction and ambiguity leads to
transformation and even resistance rather than keeping the new *mestiza* in a
state of intimate terrorism," an intimate terrorism that would be diametrical
to the experience of belonging, and perhaps also to coherence.[17]

As I showed in the preceding chapter, reconceptualizing the relation
between multiplicity and oneness is significant for the task of thinking about
national community in a creolizing way. At the level of subjectivity, this recon-
ceptualization asks us to think of difference, flux, and ambiguity not only
as aspects of the inner life of the self but also as part of an experience of
the social. But more importantly, the ways in which Lugones, Ortega, and
Anzaldúa engage with difference (and with a different idea of the subject) also
avoids thinking about difference and coherence as necessarily oppositional.
In other words, the goal of these scholars working in the Latina feminist
tradition is to acknowledge the significance of belonging, wholeness, and nonfragmentation, *as* they conceptualize subjectivity as antiessentialist, fluid, and
perhaps antistructural.[18] Lugones's insistence on the need for a nonfragmented
conception of the self captures this. Ortega's distinction between thick and
thin unease captures this. Anzaldúa's account of the new mestiza captures this.
In this chapter I argue that each of these orientations underscores Glissant's
conception of the rhizome (or, more specifically, his use of the rhizome to
ground his account of the composite community), insofar as his rhizomatic
relationality allows us to think fluidity and historical grounding all at the
same time. Glissant meets theorists like Ortega, Lugones, and Anzaldúa across
the possibility of thinking community in a relational way, of thinking antiessentialist subjectivity without rendering the identity of the subject moot, and
across the possibility of naming historical location without using history for
the sake of atavism and xenophobic closures. To frame things in the terms we
get from Cherríe Moraga, Glissant's use of creolization connects with Latina
feminist modes of theorization across the pursuit of a "broader and wiser
revolution," out of which nonfragmentary, multiplicitous subjects find plural
modes of liberatory existence.[19]

Lugones on Nonfragmentation

Ortega's concern is that the plurality of Lugones's conception of the subject
undermines that subject's capacity to experience the coherence needed to make
a home in the world. To be sure, on Ortega's account, this home-making will
be complex, given the subject's multiplicitousness; it will be a "hometactics"
that responds to the experience of being in between, and to the ambiguity of
that in-between-ness. Nevertheless, Ortega is troubled by the idea of a subject
whose selfhood is multiple, divided across several worlds, with no underlying
"I" to sufficiently gather this multiplicity. For her, this comes close to the "inti-

mate terrorism" of which Anzaldúa speaks. On my reading, Lugones's critique of fragmentation responds to this particular concern by demonstrating an important difference between a multiplicity that is reductive to a more prior unity, and a multiplicity that exists as nonfragmentation. Lugones develops this idea of a nonfragmented subject as resistance to the domination of a politics of purity. Still, her account of the nonfragmented subject seems to align with Ortega's idea of a multiplicitous self. Ortega describes her critique of Lugones's account of multiplicity as one that is grounded in concerns about "identity, self-identification, recognition of difference, and agency."[20] In what follows, I give a reading of Lugones's concerns about fragmentation that somewhat responds to Ortega's critique, but insofar as Lugones's formulation of identity is grounded in a plurality of selves, it remains open to the more metaphysical concerns that Ortega draws out.

A fragment is an incomplete part of a whole: in its being, it calls forth some large unity of which it is a part and without which it is incomplete, lacking, and perhaps also ontologically degraded as a consequence. Therefore, in its being, the fragment calls for the whole to be reassembled, or at the very least, marks that whole as more prior despite its absence. It is in this sense that, for Lugones, fragmentation is not *oppositional* to unification but, rather, "another guise for unity."[21] As part of this unifying logic, the fragmented individual (whose fragmentation signifies in (and as) the intimate terrorism that Ortega and Anzaldúa critiques) is an essential trope in those political structures geared toward control. This is because the possibility of conceptualizing a unified whole presupposes a vantage point that exists beyond and independently of the whole. The purpose of this vantage point is precisely to determine the whole by controlling the placement and purpose of the constitutive fragments.[22] For this reason, Lugones writes, "fragmentation [is] a form of domination."[23] To that end, the multiplicity in her world-traveling subject gestures toward a different sense of "more than one"; it is something other than a multiplicity of fragments. Her insistence on doing away with an underlying "I"—to then make room for an antistructural plural subject—points to this alternative conception of "more than one."[24] It is a "more than one" in the sense of being more than a unified whole that transcends the multiplicity in question. Hence, according to Lugones, this nonfragmentary way of thinking about multiplicity does not reproduce the purity implied in a more prior and transcendent whole (and by the logic of control and unification at its foundation). This undoing of the logic of purity is important for Lugones's political project, which understands purity politics to not only result in a fragmented subject but also to precisely sustain the domination of that subject as she moves through multiple worlds as a fragmented self. She writes, "[I] want to . . . understand the particular oppressive character of the modern construction of social life and the power of impurity in resisting and threatening this oppressive structure."[25] Hence, there is a vital thread in Lugones's development, which connects the possibility of resistance to thinking in terms of a nonfragmented subjectivity, in terms of heterogeneity beyond impurity, and in terms of wholeness that is beyond a dominating unity.

To reiterate, the stakes involved in moving beyond what Maldonado-Torres describes as the ego conquiro's conception of subjectivity is for difference— both at the level of the individual and at the level of the community—to signify beyond impurity, contamination, and nonbelonging contagions. Lugones's articulation of nonfragmentation gives us this reimagined account of the subject, through which structures of stasis and homogeneity are replaced with structures of fluidity and heterogeneity. These structures also facilitate the decentering of purity, a decentering that also organizes creolizing ways of being in the world. In bringing accounts like Lugones's into dialogue with those of creolization, it is important to ask, How does nonfragmentation move us away from a politics of purity? Is it possible to identify a similar nonfragmented subject at the foundation of *creolization*'s move away from a politics of purity? As Glissant demonstrated, at the foundation of creole formations are the fragments of history and cultural origins, all of which remain after the violence of the Middle Passage and the transatlantic slave trade. To be sure, the emergence of human life and resistance to colonial oppression out of these fragments is precisely what creolists identify as the hallmark of creolizing communities. All the same, we must ask, given that the creolizing process of decentering purity begins *in fragments*, how might Lugones's nonfragmentation figure into the structure of the creolizing subject? In her search for a notion of multiplicity that is *not* fragmentation, might Lugones be willing to sign on to the creolizing conceptions of subjectivity only insofar as it is possible to regard creolizing subjects, cultures, artifacts, and practices as, themselves, nonfragmented multiplicities?

How does nonfragmentation moves us away from a politics of purity? The nonfragmented subject travels among multiple social worlds, each of which positions her in a unique relationship to structures of domination. Lugones reminds us that this truth gives rise to the theory of intersectionality, which offers an account of the subject juxtaposed across multiple forms of oppression and enacting multiple forms of resistance. Though Lugones sees this multiplicity of oppressions as that to which our politics of resistance ought to respond, she asks us to replace the imagery of intersecting with that of intermeshing, for reasons that have to do with to her worry about structures of purity. With this concern in mind, she determines that the idea of a subject navigating *intermeshing* oppressions avoids the fragmentation (and consequently the dangers of purity) that continues to be coded for in the idea of a subject who navigates *intersecting* oppressions.[26] She uses her own experience to show the ways in which, out of a politics of purity, she is called to fragment herself into (on the one hand) a Latina who resists the hegemony of nativist politics, and (on the other) a lesbian feminist who resists the homophobia, sexism, and patriarchy of Latin American culture. As she travels between the two worlds to which she unavoidably belongs in some way, she finds herself split across a fragmented series of selves that remain disconnected across these discursive spaces when they are thought of as intersecting instead of intermeshing. In the sexism of Latino oppositional politics, her lesbian identity is an impurity that doesn't belong. Similarly, in the whiteness of lesbian feminist oppositional politics, her Latina identity is an impurity that doesn't belong. Under the rubric of intersectionality, these identities connect, but their meeting happens *as* fragments coming out of two disparate worlds, each of which operates through a logic of purity.

Under a rubric of intermeshing, the purity of each discursive space shows up as a disavowal of the social heterogeneity that is, in fact, essential to each space. In a broader sense, thinking about systems of oppression as intermeshing shows the ways in which the subject is multiply constituted and takes *all* of her multiplicity into her world-traveling. Without the assumed purity, these worlds are always already the locations of multiple modes of human living, which are reducible to unification only through the fragmentation of those human lives. Hence, to return to Lugones's own experience, her Latina identity ought to be one of multiple modes of enacting the resistance of lesbian feminism, which would ultimately require a more complex and heterogeneous lesbian feminist politics. Similarly, taking her lesbian identity into a Latinx oppositional politics would make that position a more complex and heterogeneous nationalist mode of resistance. As it stands under the domination of purity and unification, identities such as these signify as impure, in relation to the worlds that code for their fragmentation. In this coding as impurity, Lugones identifies the rich possibility of effective (and decolonial) resistance. In other words, in the sexist and homophobic world of Latino oppositional politics, her lesbian identity "[remains] complex, defying the logic of unity."[27] Hence, the very experience of belonging as an impurity is dually (or ambiguously) a consequence of oppression *and* an act of resistance. "Both the logic of control and unity and the logic of resistance and complexity are at work in what is impure."[28]

Impurity's production of resistance has clear resonance in the creole context. To recall from chapter 2, cultural entanglements emerge out of practices that are named "creole." That is to say, creolizing forms point to fluid entanglements among fragments, which defy all claims both to authenticity and to faithfulness to some original and pure reproduction of a predating whole. These impure entanglements are fluid, which also means that their connections to an origin are ambiguous, formed through the rhizomatic routes of Glissant's Relation. Given the entanglements in its makeup, the religious practice of Haitian voodoo stands as a noteworthy example of such creolizing movements and rhizoming movements with respect to origins. Neither wholly Catholic nor wholly West African, voodoo combines these in a nonsummative way, and in a way that asks us to think beyond the terms of fragmentation. In the voodoo ritual, it is difficult to delineate where Catholicism ends and West African spirituality begins. That is to say, the nonfragmentation that creolization instantiates is one in which a generative creole product, subject performance, or way of life exists as a whole that repurposes past fragments in something no longer measurable by a logic of purity. We might say, along with Lugones, that this repurposing produces a *non*fragmented multiplicity that is unable to be divided up into the originals "pieces" being creolized. To be sure, these pieces are recognizable in the creole artifact, but in the presentation of creolization's product, there is little to determine when one fragment begins and the other ends. In a sense, creolization is about the production of fragments *intermeshing* (as Lugones deploys this term) in a single place and moment in history. As an intermeshing, what emerges is a multiplicity in nonfragmentation, a nonadditive emergence for which split-separation no longer applies. To that end, we might say that in Lugones's account, fragmentation refers to being split among worlds (each bearing their own calculus of oppression and resistance), while the fragments that predate creolizing processes find themselves in the single world out of which creolization will take place. As chapter 2 shows, the resulting nonfragmented creole artifact does not subscribe to a logic of purity, rigid closure, or stasis. Instead, we are called to understand creoleness as becoming—always in moving, communicative relation with the diversity of the world in which such processes manifest themselves.[29]

As Ortega notes, "At the heart of Lugones's project [that proposes an ontological plurality of self and world] is an account of self as multiple but not fragmented and a disclosure of the social as heterogeneous."[30] In the third section of this chapter, I focus on the conception of community that emerges out of this understanding of the social as heterogeneous. In that account, we see that Lugones's ontological pluralism acts as a corrective to the view that sociality is unitary, homogeneous, and oriented in terms of a singular meaning. Her notion of active subjectivity accompanies this sense of sociality, since it is through this formulation that we get an *inter*subjective intentionality that unmasks the fiction of the abstract individual—one separated from connections with others, with history, and with intermeshing oppressions. In other words, the third section shows that Lugones's account of active subjectivity "[unveils] the collectivity backing up the individual [and is alive in] the activity of dispersed intending in complex, heterogeneous collectivities."[31] In the end, it is Lugones's critical exposition of fragmentation in the subject that facilitates these formulations. In other words, it is out of the centrality of the nonfragmented subject that we see the possibility of the social as grounded in difference, movement, and open-endedness.

Ortega on Thick and Thin Senses of Unease

My claim is that Lugones's nonfragmented sense of multiplicity accomplishes operations similar to what we find in Ortega's multiplicitous self. These operations of the multiplicitous self are twofold: (1) the subject is gathered across a "oneness" that makes sense of agency, rendering meaningful the identity claims at the foundation of experience; and (2) alongside this oneness, the subject is understood as living *in between* worlds, and therefore positioned in an existential condition of complexity, heterogeneity, and movement. I have traced these two operations in Lugones's development of nonfragmentation, and in what follows, I highlight those aspects in Ortega's conception of multiplicitousness that condition similar outcomes. In other words, I emphasize the ways in which Ortega's account of a multiplicitous self honors the subject's nonhomogeneity while protecting against her being split across multiple worlds, despite her being in between. To be sure, there are important metaphysical worries that stop Ortega short from adopting Lugones's account of a subject with multiple selves. In that sense, it is important to retain these important differences between her account of identity and Lugones's.

Because Ortega's account of subjectivity begins with acknowledging the existential condition of being in between, she draws a distinction between a "thick" and "thin" sense of unease. In this distinction, we find a common thread across her, Lugones's, and Anzaldúa's work—conceptualizing heterogeneity (both in the subject and the idea of community) beyond the binary of integration and assimilation or complete fragmentation. Insofar as I have noted this in creolizing conceptions of heterogeneity, the stakes involved in my current trace of Ortega's distinction (between "thick" and "thin" experiences of unease) are to connect with the ways in which creolization also asks us to move beyond the integration or complete fragmentation binary. In what ways does this distinction between thick and thin experiences of unease allow us to make connections between (on the one hand) the framing of difference in the multiplicitous self and (on the other) the framing of difference in the creolizing subject?[32] Perhaps we might ask whether the creole subject can be thought of in terms of a multiplicitous self, insofar as they are both "in process, or in the making," are relational in their structure, and subsist in a coherence that is not diametrically opposed to heterogeneity.[33]

In Heideggerian fashion, Ortega poses the question of the relationship between "mineness" (Heidegger's concept of *Jemeinigkeit*) and the ambiguity that often accompanies the experience of having to engage with multiple communities of sense, and perhaps also the outright contradiction in that existential sense of being in between. Given this movement, ambiguity, and contradiction, in what sense can I hold on to a notion of "mineness," or existentially encounter a self that is mine? A possible consequence of my being in between worlds is that I am called to be someone of a certain comportment in one world, and then have to take on a radically different (and sometimes contradictory) comportment in another. Where am I in such transitions, or, more importantly, *who* am I in such being-in-between? As one can imagine, it is difficult to imagine having such an experience while being at ease in the world. That is to say, Ortega calls her readers' attention to a relationship between a subject's access to the experience of "mineness" and that subject's access to the experience of being at ease, such that a compromised experience of the coherence that "mineness" offers underscores a comportment of unease in the world. Hence, if the existential condition of being in between worlds comes at the cost of existential coherence (or unity), then the multiplicitous self is one for whom being at ease is a foreclosed possibility. Ortega writes that "being-at-ease is a function of one's ability to be nonreflective about everyday norms in the sense that Heidegger indicates and of having familiarity with the language, as well as sharing a history with people [in those communities of sense]."[34] Here she draws our attention to the ways in which existing easily not only emerges out of a sense of "mineness" in the world but also means that one does not have to think about the implications of being in that particular world, or about the implications of how one might be faring in that world. In other words, the question of personal coherence or oneness—the question of mineness—does not rise to the level of explicit reflection when one is maximally at ease. The experience of being in between worlds opens up the multiplicitous self to the possibility of not having access to mineness and, as a consequence, to not being at ease in the world. For this reason, Ortega develops the distinction between a thick and thin sense of not being at ease, to determine such possibilities (of the subject's access to the experience of mineness and coherence in her multiplicitousness).

Ortega joins both Lugones and Anzaldúa in her recognition of the importance of being in the world critically and reflectively, noting that "Anzaldúa recognizes the creative potential of a life of not being-at-ease."[35] Lugones similarly finds, in this "not being-at-ease," the inclination to world-travel, which ultimately increases the subject's capacities for creatively reimagining what it means to be a human in the world. Ortega similarly understands that the experience of being in between worlds (much like the experience of navigating ontological plurality that Lugones describes) is explicitly shaped by those political structures of domination that determine citizenship and belonging in a post-neocolonial age of migration. *Critical* being-in-between allows for creative modes of sociality in resistance to those dominating structures. So as Ortega theorizes the two distinct senses of not being at ease, she is mindful not to undermine the resistive potential of this critical comportment in the lives of those living under the domination of colonial hegemony. Following a Heideggerian understanding of what it means to encounter ruptures in one's world at the level of everyday existence, she writes, "Being-at-ease might be a welcomed way of life, but it is also an avoidance of change and transformation."[36] This is because, for Ortega, being at ease in one's world makes it unlikely that one will cognize unjust political structures and, ultimately, unlikely too that one will be motivated to imagine a world otherwise. To borrow from Lugones, a subject who is at ease in the world is one for whom the need for world-traveling is absent—thus, one who will not encounter other subjects adversely "affected by relations of power influencing . . . and [regulating their] social identities."[37] The fourth section of this chapter will focus on the various formulations of home and belonging found in Lugones, Ortega, and Anzaldúa and bring these into conversation with what I hold to be a creolizing idea of home. But I note here that, in reconceptualizing a notion of belonging that includes the kind of critical reflection needed for political transformation, I call into question this relationship between unease and the potential for resistance and transformation: I claim that in creole modes of belonging one finds a being at ease in the world that is simultaneously resistive (or, at the very least, subversive). More broadly, I am wary of analyses of marginalized experiences that mark the price of "home" as that which must be paid for the prize of resisting dominant structures and of working out alternative ways of being, experiencing, and identity formation.[38]

For now, I return to Ortega's position, which holds that too much ease in the world undermines possibilities for critical resistance against oppressive relations of power. To articulate this position, she develops the idea of a thin sense of not-being-at-ease to describe "the experience of minimal ruptures of everyday practices."[39] In contrast, a thick sense of not being-at-ease points to "the experience of a deeper sense of not being familiar with norms, practices, and the resulting contradictory feelings about who we are given our experience in the different worlds we inhabit and whether those worlds are threatening or welcoming."[40] This distinction allows Ortega to argue that a level of unease (what she describes, following Heidegger, as a certain "un-readiness-to-hand") is needed for subjects to desire alternative and more just ways of living, without valorizing the kind of "intimate terrorism" that Anzaldúa articulates in her experience of interstitial living.[41] A thick sense of not being at ease maps onto this kind of intimate terrorism, while a thin sense would simply capture the existential condition of a multiplicitous self who moves between worlds. For Ortega, it should not be the case that my movement between worlds and my existing liminally undermine my ability to encounter myself as coherently one and to recognize my experiences as, indeed, mine. This would amount to a thick sense of unease, whereby the subject does not know *who* she is as she moves between worlds. At the level of thin unease she navigates uncomfortably, or haltingly, but her journey is accompanied by a sense of coherent mineness that, for Ortega, is necessary to her thriving in her being-in-between.

At stake in this differentiation is Ortega's concern with the multiplicitous self's capacity to make a home for herself in the world. I address this more fully later in this chapter. However, for my current trace of her alternative account of subjectivity, it is important to note that, in a thin sense of not being-at-ease, Ortega identifies conditions for the possibility of existential unity. This is *not* the kind of unity that informs the politics of purity that Lugones critiques, nor is it the kind of unity that grounds a notion of the subject as homogeneous onto itself. Instead, the existential unity Ortega has in mind incorporates the ambiguity, movement, and relationality that is included in the idea of a multiplicitous self. This self is *multiplicitously one*. She is "thinly" ill at ease in her movement, insofar as she encounters a particular world as somewhat unfamiliar and as a discursive space in which she must engage with other subjects in the acts of world building and sense-making. This subject's thin sense of not being at ease equips her with a readiness to respond to difference, given that she is both critical of structures that code for that difference as illegitimate and reflective of the implications, for her own liminal existence, of such political codes that vilify impurity (codes that determine difference as illegitimate). A thin sense of not being at ease means that, as multiplicitous, this subject is positioned to explicitly cognize structures of domination (and to then resist them) and to be attentive to the alternative modes of sociality coming out of spaces of liminality.

In Ortega's account of a thick sense of not being at ease, we read dangers similar to what Lugones finds in fragmentation. In being ill at ease in a thick sense, I find myself split apart among contradicting versions of myself in ways that are unreconcilable and that undermine my capacity to encounter my experiences as, indeed, mine. This splitting does the work of fragmentation, insofar as it robs me of the kind of coherence needed to both name my identity as one shaped by political domination and resist that domination for the sake of a more liberatory kind of existence. Ortega is clear that because her account of a multiplicitous self does *not* imply this thick sense of not being at ease, it does not call for sacrificing a sense of oneness and existential unity that (on her account) *should* be at the foundation of being-in-between-worlds.

The need to retain a notion of identity for the purpose of political resistance is a position across which Latina feminisms (along with broader third-world feminisms) contend with postmodern interpellations of identity.[42] Ortega holds that some conception of identity—along with its grounding in sociohistorical location—is needed for the kind of political resistance and transformation that marginalized communities need to enact for their survival and flourishing. In other words, subjects for whom liminality is central to their existence must anchor their political work in their relation to historical power (a relationship shaped in the grid of colonial domination). Hence, although Ortega includes a clear account of ambiguity and movement in her notion of a multiplicitous self, she does not see such movement as undermining the possibility of naming identities as such. She writes, "The problem is not identity politics but how identity is conceived. The concept of identity politics needs to be reframed in such a way that it allows for political solidarity while recognizing the multiplicity of political identifications that are available to the multiplicitous self."[43] Here Ortega identifies as false the dichotomy between (a) rejecting identity for fear of its regressive essentialism and (b) embracing ambiguity and fluidity at the expense of understanding identity as historically located and of forming solidarity out of those shared historical locations. Multiplicitous selfhood—much like Lugones's nonfragmented plural subject—is *both* a locus of historically grounded identity claims *and* ambiguously fluid (antiessentialist) in its existential orientations.

Cristina Beltrán is critical of attempts to etch out a politics of resistance or subversiveness out of experiences of border living. She writes that "when hybridity becomes a kind of foundational or 'fixed' identity that forecloses more creative and productive defiant approaches to identity and subjectivity," then we return to the atavism that has produced oppressive conditions for those hybrid identities.[44] In other words, Beltrán is wary of the tendency for a "politics of hybridity"—political resistance that comes out of identity claims of hybridity, in-between-ness, border living, or interstitial existence—to position itself as ultimately another politics of purity, producing its own hierarchy through which hybridity is valorized over against its other. In this move, hybridity becomes the essentializing and closed-off "purity" against which white and European modes of identity signify as inferior. "*Mestizas* are in flux, Others are not; *mestizas* represent the next step forward, while Other subjectivities are less capable of evolution."[45] Lugones's conception of separation-as-curdling (which I address in the fourth section of this chapter) seems to be called for here, since it is precisely through the metaphor of curdling that she guards against the critique offered by Beltrán. In other words, Lugones's conception of separation-as-curdling offers a mode of resistance against oppressive structures that avoids what is of most concern in Beltrán's reading—a version of political resistance that comes out of hybrid (mestiza and multiplicitous) identity claims and uses hybridity *not* for its impurity but, rather, for what is *pure and authentic* to that identity.[46] This version of hybrid politics is but another version of a politics of purity which, for Lugones, reproduces the fragmented subject split between (or among) oppositions. Instead, separation-as-curdling demands a separation from a politics of purity and a genuine anchoring in the *impurity* of impure identities.

In other words, Lugones's metaphor of curdling imagines a political resistance that grounds itself in a specific identity claim—identity as impure—without reproducing the essentializing hierarchy of which scholars like Beltrán are critical. Allison Weir's conception of transformative identity politics can also help us avoid the dangers that Beltrán identifies.[47] In transformative identity politics, Weir asks us to understand identities as being situated across and in terms of historical power. Out of those multiple historical locations, they can form relationships across lines of power: identities can come together in a collective "we" for the sake of political resistance and transformation. But in that crossing for the sake of coming together, differences are encountered in terms of their originating historical location, so reflection and self-critique occurs, such that the identities involved in the encounter (in the "we") are themselves transformed. In other words, historical location is understood as vitally informative, but not as absolute or naturalized insofar as the identities occupying these locations are available for transformation through the dialogic process of being in community.[48] Weir writes, "Identification becomes a process of remaking meaning [grounded in] an ethical, relational model of identity as a historical, dialogical process of meaning making."[49]

We can understand Ortega's account of the unity and multiplicitousness of the subject in the vein of Weir's transformative identity politics. The multiplicitous self is open to transformation (as she moves between multiple worlds), but also squarely located in historical relations of power. In other words, the multiplicitous self claims a social identity through which she makes sense of her multiplicitous experiences across plural communities. However, any political resistance coming out of the idea of this multiplicitous self would avoid the atavism against which Beltrán warns, since, for Ortega, oneness at the expense of multiplicitousness generates a politics that "[falls] into the trap of translating [that] sense of oneness into a call for sameness."[50] In other words, Ortega's understanding of the unity of the subject is not one that participates in the homogenizing of difference. It is not a unity that participates in what Lugones identifies as the logic of purity politics. Out of her distinction between thick and thin senses of not being at ease in the world, Ortega shows us how the identity of the subject can honor multiplicity, difference, and ambiguity *as* she encounters herself (her identity) as unified.[51]

In taking this formulation to the level of community, this model of "multiplicitous-as-one" points to the possibility of collective existence that is unified socially, politically, and culturally, without that collective existence resorting to postures that serve the interests of closed-off community borders. In other words (and to anticipate what I discuss in chapter 6), Ortega's model allows us to conceive of a collective national existence without resorting to ultranationalism. Hence, I note the ways in which Ortega's account of the subject positions us to think differently about community. More importantly, what her accounts gestures toward echoes how Glissant adopts creolization to theorize the possibility of a differentiating (rhizoming) community that is coherent despite its rhizomaticity. In both instances, the subject and the community are structured as neither fragmented confusion nor reductive integration. Instead, subject and community stand as some alternative "third" way, one that avoids integrative practices that undermines ambiguity and flux, but also facilitates coherence in the midst of that ambiguity and flux. To recall, processes of creolization generate ways of being in the world that very much mirror Ortega's and Lugones's respective assessments of existential multiplicity—ways of being in the world through which this subject is "caught in between norms and practices of different cultures . . . races or 'worlds.'"[52] Any integration that happens in creole processes are alongside (and thus not at the expense of) diversities in relation. To that end, the structure of subjectivity coming out of creolization aligns with the dimensions of Ortega's multiplicitous self, insofar as creole oneness also simultaneously accounts for movement, ambiguity, and in-between-ness.

Anzaldúa's New Mestiza

Gloria Anzaldúa's work on the experience of living in the borderlands poses similar questions for conceptions of subjectivity. Out of her seminal work on the new mestiza, she asks her readers to think through the possibilities of naming for the sake of ambivalence and of making home out of suspensions, in the thresholds between political and cultural worlds. Anzaldúa's new mestiza captures this alternatively imagined subject—a subject whose way of being in between, in the border, is one of such ambivalence. In what follows, I focus on how Anzaldúa's conceptions of mestiza identity, *la facultad*, and the *Coatlicue* state work not only to demonstrate the idea of a subject grounded in difference and movement but also, ultimately, to put this way of theorizing borderland subjectivity into conversation with accounts of creolization.

Of the mode of knowing that she names "la facultad," Anzaldúa writes, "Those who do not feel psychologically or physically safe in the world are more apt to discover this sense. Those who are pounced on the most have it the strongest—the females, the homosexuals of all races, the darkskinned, the outcast, the persecuted, the marginalized, the foreign."[53] In this account of la facultad, we hear resonances with Ortega's descriptions of being ill at ease in the world, of not being able to fall into the kind of Heideggerian nonreflectiveness about the world precisely because its structures are not designed for your thriving. Instead, for the subject who is "pounced on," the world is encountered as alien (as unlivable) due to its mainstream politics and cultural practices. Anzaldúa tells us that from that outcast position the subject develops an extra sense that allows her to navigate through and survive in structures that undermine her ability to be fully human. Hence, this extra sense—la facultad—is to be understood as a survival mechanism that is developed out of necessity by liminal subjects (like Anzaldúa herself). "[We] are forced to develop this faculty so that we'll know when the next person is going to slap us or lock us away. . . . It's a kind of survival tactic that people, caught between the worlds, unknowingly cultivate."[54]

Though there is a correlation between possessing this faculty of sensing and the experience of not fully belonging, we might ask how la facultad is in relationship with Ortega's distinction between thick and thin senses of being ill at ease in the world. Does the conditioning borderland experience of this extra sense constitute the thick sense of unease, of which Ortega is critical? Or might it qualify in terms of the thinner sense, the sense that, in Ortega's account, still makes possible the work of home-making in the in-between spaces of the borderlands? Such questions are important as I determine what it might mean for the subject in possession of la facultad to create spaces of belonging (or mechanisms of alternative belonging), despite her being in suspension between worlds. I want to keep these questions at the forefront as I place Anzaldúa's new mestiza alongside Lugones's account of the plural self, and alongside Ortega's account of the multiplicitous self.

According to Anzaldúa, the antihabitual existence of the subject in possession of la facultad shapes the kind of consciousness out of which emerges the new mestiza—the subject who must live in the borderlands across which cultural worlds collide. Out of this liminal space, the mestiza pieces together fragments of worlds found in these liminal spaces, to then generate conditions for being human in ways that ought to be impossible, given the dominant structures of those worlds. For this reason, Anzaldúa uses the metaphor of "a morphogenesis" to describe this generative work of mestiza consciousness, referencing the work of chemist Ilya Prigogine: "Prigogine discovered that substances interact not in predictable ways as it was taught in science, but in different and fluctuating ways to produce new and more complex structures, a kind of birth he called 'morphogenesis.'"[55] In a similar vein, she asks us to understand the work of mestiza consciousness in terms of this unpredictability and creative emergence. Something new and different is produced as a consequence of living in the borderlands, and of being called to negotiate the fragments of worlds from which one is outcast and in which one is "pounced on."[56] Integral to this creative process is la facultad, given that it is across this sense that the mestiza encounters her dissonant relationship to the mainstream. The urgency to articulate something new arises out of this dissonance, so for Anzaldúa, the increased awareness that comes out of the experience of living in the borderlands produces the kind of mestiza consciousness that would then engage with the world in this morphogenetic way.

As I have shown in chapter 2, processes of creolization are marked by this unpredictable joining of fragments of worlds—linguistic worlds, religious worlds, culinary worlds. However, even more fundamental that this, Anzaldúa identifies, in the morphogenic creativity of mestiza consciousness, possibilities for joining what she reads as a bifurcation produced out of Western modernity's metaphysics—spirit disjoined from body, reason from passion, light from dark.[57] Out of the consciousness of the new mestiza, she finds the possibility of crossing beyond such separations to generate alternative modes of being human through which the subject is no longer split between falsely oppositional metaphysical regions. Instead, her critical understanding of the harm coded for in these binaries positions the mestiza to enter into a more complete (less fragmented) sense of self. In writing that is both personal and sensual, Anzaldúa's account of "la Coatlicue" captures this experience of crossing. It is a mode of writing that *itself* crosses the often-assumed binaries between the personal/testimonial (on the one hand) and the philosophical (on the other).[58] My current trace of the alternatively imagined conception of subjectivity in Anzaldúa's work will not include all of the richness of the Coatlicue state, given that it takes me away from my goal of identifying fruitful connections between creolizing and Latina feminist conceptions of self, belonging, and community. Nonetheless, it is important to note that, for Anzaldúa, this Coatlicue state "[disrupts] the smooth flow (complacency) of life. . . . *Coatlicue* is a rupture in our everyday world."[59] In one sense, the world of the mestiza is marked by rupture to the degree she is unable to fully belong in mainstream structures of the world. But in another sense, and perhaps more fundamentally, the Coatlicue state is what allows the subject situated in the borderlands to *transcend* the alienation she encounters in the mainstream. In other words, the rupture in the Coatlicue state gives birth to a kind of reconciliation, to a new (more whole, less ruptured) way of being that is no longer the alienation and dissonance experienced at the hands of dominant structures. "*Coatlicue* is the mountain, the Earth Mother who conceived all celestial beings out of her cavernous womb. Goddess of birth and death, *Coatlicue* gives and takes away life; she is the incarnation of cosmic processes."[60]

Does the more prior unity, toward which this Coatlicue state moves, succumb to the critique we find in Lugones's argument for nonfragmentation? In other words, does Anzaldúa's Coatlicue recenter a logic of purity in its move toward repairing the subject's alienation (her splitting) across disparate worlds? Though the Coatlicue state works against the subject's supposedly irreconcilable fragmentation—across the Mexican, the Indian, and the American in her—by taking her to a higher completion, this completion is not a being-at-ease in the world. To the contrary, Anzaldúa notes that "*la Coatlicue* is the consuming internal whirlwind" that continues to call her to encounter and live in the vulnerability of the contradictions of light and dark, mind and body. Hence, on my reading, the Coatlicue state would not participate in the purity logics that Lugones critiques. In this state, Anzaldúa identifies the replacement of autonomy with the vulnerability that one might expect from the experience of painful growth and transition, or of becoming other to oneself. Of the autonomy that often structures a Western notion of subjectivity, she writes, "I spent the first half of my life learning to rule myself. . . . Now at midlife I find that autonomy is a boulder on my path that I keep crashing into."[61] This Western-constituted autonomy centers the subject as the controller of her universe and as the controller of all that is other than her in that universe. On the other hand, the vulnerability central to the Coatlicue state *unhinges* the subject's control of herself and places her in the midst of contradicting (*impure*) states. Hence, any transcendence of alienation that takes place is less of a reconciliation (if by "reconciliation" one means the replacing of dissonance, ambiguity, and movement with stasis, purity, and transparency), and more of a crossing over into a new center, a center that brings about completion *in* (and not despite) the vulnerability of contradiction and movement.

For the purpose of bringing Anzaldúa's account of subjectivity into conversation with creolization, I note the ways in which the centrality of this vulnerability reveals what, in the Coatlicue state, can be read as a state of suspension—neither completely spirit nor completely body, neither light nor dark. This is important for how Anzaldúa wants us to understand the new mestiza to be similarly suspended in the nonplace (or not-yet-place) of the border. If the border is a line, a conceptual region where the safety of the home space ends and danger of the unhomely space begins, then we can also think of the being of the border as nonspaced insofar as it is neither of the two. It is without dimension, so that it might give dimensionality to spaces of "home" and "foreign territory." Insofar as it functions to separate domestic from foreign, the border signifies as neither, existing in suspension as it functions to delineate between the two. As neither, though, its ontology participates in an ambiguity that conditions an impossible naming. We might think of this suspension of dimensionality, of place-in-space, to also inflect the subject—Anzaldúa's new mestiza—occupying the borders. Not fully American, Mexican, or Indian, the mestiza is culturally ambiguous, and similarly impossible to name as she navigates multiple worlds in which she never fully belongs. This ambiguous suspension of categories is what the Coatlicue state underscores. And it is through being centered "in suspension" that the mestiza is able to find reprieve from her experience of alienation.

Much as in Lugones's and Ortega's work, Anzaldúa identifies one sense in which the ambiguity of mestiza identity manifests itself as everyday existential violence. But there is also another sense that signifies as the promise of an emergence, of generating a way of being human out of the foreclosure determined in structures of domination. Alternative ways of naming and identity formation matter in this negotiation of domination and liberation, so all three thinkers (Anzaldúa, Lugones, and Ortega) explore modalities of naming that might respond to the violence of being in between, without reproducing the very logic of essentializing out of which that violence grows.[62] I locate this at the conceptual heart of a creolizing way as well—ways of attending to the importance of historical location, without deploying that historical ground for the exclusionary politics that often underscores cultures of ultra-nationalism.[63] On this question of the possibility of alternative practices of naming, Anzaldúa reflects on past nationalist Chicano movements as follows: "Chicanos did not know we were a people until 1965. . . . With that recognition, we became a distinct people. Something momentous happened to the Chicano soul—we became aware of our reality and acquired a name and a language . . . that reflected that reality. Now that we had a name, some of the fragmented pieces began to fall together—who we were, what we were, how we had evolved."[64] I cite Anzaldúa at length here not only because she stresses the political violence of being suspended in between (of living with an impossible naming) but also because she points toward the relationship between the personal and the more overtly political negotiations of domination. What happens at the level of politics both constitutes and is constituted by those radically resistive orientations of "the soul," orientations that change the cadence and direction of language and ultimately change the politics called for by that (new) language. This should remind us of Glissant's more fundamental claims about the need for a new imaginary *first*, before there can be anything new at the level of the political. Anzaldúa notes that despite the politics of Chicano nationalism, "the struggle of borders is our reality still."[65] In other words, the *political* gestures toward establishing a name (an identity) for the mestiza experience of the borderlands is but one articulation of that struggle. Alongside it remains the cultural ambiguity that shapes the existential level of the everyday, an ambiguity with which *Borderlands* ultimately grapples.

To be sure, it is *because* the subject is positioned in this impossible naming (suspended in an ambiguity) that she is coded as fearful and as what is "pounced on." A consequence of this ambiguity is that the subject either floats between, or is in tension across, the known identities of "the one who belongs" and the "one who doesn't." Mexican Americanness is a moving signifier, in this regard—both Mexican and American, and neither of the two, all at the same time. In this spirit Anzaldúa writes, "I am visible—see this Indian face—yet I am invisible. I both blind them with my beak nose and am their blind spot."[66] There is much resonance here with the ways in which creolizing cultural forms exist in an ambiguous relationship to dominant structures and play with a visibility under the colonizing gaze *as* they simultaneously hide in the plain sight of that gaze. Those traditional masquerade characters that slaves donned in their pre–Ash Wednesday carnival festivals are a powerful manifestation of this. Many of these figures mimicked the colonizing stereotypes of the lazy, devilish, and irredeemably childlike African, but in the performativity of the masquerade, there was often a mockery of those stereotypes that happened in the plain sight of the colonial space. Anzaldúa captures this as she meditates on her own culturally ambiguous borderland identity, in tension across the invisibility and hypervisibility of the cultural politics of a neocolonial global structure. Across this tension is the perpetuation of the suspended/impossible naming that persists at the level of the existential, both as source of violence *and* as promise of creative resistance.[67]

For the purpose of bringing this account alongside the process of creolization, it is important for us to read Anzaldúa's meditations on "the stress of living with [this] cultural ambiguity" alongside her critique of a white culture that has stood in the way of Chicanas and Chicanos fully becoming themselves.[68] In response to this violence, her desire is for her community to "[take back] or [uncover their] true faces.[69] What would these "true faces" be, in light of the centrality of the cultural ambiguity of living in the borderlands? Is Anzaldúa's program one that calls for a replacing of this ambiguity with clearly defined (read, here, *essential*) modes of naming? Alongside similar formations that come out of creolist expositions of identity politics, it is possible to locate Anzaldúa's desire for "true faces" in an antiessentialist register. In their essay "In Praise of Creoleness," Jean Bernabé, Patrick Chamoiseau, Raphaël Confiant, and Mohamed B. Taleb Khyar reference a true Caribbean way of being, but this true identity is one that already opposes the logic of "Same and the One. . . . It opposes to Universality the great opportunity of a world diffracted but recomposed, the conscious harmonization of pre-served diversities: DIVERSALITY."[70] It is in a similar vein that I hear Anzaldúa's call for a clear sense of Chicanx identity. As a call to resist erasure by white culture, it is also one that envisions that resistance in terms of the unpredictable morphogenic activity of the new mestiza—activity that creatively joins together fragments in the cultural collusions of the borderlands in a way that centers movement and fluidity. In other words, the truth of mestiza is named in the midst of ambiguity, or *as* this tolerance for ambiguity, thus without resorting to essentializing frames of purity, origin, and authenticity.

Authenticity almost always signifies in opposition to a frame that understands borders as leaky or fluid. Out of such accounts, the authentic subject is certainly not one who exists liminally, and in terms of movement and change (as with Anzaldúa's new mestiza, or Ortega's multiplicitous self, or Lugones's world-traveler). How Anzaldúa's account troubles this conception of authenticity also takes us to the complex relationship between location (particularly "location" in its function of original and founding place) and relation, which comes out of Édouard Glissant's conception of the rhizomatic community. Chapter 3 outlined this concept of Relation in Glissant's work, but I want to reiterate here that his deployment of the metaphor of the rhizome precisely captures an attendance to the location and historicity of a community as it problematizes the centrality of origin, purity, and stasis. We find in Glissant what I argue is also true for Anzaldúa—namely, a way to understand how a vital connection to place and history can also account for the equally vital movement of a relationally constituted subject and a relationally constituted community. In this alternative signification of historicity, both the subject and community are no longer grounded in temporal and spatial origin narratives that function for the sake of stasis and closure.

This reformulation is particularly clear in Anzaldúa's meditations on the linguistic in-between-ness of the new mestiza. She writes, "Chicanas who grew up speaking Chicano Spanish have internalized the belief that we speak poor Spanish. It is illegitimate, a bastard language."[71] She underscores the importance of having pride in this borderland way of speaking, despite its being at the fork of twin identities.[72] I would add that Anzaldúa demands a pride in this linguistic identity despite its "illegitimate" signification, insofar as its bastard nature points to a way of naming (of articulating one's subjectivity) that is void of the essentializing forces of origin. Much like identities that have emerged through creolizing processes, the identity that is bastard is without linear genealogies, without single roots, and without purity. It means to "be" in the world through complex and zigzag connections to what came before; to "be" ambiguously, opaquely, in a way that is out of line with the legitimized order of things (out of the line that would clearly trace back to points of origin).[73] To that end, a bastard identity (or language or culture) conditions the possibility of generating "a new story to explain the world and our participation in it."[74] That alternative world participation complicates the story of roots and origin *as* it marks historical location for the sake of resisting the domination produced out of such stories of roots and origin.

Implications for Difference, Borders, and Community

The alternative conceptions of subjectivity offered by Lugones, Ortega, and Anzaldúa all demand this new mode of participation in the world. They all mark the urgent need to theorize differently about productions of community that would account for this new participation in the world and for their own existential truths of multiplicity, movement, and liminality. In the following two chapters (comprising part 3 of this book), I determine what such structures of community would be if we started with "subjectivity otherwise" and attended to how a subject grounded in fluidity and heterogeneity might encounter difference differently.

My goal in part 3 continues to be one of highlighting how these articulations might be brought into conversation with creolization. To that end, chapter 5 turns to Lugones's conception of curdling in order to trace its implications for the possibility of community as both unified and heterogeneous. I simultaneously bring this account of social heterogeneity into those creolizing modalities of community as One in and as many. But more broadly, chapters 5 and 6 are concerned with how these combined resources (offered in creolization and Latina feminist conceptions) might be taken into overtly political registers. In determining how all this—Lugones's curdling subjectivity and social heterogeneity, Glissant's composite relationality and rhizomatic errantry—might offer a *politics* of community otherwise, chapter 6 will turn to the work of Frantz Fanon. Namely, in response to Fanon's critical reflections on a narrow nationalism and to his call for a decolonial account of nation, chapter 6 will offer a properly creolizing conception of the nation—a conception grounded in the poetic imaginary developed by Glissant.

Though I don't address this explicitly in what follows, I want to acknowledge that, in thinking subjectivity and community otherwise, we are taken to the question of belonging. In other words, in these reimagined formulations of subjectivity, of difference, of community, we might ask: How much "contradiction and ambiguity" is needed for generating resistive ways of being and for transforming structures of domination? Additionally, how much grounding (stability, home) is needed to support that invariably difficult work of resistance? I am drawn to processes of creolization because I find, in those processes, an attention paid to both of these questions. In other words, in creolization there is this possibility of being critically resistant to structures of domination while determining, in the interstices of those structures, alternative spaces that can serve as homely spaces.[75] In taking these formulations to the more politically constituted questions of community (and solidarity), this possibility of home-making and belonging is central.

Part 3

✦

The Poetics and Politics of "Community" Otherwise

Part 3 of this book begins from the reimagined conceptions of subjectivity traced in chapters 3 and 4. Its orienting questions are those of community and borders: namely, how our understanding of community and border formation shifts in response to the subject as liminal, fluid, and in between. These reformulations will be tested (so to speak) on explicitly political terrain in chapter 6, where I bring Glissant's account of the composite community to bear on Fanon's development of an alternative and decolonial conception of national culture and identity. Through such assessments, what remains to be gauged is whether or not it is possible to think the resistive generativity of Lugones's curdling separation (discussed in chapter 5), and of Glissant's creolizing community, in terms that allow for signification on political terms. What do we lose when we frame sociality as complex, antiteleological, and permeable? To ask this differently, what remains of nation-ness in reformulations that are without the essentialist structures and logic of rigidity and purity that chapter 1 of this book outlined?

Chapter 1 gave an overview of the temporality and spatiality of standard articulations of nation, grounded in singular historical roots and linear organizations of an imagined community. The chapters that followed then traced the ways in which the process of creolization calls for alternative organizations of space and time, organizations that utilize creolizing conceptions of subjectivity, relationality, community, and borders. In this culminating section, I offer these creolizing conceptions as potential responses to Fanon's aspirational demands for a radically new (and decolonial) understanding of the nation that, in moving beyond the structures of colonialism and its legacy, offer something otherwise than a colonial narrative of the human. Hence, chapter 6 imagines how Fanon's analysis might open up possibilities for Glissant's composite community to signify in the political realm.

But before that, chapter 5 clarifies the ways in which intersections between Glissant's theorizations and those of Latina feminisms call for alternatively structured conceptions of community. Specifically, the chapter pursues the question of difference, or what conceptualizations of difference emerge out of mestiza consciousness, ontological plurality, and multiplicitous selfhood. I pursue this question of difference using Lugones's account of curdled identities, given its powerful reimagination of the relationship between the one and the many. I bring her conception of curdling to bear on a creolizing process, a process through which one also witnesses reimagined ways of understanding the one/many relationship. Because chapter 5 is oriented around the question of community and its relationship to borders, Anzaldúa's conception of nepantla also features prominently in its analysis. This is because Anzaldúa's notion of nepantla gives us a framework from which to name the meanings of liminal existence, the ways that borders can be dwelling places despite also being nonlocations, and the composite pain and potential for creative transformation (for the generation of "new stories") that emerges from the border.

As chapter 6 will show, Fanon's work is explicitly grounded in the anticolonial struggles of peoples across the continent of Africa, Asia, and the Caribbean. On this account, his work is attentive to the urgent need for a conception of the human *other than* what we find under colonial violence. In other words, Fanon's decolonial thinking centers on a demand not only for a rupture *from* colonial violence but also, and perhaps most importantly, for the difficult work of determining a radically other way of being, doing, and living (that would not simply reproduce what colonialism had historically offered). How do such newly independent nation-states articulate their sovereignties otherwise? How might their democratic strivings articulate a truly decolonial arrangement of the social, the cultural, and the political?

These are the questions around which chapter 6 brings Fanon into conversation with Glissant. Its central argument is that, in more explicitly political ways, Fanonian conceptions offer an account of the social similar to what we find in Glissant (and in Glissant's intersections with Anzaldúa, Lugones, and Ortega). In other words, when it comes to questions of the nation, a similar account of a complex and fluid sociality is at the foundation of how Fanon conceptualizes the decolonial nation, since it is a conception ultimately shaped by the possibility of free life. Using Glissant's account of the composite community allows us to underscore this in ways that are productive not only for reading Fanon's work, but also, more broadly, for thinking imaginatively about alternative (decolonial) ways of being in community with others.

Chapter 5

✦

Difference, Borders, and Community

In creolizing the nation, my attempts have been to locate a Glissantian conception of relationality at the heart of the culture and spirit of national community. This move calls for an account of the subject as relational in nature, entangled with the other in a heterogeneous complex. Chapter 4 identified such conceptions of subjectivity in three pivotal Latina feminist scholars—Gloria Anzaldúa, María Lugones, and Mariana Ortega—and established significant intersections between their conceptions of subjectivity and corresponding accounts in creolization. This chapter remains at these intersections and draws out the implications of these accounts of "subjectivity otherwise" for social, cultural, and political registers of difference. I also argue, in this chapter, that these implications ask us to think differently about the functionality of borders, as well as the communities demarcated by those borders as they are differently imagined.

As I engage with these conceptions of difference, borders, and community, I mark the following tension in my exposition by returning to Anzaldúa's account of the new mestiza. Of the Mexican philosopher José Vasconcelos, Anzaldúa writes, "Opposite to the theory of the pure Aryan, and to the politics of racial purity that white America practices, [Vasconcelos's] theory is one of inclusivity. At the confluence of two or more genetic streams, with chromosomes constantly 'crossing over,' this mixture of races, rather than resulting in an inferior being, provides hybrid progeny, a mutable, more malleable species with a rich gene pool."[1] Here Anzaldúa notes the superiority of the new mestiza in terms of the inclusivity represented not only in her biological or genetic position but also in the cultural "crossing over" that accompanies this chromosomal heterogeneity. "[La] mestiza is a product of the transfer of the cultural and spiritual values of one group to another."[2] Anzaldúa claims that, in the identity of this new kind of heterogeneous subject, multiple cultures and ways of being are included. As a consequence, the (genetic and cultural) impurity of the new mestiza positions her to undermine the political hold of the self/other divisions out of which racial purity politics emerge.

How one reads this inclusivity and, more broadly, its implications for relationality and heterogeneity is of great consequence to what it means to creolize the nation. If, in being me (in giving an account of who I am), I am already giving an account of what is also other, or different, then the risk of such a radical notion of inclusion is that differences among historical positions—and, along with them, the political significance of their material histories—are erased. To be sure, interpretations of Glissant's conception of the rhizomatic community that dismisses the centrality of opacity in his notion of Relation identifies this risk as well. The analysis of this chapter (as, hopefully, of the book overall) avoids renditions of heterogeneity, antiessentialism, and impurity that result in a flattened account of history. I want to keep at the forefront of my analysis the stakes of my proposal to creolize the nation, which are to determine ontological ground for decolonial conceptions of the subject, of difference, and, ultimately, of the culture and spirit of national community and belonging.[3] Developing such decolonial conceptions requires explicit attendance to the neocolonial implications of colonial history or to our obligations to be critical of (so that we might undo) the coloniality that structures contemporary arrangements of individual lives, communities, and their place in the world. As such, my current exposition of difference—how difference might be reimagined to account for the conceptions of subjectivity laid out in the previous chapter—retains the rooted depth of history along with the breadth of heterogeneous impurity.[4]

Difference in and as Relationality

Linda Martín Alcoff's account of the self in *Visible Identities: Race, Gender and the Self* discusses the implications of a certain account of ontological freedom that understands the freedom of the self as an explicit measure of its *lack* of identity. She is critical of this account insofar as it measures freedom in terms of the extent to which the sociopolitical structures that pertain to identity are voided out (so to speak) of the self, so that the self exists beyond the constraints of those structures.[5] Ortega expounds on this account, pointing out that in this formulation "identities are seen as artificial, oppressive constraints on the self's natural indeterminacy."[6] In chapter 4, I address this reading of postmodern accounts of identity and position my own understanding of creolizing identities in opposition to them. However, for my current purposes of tracing the meaning of difference in the conceptual apparatus of creolizing relationality, I note Ortega's synopsis (one that she also shares with Allison Weir) that this move away from the determinative forces of identity is ultimately grounded in a "fear of the power of the other."[7] Out of that fear, the other's alterity signifies as diametrical to an ontological freedom, and all of this bears out at the sociopolitical level as the purity politics of which Lugones is critical. More importantly, fear of the power of the other stands diametrically opposed to the kind of Glissantian relationality on which I aim to ground a creolizing sense of the nation. We might hear such a fear foregrounded and then called into question in Anzaldúa's assessment (quoted earlier) of her lived experiences of her autonomy: "I spent the first half of my life learning to rule myself. . . . Now at midlife I find that autonomy is a boulder on my path that I keep crashing into."[8] Here I read "autonomy" to reflect the kind of subject who is free of those external influences of the sociopolitical—influences marked by the other. In this sense, autonomy describes the subject as self-authored and entirely responsible for the determinations of her inner (and, ultimately, social and public) life. That Anzaldúa encounters this autonomy as an obstacle suggests that it stands in opposition to the fluid and heterogeneous structures of the new mestiza, structures that mirror, in significant ways, the relationality of the rhizome that moves processes of creolization.

In chapter 1, I traced the role of origin narratives in the cultural and discursive formations of the nation. To recall, under standard conceptions, nations emerged with an understanding of themselves as entities with antiquity, rooted in a sacred past that was transcendent to the contingencies of its material history. As Étienne Balibar reminds us, "[The] formation of the nation . . . appears as the fulfillment of a 'project' stretching over centuries," offering a national time—a mythological temporality stretching from a conceived time of origin in the past to the present—to be encountered as linear, uniform, and constant.[9] Because these temporal constructions allowed national collectives to replace their accident of birth with a necessary existence (indeed, a necessary being), the role of linear time in the shaping of the nation is, ironically enough, to give the nation a timeless character, one whose contingent existence becomes constituted as absolutely necessary. To this end, narratives centered in a traceable path back to a single moment in time often ground nativist conceptions of the nation-space, which are rigidly bordered so as to enclose only those whose identity maps onto the single originating moment in question. Chapter 1 showed that, through this organizational framework, difference often shows up as a bastardization of this temporal lineage. That is to say, what shows up as a deviation from the line that leads back to origins in time and place, what cannot be determined to emerge out of the nation's single originating moment in time, is cast as the nonbelonging other, vilified as a consequence of her falling out of the legitimizing linear order.[10]

In the preceding chapter, I discussed Anzaldúa's reflections on the bastard nature of the language of the new mestiza in order to emphasize the significance of this "fall" out of the legitimacy of order for her reimagined account of subjectivity. I reiterate it here to orient the notion of difference in terms of the opacity out of which such bastardized, illegitimate identities are made to (un)signify. In so doing, I hope to address the following question: Does a decentering of narratives of clear lineage and single origins in time make room for us to think about difference as opacity, as what is there without making itself known (or knowable) insofar as it presents itself ambiguously? For difference to signify in this way—as points of opacity—our understanding of difference would require grounding in both epistemological and ontological accounts that are capable of retaining an ambiguous relationship to the "order of order," or to the dominant logics of order and lineage (source, or origin). In what follows, I identify moments in Lugones's work that, by gesturing toward such epistemological and ontological grounding, offer such an account of difference. To be sure, my discussion of Glissant's work (in chapter 3) showed the significant role of opacity in his conceptions of the rhizome and the composite community. In identifying moments of opacity in Lugones, I also highlight ways in which her work might be brought into dialogue with Glissant's formulation of opacity as that which is essential to a community that "rhizomes" itself.

Opacity in Lugones's World-Traveling Subject

Chapter 3's account of the rhizome showed that, for Glissant, a relationality that grows out of an opacity of the other guards against her (epistemological and ontological) reduction to dominant structures. Hence, to be in relation in the composite community would be to "give on and with the other" *as* she remains not entirely known (or not entirely knowable). Glissant theorizes this in his conception of errantry—a mode of knowing, being, and existing that is contemporaneous with the absence of the other's disclosure. As I highlighted in chapter 3, errant thinking produces knowledge that does not totalize for the sake of understanding but instead acknowledges the irreducible difference that emerges through the dynamism of becoming. The subject who moves in the world errantly "challenges and discards the universal. . . . He plunges into the opacities of that part of the world to which he has access . . . but willingly renounces any claims to sum it up or to possess it."[11] Hence, because it is no longer the onto-thinking that reduces all difference into the totalizing frame of a universal, the movement of errantry encounters and retains the opacity that structures Glissant's rhizomatic community. Errantry and opacity work in tandem for difference to register neither as the fearful other nor as what is reduced to or known in terms of sameness (options that participate in a calculus of purity). So, in grounding difference in the opacity of the other, we arrive at a way of thinking about relation, community, and ultimately the nation that conditions human living in the impurity of plurality (heterogeneity), movement, and ambiguity. Difference as opacity moves beyond the same/other duality that grounds a politics of purity (which determines difference in allergic terms) while allowing the alterity of the other to signify. Indeed, it is precisely because this alterity signifies out of a frame of opacity that Glissant's composite community is able to present an alternative conception of community.

In Lugones's development of world-traveling, we find a similar signifying frame for the question of difference. That is to say, the travel of Lugones's plural subject, between multiple worlds, also includes a negotiation of that which is opaque in traveling through ontological plurality. To be sure, like her conception of the plural subject (discussed in chapter 4), Lugones's account of world-traveling is very much motivated by her need to offer a politics of resistance, which would capture the lived experience of those who must exist in between multiple cultural and discursive spaces. In other words, the consequences of the opacity of multiple worlds that shape the experience of world-traveling are explicitly political for Lugones, insofar as it is out of that opacity that oppressed subjects are able to find inventive ways around their oppression under structures of domination. Though my treatment of Glissant's conceptions of relationality and opacity identify the political implications in their formulations, Glissant's work is not explicitly political.[12] However, I identify the following significant resonances between his formulations and Lugones's— difference as and in opacity, ways of knowing and being with the other that preserves that opacity, and generating communal structures that condition inventive possibilities of resistances amid structures of oppression. To that end, I argue that in pairing the travels of the rhizome with that of the plural subject, we find ways to historically ground Glissant's spreading, nontotalitarian rhizome in ways that position the composite community in a register of political resistance. These resonances—across the idea of opacity—suggest that the political negotiations of the world-traveling subject might be supported by the poetic errantry of the rhizomatic encounter with difference. In a similar vein, the political implications of Glissant's poetics of errantry are foregrounded in how opacity centers Lugones's politics of resistance.

On her development of ontological plurality, Lugones writes, "I think that there are many worlds, not autonomous, but intertwined semantically and materially, with a logic that is sufficiently self-coherent and sufficiently in contradiction with others to constitute an alternative construction of the social."[13] She names this alternative construction "heterogeneous" and, in so doing, asks her readers to understand sociality as a historically differentiated space, consisting of a plurality of discursive practices and meaning production. On this formulation, the social is constituted *in* difference, and those differences acquire meaning in history. This way of encountering the social is part of the concrete existence of the plural subject, since (as we saw in chapter 4) it is out of her liminality that the social shows up as heterogeneous, or as consisting of worlds into which she either differentially or partially belongs. The potential for this plural subject to find ways of resisting dominant structures is embedded in sociality's heterogeneous complex, insofar as that complex consists of entanglements of domination *and* liberation. It is in her world-traveling that this liminally positioned subject is able to pursue possibilities of resistance right alongside her oppression.

When it comes to the question of difference, we see that out of this frame of heterogeneous sociality, differences that are socially and politically relevant show up as plural negotiations of history: the other's difference comes out of her concrete experience of navigating structures of domination, and of devising ways to resist those structures, as a consequence of how history has shaped the social through its matrices of power. Hence, our differences are not exterior to the totality of the world (of its history); rather, they precisely reflect how we have been shaped by our public and private navigations of that history. What this means is that, on Lugones's account, to reckon with difference is always already to acknowledge and deeply engage with historical locations and with how the multiplicity of those locations constitute the social as heterogeneous. The social is a complex multiplicity shaped by a plurality of such encounters with history, with each encounter constituting a world—a semantic and discursive ground for meaning production and ways of being. But, as Lugones notes, these historical positionalities are neither monadic nor absolutely isolated from each other. Framing social heterogeneity in this atomistic way simply reinstantiates the fragmentation and calculus of purity of which she is critical. Furthermore, it replaces one socially homogeneous space with *multiple* socially homogeneous spaces, a move that does not yet capture the way in which Lugones's account of social heterogeneity conceptualizes difference to be *constitutive of* the social.

In other words, this reconfiguration grounds sociality in an antiessentialist logic, or in what Lugones calls a politics of impurity. Hence, as we attend to history in order to encounter the concrete meaning of differences, we must also see that historical positions are not mutually closed-off, essentializing categories of human experience. In Lugones's words, "The [historically constituted] categories are real even if one can criticize them as essentialist."[14] Given the living and dynamic nature of the social, these historical locations are not impermeable. The point of the world-traveling subject is that she moves in and out of worlds (or communities of sense), because this movement is indeed possible. World-traveling is facilitated by a comportment of liminality, in particular, because liminal encounters with sociality generate a communicative crossing between historical locations. The world-traveling subject both moves among worlds and conditions the possibility of permeability between those worlds in her act of world-traveling. Hence, when Lugones describes the plurality of the social in terms of many distinct worlds, "not autonomous, but intertwined semantically and materially, with a logic that is sufficiently self-coherent and sufficiently in contradiction with others to constitute an alternative construction of the social," we see her grappling with the need to both acknowledge the significance of historicity, without using that historicity to support a pure, essentialist understanding of the social as consisting of many impermeable worlds.[15] In so doing, she is able to present a reading of the social as dynamic, fluid, and in the process of transforming as a consequence of the concrete, "on the ground" engagements among plural, world-traveling subjects. Most significantly, this transformation happens out of a grounding in histories, not despite them.

On my reading of Glissant's formulation of the composite community, this is also how creolizing processes are captured in the metaphoric movements of the rhizome. In chapter 3, I accounted for this reading by emphasizing the important sense in which creolization, as a way of being in the world and as a process out of which new syncretic linguistic and cultural artifacts emerge, is always already grounded in a specific historical experience. That history (the rupture and forced transplantation constitutive of the transatlantic slave trade) informs the inventive transmutations that are creole in kind. However, insofar as these creole emergences are *inventions*, they attest to the nondeterminative force of that history.[16] History shapes, in other words, but not in definitive ways. Lugones's conception of sociality (as a heterogeneous complex grounded in history) is a clear and explicitly political rendition of this, and like Glissant, she gives opacity a pivotal role in this formulation.

In Glissant's rhizomatic movements, opacity serves as resistance to epistemic imperialism. The other is encountered not to be reduced to some common cultural denominator for the purpose of transparency but, rather, as someone with whom I can be in community, despite my inability to fully understand her concrete historical experience. Furthermore, the horizontal spread of the rhizome captures the sense in which I might even become other to myself in my engagement with an opaque other: my being in community with her has the potential to transform who I am in fundamental ways. This "becoming other unto oneself" is what Glissant captures in the dynamic nature of the rhizome's horizontal spread. Opacity is central here, insofar as it guards the composite community (the community that will model the spread of the rhizome) from remaining, quite statically, an unchanging version of itself. Without the guard of opacity, the treatment of difference (within the cultural and discursive frames of the community) would be such that the other signifies in her likeness to some common (unifying) denominator. In this case the community as a whole would remain in the space of an unchanging commonality, a commonality that could then be used to differentiate legitimate and illegitimate belonging. On the other hand, if we begin from opacity, differences are left to signify as such. Relationality would be grounded in transformation and movement as subjects within the composite community determine, at the concrete and intimate levels of community life, what it means to become other to themselves, or to "give on and with" each other. Beginning from opacity, the community as a whole becomes what Lugones calls a moving heterogeneous complex of change.[17]

In the world-traveling of the plural subject, Lugones also recognizes potentialities of becoming-other. She describes such potential in terms of "epistemic shifts to other worlds of sense," shifts that happen when the plural subject moves in and out of various communities (of which social multiplicity consists) in travel that is precisely not motivated by imperialist endeavors.[18] In other words, like Glissant's errant thinker, Lugones's world-traveler does not seek to understand for the sake of conquering (or to conquer for the sake of understanding). Rather, very much in the spirit of Marilyn Frye's account of the loving eye, Lugones conceives world-traveling as travel led by "the eye of one who knows that to know the seen, one must consult something other than one's own will and interests and fears and imagination."[19] Hence, in both the errant thinker (constituted through the relationality of the composite community) and the world-traveler (moving through a heterogeneous sociality), there is a decentering of the epistemic comfort and ontological wholeness of the subject. Her seeing of the other is an encounter that grapples with certain blind spots (if you will) and resists the need for full disclosure (a need that belongs to an arrogant will, or to an arrogant perception). The errant thinker is in relationship with the other despite this absence of full disclosure, and the world-traveler moves in and out of permeable worlds despite their preservation in opacity. Indeed, without that opacity world-traveling returns to the travel of "tourists and colonial explorers, missionaries, settlers and conquerors."[20]

Community without Telos

In her development of the notion of complex communication, Lugones describes the liminality across which world-traveling happens as a "communicative opening and impasse."[21] That is to say, the borders that separate multiple communities of sense-making condition the possibility of communication—and solidarity—as they also determine the limit of that possibility. Lugones makes sure to point out that, because the social is multiply constituted, liminalities are also multiple. That is to say, plural subjects are pushed into existential negotiations from the borders—where their experiences are in terms of marginalization—across a variety of dominant structures. It is out of these multiple liminalities that Lugones asks us to see, quite simultaneously, the possibility of communicative openings and their *im*possibility (the communicative impasses) within the borderlands of sociality. Communicative openings emerge across worlds as plural subjects find themselves in community as a consequence of their respective experiences of liminality. However, there is also impasse in communication to the degree that my knowledge of my own liminal experience does not guarantee that I am able to understand the other's, especially if we are pushed into the borders by different matrices of oppression. For Lugones, this opening-impasse dyad does not undermine the possibility of community or coalition; rather, it means that such community formation must take place in the absence of complete transparency among subjects. These complex communications emerge across and despite opacity, insofar as what they call for moves beyond the either/or of "opening" and "impasse." Complex communications (perhaps much like the rhizome's errant movement) brings forth a third possibility, which promises to condition what a community of "subjects otherwise" might look like.

For Lugones, complex communication names this third possibility, beyond the opposition of opening and impasse. It grounds a mode of coalition building that captures the possibility of solidarity across multiple and (opaquely) different social locations, as that solidarity attends to differences across historical locations.[22] Through complex communication, Lugones offers a model for what it might mean to form deep relationships across differences that are sustained in their opacity. Much like Glissant's rhizomatic community, complex communication allows for solidarity and community that is transformational and fluid instead of rigid and static, as it grounds itself (in an antiessentialist way) in history. To make such complex communication possible, Lugones calls for the replacing of monologism (which understands successful communication in homogeneous and pure linguistic frames) with polyglossia (through which successful communication happens in heterogeneous and impure linguistic frames). With the latter, communication and community formation emerge as a "dialogic resistance [that] disrupts the communicative barrier without necessarily securing intelligibility in any transparent sense."[23] Much like the movement of the rhizome, polyglossic communication finds its realization in opacity itself, not in opacity's reduction. Might we understand Glissant's errant thinking as a kind of polyglossia, as a mode of dialogic resistance through which the errant thinker's relationship with the other neither aims for understanding in order to reduce nor reduces in order to understand? If this is the case, then both errantry and the polyglossia of complex communication encounter these "communicative barriers" not as a foreclosure of the possibility of communication, community, or coalition but, rather, as their generative condition of possibility.

Much like the transgressions in creolizing generativity (of inventing conditions of possibility against the grain of power and dominant structures), complex communication "[does] not precede the encounter among liminal subjects."[24] That is, the dialogic resistance of both creolizing processes and complex communication does not happen in a historical vacuum. Rather, it happens in the concrete time of relationality and cannot be predicted (in advance of that concrete time) by structures that code only for the communicative impasses that, according to Lugones, sustain the mainstream's production of oppression. These elements of creativity and collective possibility are all part of the community formations that emerge out of creolizing processes, processes that are open-ended in their rejection of the teleologies set up by dominant structures—abjection, dehumanization, and social death. Indeed, this is the salience of Glissant's rhizome metaphor, insofar as its spread is neither determined in advance of its unfolding (on the ground) nor available to some universal systematization of the patterns of its growth at any one moment. This creolizing open-endedness (or antitelos) gives meaning to the process's antiessentialist relationship to history. More importantly, the resulting community without telos seems to find resonance in Lugones's assessment of the ways in which polyglossic forms of communication and solidarity formation work to perpetually undo closure, tendency toward closure, and categorizations that work to reinstitute a logic of purity. This polyglossic form of complex communication, Lugones writes, "may be both meant and heard as an invitation to open up, to complicate, the polyglossia."[25] There is an undoing of the polyglossic communication itself as those openings and impasses are negotiated through, toward the formation of community, in that formation's concrete time. At any given moment, the status of that community (its members, the meaning of its political stakes, the trajectories of its communicative acts) is reopened, renegotiated as new impasses and openings emerge.

This is not to say that the outcomes of complex communication, or the implications of world-traveling from one community of sense into another, are ungrounded, unaccountable to the implications of history's power arrangements. Lugones anchors the moving heterogeneity and open-endedness of the polyglossic form in those power arrangements, and for me the rhizomatic form of Glissant's composite community operates in a similar sense. In both cases, there is a move away from essentialist and homogenizing instantiations of difference and community; at the same time, those antiessentialist instantiations remain rooted in historical positionality, historical memory, and social location.[26] As I turn to Lugones's conception of play—and how that conception might work in conjunction with a Glissantian errantry—it is important to stay close to this formulation of emergent transmutation as historically grounded. We see this in the way the playfulness of Lugones's world-travel signals its difference from the travel of the arrogant perceiver. "[Playful world-travel] is not the Western, middle-class idea of the chosen and leisured journey[, nor is it] the epistemic imperialism and aggressive arrogance [of] colonial conquest."[27] How this attitude of play performs this role, while keeping at its center an attention to historical location, will be important in my overall goal of developing a creolizing account of the nation.

Playfulness and Errantry

The plural subject's proficiency with world-traveling is a consequence of her not fully belonging to any one world. More than this, proficiency with world-traveling often grows out of being *marginalized* in multiple worlds in which political structures code for varieties of oppression that one has to then figure out how to resist. And it is, indeed, these inventive ways of resistance that emerge out of world-traveling. The world-traveler does not simply move from one space to another. Rather, she travels in order to generate, in very novel ways, conditions for the possibility of free life, belonging, and being fully human in one community of meaning in ways that are foreclosed in another. Hence, acts of world-traveling are very much acts of sabotage against oppressive structures, and by "sabotage" Lugones means that, as a liminal subject, I concretize resistance right alongside my oppression. I upset the architecture of a power grid out of which I *should* have only encountered oppression, not by *destroying* that power grid but by "tricking" it (living alongside it—and despite it). For Lugones, this must be accomplished through an attitude of play. It is not that the sabotage of world-travel is without stakes. Rather, the plural subject, positioned as she is to create resistive pathways against her oppression, must encounter those dominant structures coding for that oppression as structures without the last word. She must encounter their totalizing logic of purity as open to contestation (therefore not totalizing after all) and as open to subversion and decentering. All of this happens as the very serious stakes of those dominant structures are acknowledged for what they are—their power to oppress, marginalize, and dehumanize the human.

Hence, in describing world-travel as playful, Lugones accounts for a navigation of ontological plurality that divests from ossification, from reified modes of being, and from static conceptions of what it means to be human. To reiterate, this is not because the world-travel of liminal subjects are devoid of serious stakes. A playful attitude allows for disinvestment from the normativity of historical power because it "[stands in] an openness to uncertainty," ready for the dynamism of complex communication and its polyglossic forms.[28] In this formulation, Lugones very purposely invokes the attitude of children at play, while *explicitly* opposing her definition of playfulness to what she calls "infantile judgement," where I make judgments about the world "in fear of hostility, and hostile in my fear." Such infantile habits of being are in *flight* from critique, from transformation in relationships with others, and from having to possibly change views of the world. The playfulness of world-travel, on the other hand, "involves openness to surprise, openness to being a fool, openness to self-construction or reconstruction and to . . . reconstruction of the 'worlds' we inhabit playfully. [Playfulness is an attitude that is] an openness to risk the ground that constructs us as oppressors or as oppressed, or as . . . colluding with oppression."[29] So in playful travel to another's world—to meet the other in that alternative community of sense—the plural subject is already primed to let go of reified conceptions of what it means to be human. It means that she is primed to transgress her position on the power grid and to entertain the possibility that she can take on a role other than the one prescribed for her by that power grid.

Can we locate this account of playful world-travel in the register of Glissant's conception of errantry? Does the rhizomatic movement of errantry model the *playfulness* of the world traveler? If we think about the subject's rhizoming as her becoming-other, but then locate this movement in a space that is already constituted in terms of a logic of oppression (in terms of worlds in various oppressive relationships to power), then the becoming-other of the rhizome is about moving across ground that is already "in the world"; the ground across which the rhizome spreads is itself deeply rooted in and through history. To that end, the nontotalitarian spread of its growth—nontotalitarian in its openness to transformation, to concrete relational inventions that are not precoded in mainstream structures—can be framed as the playfulness of the plural subject's world-traveling without undermining its conceptual role in Glissant's developing of composite community. In that attitude of play, moreover, subjects in community "are not wedded to a particular way of doing things," which then allows for the creative emergences of complex communication.[30] Thus, we might think about each node of the rhizome's becoming-other-to-itself as an instantiation of some epistemic shift in the playful world-traveler. In the unpredictability of the rhizome's spread, much like the open-endedness of the playful traveler's movement in and out of communicative openings and impasses, the possibility emerges to move beyond mechanisms of power and domination, as those mechanisms are taken into account (or reckoned with) by such antiteleological transformations.

This move beyond is *in* the world of power and domination, and (as Lugones points out) "involves acute fluency in the mechanisms of oppression."[31] Hers is a deep engagement with the logics of oppression being resisted and transcended, which means that the emergent "otherwise"—in the composite community grounded in creolization, in the playful world-travel facilitated by polyglossia's complex communication—is very much immanent to the world of historical power. The playful attitude is open to transcending history in a way that is informed by the depth and shaping force of that history.[32] For this reason, Lugones will claim that the attitude of play is ultimately saturated with political urgency and that it remains attuned to the implications of historical forces precisely so that those forces can be reckoned with in the playful attitude. Ortega raises important concerns with Lugones's formulation of play, pointing out that because her movement in and out of worlds is playful, the world-traveler is unable to engage in this double move of seeing history in order to then risk its hold on her (the world-traveler's) world.[33] According to Ortega, world-travel that happens playfully runs the risk of losing sight of the kind of vigilance needed not only to understand the workings of oppression but also to see how deeply implicated our subjectivities are in those networks of power. In place of *playful* world-travel, Ortega calls for a practice of *critical* world-traveling, which "requires that the world-traveler be engaged in an ongoing process of evaluation and interpretation of not only what is learned through traveling but also of the very practices of traveling across worlds."[34] In this reframing, Ortega attempts to arm a playful attitude's readiness to imagine the world differently with an ongoing attentiveness to how its own embodiment is situated, as that reimagining of power unfolds. She writes, "Critical world-traveling [is] the type of travel in which one is aware of the baggage that one is bringing along."[35] This awareness is key to the plural subject's capacity to understand how her own liminality aligns with the multiple liminalities of other subjects in the borderlands, and it significantly shapes the effectiveness with which she builds a coalitional limen with others. On Ortega's critique, playfulness runs the risk of concealing the so-called baggage I bring with me into the limen, and I thereby run the risk of becoming complicit with systems that further the oppression of my fellow world-travelers.[36]

I want to offer a reading of playfulness through which we might make more explicit the critical attitude that Ortega rightfully identifies as necessary for effective world-travel and coalition building. This reading presents the playful attitude as already including a comportment of being open to judgment about my baggage, and an attunement to potential blindness to my "dominator iden-tities." In other words, the distinction that Lugones makes between the playful attitude and infantile judgment suggests that it is through the attitude of play that I'm able to consider my initial judgments to be wrong and to commit to the difficult transformative work of correcting them. Ortega is right to bring our attention to the criticality that must be at the center of world-traveling if this practice of dynamic, antiessentialist community building is to result in something other than a mere reproduction of colonial or imperial relations. On my reading, though, Lugones's formulation of play—and how I imagine this formulation being used to position Glissant's poetics in a more overtly political register—is very much in the spirit of this kind of vigilance. Hence, it is possible to understand the critical nature of world-traveling not in opposi-tion to its playfulness but as a consequence of it. This is because play describes a confrontation with the stakes of history and with how we ourselves are implicated in those stakes, a confrontation enabling us to move beyond its dominating effects via creative, resistant, and (most importantly) collective pathways.[37] To this end, the playfulness of the world-traveler is attuned to history but is also able to imagine—and to work toward—radically alterative (more liberatory) relationships to the historical.[38] Like the movement of the rhizome, this playful world-travel conditions the possibility of community that is fluid, antiessentialist, and open-ended.

To think of community in this sense is, invariably, to reframe the way we think about the border's role. Anzaldúa writes that "[borders] are set up to define the places that are safe and unsafe."[39] They set up, to then keep sepa-rate, modalities of living that are meant to coexist but never touch, to parallel each other but never engage.[40] In this regard, the accounts of complex com-munication and playful world-travel are in diametrical opposition to what we think about—what Anzaldúa describes above—when we imagine the border's relationship to the community. To recall from chapter 4, if the bor-der is a line, a postulated or imagined region across which "safe" ends and "unsafe" begins, then we can also think of the being of the border as that which is without dimension (suspended between places, itself a nonplace). I have noted how this suspension of being determines *as indeterminate* the subject living in the border (she is ambiguous, not yet defined). I now turn to Lugones's account of curdling to provide conceptual language that might allow us to think through the implications of this ontology of ambiguity as it pertains to the border. In that turn, I note the importance of the ways that both Lugones's heterogeneous sociality and Glissant's composite community retain the vital historicity of difference. As they center their accounts on movement and fluidity, an attendance to (and not forgetting of) difference is what anchors the antiessentialist community *in history*. Complex communication must grapple with the other's experience of liminality across an opacity that, through some formulation of a border, sets my world apart from hers. I propose that Lugones's account of curdling gives us ways to think about borders in this dual sense. That is to say, I find, in curdling, a conception of borders that (1) facilitates transformation to the degree that the implications of social location do not result in stasis, and (2) is politically meaningful insofar as social location gives meaning to *how* the community emerges as fluid.

Curdling Borders, Curdling Communities

On Lugones's account, the concept of curdling is valuable insofar as it allows us to think of separation that is not for the sake of a politics of purity.[41] I am drawn to this (impure) way of understanding separation to the degree that it is useful for theorizing how processes of creolization reconstitute the meaning and functionality of the border. What conceptual language might we use to attend to the modes of relationality that emerge from rhizomatic transformations between self and other? In what sense would the border signify in Glissant's composite community, simultaneously grounded in history and fluidly against the essentialist force of historical identities? In this section, I examine Lugones's account of "separation as curdling" for an avenue through which to develop such conceptual language.

Lugones uses separation to mark as distinct two modes of sociality. The first is a conception of the social as ordered or neatly demarcated with respect to power and history. Social identities are static in this model, and they exist in relationships that resist transformation. The second conceives the social as plural, ambiguously ordered, and consisting of pockets of liminality out of which distinctions across social groups (and social locations of power) are fluid and intermeshing. Lugones understands both of these to be simultaneously operational—the first supporting the fragmented identities that systems of domination need in order to sustain and reproduce their effects of domination on subjects, while the second enacts resistance against that fragmentation and thereby generates ways to undermine those systems of domination. For Lugones, separation as curdling offers a metaphor that could be used to visualize how living against the grain of purity, fragmentation, and stasis might happen in the midst of a political architecture that orders human life in accordance with all of these (purity, fragmentation, and stasis). As I outline Lugones's conception, I pay special attention to how the border comes to signify in that concrete time of curdled separation. In other words, I am interested in what emerges *as* a border as the curdled subject—the world-traveler, the mestiza, the creolizing subject—lives out her politics of impurity, producing a sociality that is no longer a rigidly divided (and homogeneous) grid of historical locations.

As Ortega describes it, "Curdling is necessary so as to rule out a vision of a subject whose various identities could be neatly separated, thus leading to a fragmented self and narrow identity politics that privileges homogeneity and exclusion."[42] Through separation as curdling, it is possible to engage with historical locations, and the regions that delineate those locations, in ways that acknowledge difference by way of resisting, not enacting, xenophobia. We might think of the consequence of curdling in terms of what Allison Weir describes in a model of solidarity that can "take account of change: a model of *transformative identity politics*."[43] Insofar as it is grounded in the premise of change, separation as curdling is about separating *away* from the purity politics of the mainstream, so as to live the social as impurity and movement. This gives us a sense of how borders are *not* encountered, in those lived moments of curdled subjectivities and socialities. But, more positively, how borders *are* negotiated in this process of muddled and ambiguous relations between self and other remains to be seen. The task at hand here, as in the case of creolizing processes, is a reimagining of the relationship between "one" and "many," as that relationship plays out in resistant socialities and community formation. What takes the place of "a world of precise, hard-edged schema" when errantry grounds the community?[44]

Lugones describes the impurity of the impure as that which "threatens by its very ambiguity the orderliness of the system, of schematized reality."[45] In other places, she uses the concept of "impure" to "mark the *disruption* of dichotomies in resistance to domination."[46] Does the positivity of curdling separation lie only in its disruptive force, in its "gadfly effect" (if you will), of perpetually resisting the closure of purity politics? The purposive aspect of creolizing ways of being—of disrupting and undermining mainstream structures and cultural formations—is often read in this register as well. In creole processes, distinctions between same and other, old and new, are made ambiguous through the generative emergences of lifeworlds. Nonetheless, these distinctions remain *in* their ambiguous state, within the creole artifact. New and perhaps more generative relationships between these dualities (old/new, same/other) emerge, across liminal points that facilitate this moving negotiation between the "many" of the creolizing "one." That is to say, what makes the creolizing process not only resistive but also creative—what made the creole artifact signify as, positively, something new—is the fluidity of the relationships between and among its parts. Furthermore, the conditions for the possibility of this fluidity lie in understanding the borders between and among those parts as liminally constituted in order to shift in response to the living relationalities (the complex communications across rhizomatic nodes, perhaps) of the community in question. Hence, with impurity at the center, creolization enacts an ongoing process of shifting relations both among subjects and between the subject and the sociopolitical structures that sanction categories of life. So though those sanctioned categories follow a calculus of purity, it nevertheless becomes possible to relate to that calculus in a more liberatory way, living separately and alongside that calculus as one resists its demands for stasis.

Hence, what is produced in the creolizing process is a radically new relationship to the idea of relation. If I am right in identifying important resonances with Lugones's curdling separation, then her account of curdling might also offer more than a disruptive force against purity politics. Indeed, there *is* this disruption. But an engagement between curdling and creolization shows that, more positively, the notion of curdling produces a relationship to the border (to the spaces and times that, under other conditions, might have divided the social into discrete categories) through which these spaces show up as liminal (ambiguous, not yet determined) moments of creative possibility. Through curdling, there is resistance against or disruption of a politics of purity; more importantly, though, new modalities of "borders" and "relations" emerge. In these resulting new relationships to the very idea of relation, borders are encountered as spatiotemporal modes to be moved in response to living and complex communicative practices among subjects. For Lugones, the kind of subject who resists through curdling-separation is one who lives in between the sanctioned categories of a purity politics. This subject does not easily belong to purity's "precise hard-edged schema," so out of that condition of liminality, the relationships among these pure categories are experienced as fluid regions to be negotiated. That is not to say that the liminal subject dismisses the historical materiality of these in-between spaces. To the contrary, her liminal experience points to the gravity of this history. However, as this liminal subject encounters these regions in their telos of sustaining the fragmented nature of pure categories, her concrete experience of not easily belonging to any of these categories means that the regions between these spaces (the borders) will signify in order to be shifted. The "there-ness" of the space between these unlivable categories will present itself as potential ground for responding to the concrete and political urgencies of subjects for whom "border-as-stasis" was never a reality to begin with (and for whom purity is always already disarranged).

Like creolization, the generative resistance in separation as curdling points us to its operational antiteleology, or to what Lugones describes as its "lack of script."[47] To fully account for the creative potential of liminality's encounter with the border, and for the "act of social creative defiance" that a liminal way of being signifies in Lugones's account, is to understand the movements of curdled separation as necessarily unclassifiable or unmanageable.[48] There is no deciding in advance the outcome of those concrete navigations of world-traveling subjects, who insist on their impurity through determining modes of living in the midst of dominant structures of purity. Indeed, it is in these (mainstream) structures of purity that we find the calculus to predict life in advance of actual, concretized living. Living that resists these codes will always signify as unexpected, as a surprise (so to speak), because it has been prefigured as not-possible.

I want to pose the question of what this means for the proposal to creolize the nation. Given the similarities that I've traced between creolizing processes and Lugones's metaphor of curdling, is it possible that, in creolizing the nation, we are also envisioning a modality of "nation" that includes curdled separation? How might we understand the relationship between the structural teleology of nation-ness alongside the antitelos of curdling acts? How do we code for enactments that are, by definition, uncodable in their generativity? More pertinently, could such antiteleological (uncodable) enactments be aspects of the nation?

Chapter 6 takes on these questions directly, in bringing Glissant's conception of a composite community into engagement with Fanon's decolonial politics. But for the moment, I return to Glissant's description of the rhizomatic movement of the composite community as "neither fusion nor confusion," so as to reiterate that Glissant asks us to imagine ways in which order (in the context of the composite community) might be thought of in terms other than control. Though it avoids the "fusion" effects of reductionist universalism (of purity politics), in other words, the living dynamism of the composite community does not drag the community into chaos either. Perhaps such composite relationalities abide by a kind of coherence that doesn't slip into the managed classifications that, for Lugones, results in fragmentation and stasis. In chapter 4, I traced notions of multiplicity or plurality at the level of the subject that do *not* result in the erasure of identity (in a postmodern, postidentity sense). In a similar vein, the complex alliances that Lugones calls for (in her account of curdling separation) do not result in the absence of community as such. Likewise, Glissant's account of "giving on and with," at the foundation of the composite community, does not mean that *no* boundaries exist, or that the composite community is fully open (and thus not really a community at all). To recall, rhizomatic growth, though horizontal, does participate *in* the actual world. Likewise, separation as curdling happens within a lived grid of structural domination. In both cases, the meaning of borders, relations, *and* power are all negotiated in the grounding of history. How and to what end the movement of curdling (or rhizoming) happens remains open for critique, deliberation, and complex negotiation between and among thick and thin members of the community, between liminal subjects and those who more solidly belong.[49] Hence, Lugones's conception of a heterogeneous sociality, Glissant's composite community, and Fanon's "humanist" nationalism (chapter 6) all participate in a multiplicity and fluidity that, though antiessentialist, nonetheless has a coherence that makes community possible. In the analysis of the following chapter, I offer support for the claim that such antiteleological (uncodable) enactments can indeed be aspects of the nation.

Escaping the Escapable

Given Lugones's understanding of the social as heterogeneous, the creative defiance produced in the limen (the space between the "worlds" of the social) is presented as "a fragment indicative of interworld contestation between actual, co-temporaneous, overlapping constructions of social relations, including relations of power."[50] My project to creolize the nation situates the creole artifact in a similar register, such that moments of creolizing produces networks of a disrupting ontology at the level of the everyday, between those lifeworlds of which the social is constituted, and across which the creolizing process determines new modes of living. These new modes emerge in order to resist power dynamics that foreclose the possibility of full human life, to enable living as fully human despite those dominant relations of power. Hence, we can use Lugones's account of interworld contestation to think about Glissant's rhizome movements as practices enacted by the composite community to produce resistant and liberatory networks alongside, within, and in between power's insistence on purity. The consequences of the rhizome's spread might be those of curdled separation, insofar as both generate new ground for living impurely and "against the grain of power."

Lugones is careful to note that out of these liminal enactments of impurity, we arrive at a conception of oppression that always already includes escape from that oppression. To make liminality part of the narrative of the social is to make possible a fuller narrative of the experience of marginalized, nonbelonging subjects' manipulation of oppressive structures for the sake of their own liberation, so that these structures, despite their mainstream location, in no way have the last word. When we bring the conceptual language through which Lugones develops this account of resistance in the midst of oppression into dialogue with the tools through which Glissant builds his own account of creolization, it becomes possible to read, in creole ways of navigating power, a similar story of power not having the last word. The rhizomatic spread that makes possible the emergence of new (creole) ways is also an account of escaping what should be inescapable.[51] More importantly, the avenues of escape are not some otherworldly, transcendental possibility; they exist at the level of the concrete, and in full engagement with the real time of historical power.

Hence, creolization calls for a picture of the social as heterogeneous, as a space of complex multiplicity. And this "tense multiplicity" calls for a recognition that, through creolization, subjects are always in the practice of "inhabiting [the power grid] in great resistance."[52] For their full efficacy, dominant maps of power depend on clear boundaries between empowered and disempowered positionalities. In undermining this demarcation—in blurring boundaries by creating conditions of empowerment out of positions of disempowerment—creolization and curdled separation are processes that contest this efficacy. In their insistence on impurity, they have already undermined power's mode of subject production.[53] What this means is that there is never just a unitary and homogeneous world within which subjects shaped by oppression must remain and live. Instead, out of their in-between-ness, and as a consequence of their being marked as impure, these subjects exist in a multiplicity of worlds as they produce their own complex relations to the calculus of power. Through these complex relations emerges an escape that works to undermine the totality of that oppression—or, in effect, an escape from that oppression.

This seems to articulate the intimate resistance of which creolizing processes are comprised, as processes that generate liberatory living—avenues of escape—*in the midst* of (what ought to have been an escapable) cultural domination. There are clear resonances here with Lugones's own articulation of curdled separation as a scheme through which "the actual world [is] constituted by multiple spatio-temporalities in tense power relations and in tense semantic relations."[54] These accounts of what it means to escape the inescapable have implications not only for enacting one's subjectivity otherwise but also for enacting the nation otherwise. In chapter 6, I turn to the architecture of Fanon's postcolonial nation, bringing it into dialogue with Glissant's composite community in order to develop this possibility of conceptualizing the nation otherwise.

Chapter 6

◆

The Composite Community in
Fanon's Postcolonial Moment

In this chapter, I bring Fanon's caution against a regressive form of national-ism into conversation with Glissant's conception of the composite community. The former comes out of Fanon's need to imagine a humanism radically dif-ferent from the one around which colonial violence organizes itself. The latter emerges out of the process and practices of creolization that, for Glissant, characterizes the history of the Caribbean. In thinking through Fanon's deco-lonial nationalism and Glissant's creolizing composite community together, I hope to put forward an explicitly political groundwork for imagining the nation as creolizing, as an open community that supports plural modes of the human, and as orienting itself against the stasis of coloniality and toward the dynamic syncretism of a living culture and a living democracy.

Fanon's concern was about the conditions that might enable previously colonized societies (across the continent of Africa, across Asia, and in the Caribbean) to pursue their respective postindependence nationalisms in ways that avoid the orientation toward essentialism and xenophobia that grounded much of the violence of imperialism. Glissant, though not explicitly driven by the question of the nation, conceived of the composite community as a model for living with the radical diversity characteristic of communities in the Antil-les.[1] I bring these two together (Fanon's critique of a narrow nationalism, and Glissant's vision for a composite community) because they ground themselves on alternative ways of thinking about human relationality, and about how the emergence of the "new" is conditioned by thinking differently about human relationality. In both Fanon and Glissant, one finds a meaning of national community (and nationalism, more generally) that merits the attention not only of scholars of the human condition but of all citizens of a world that is, in the words of Paul Gilroy, "increasingly divided but also convergent."[2]

In bringing Fanon and Glissant together this way, I also acknowledge an important difference between their respective critical projects. Fanon's was a commitment to anticolonial political struggle, while Glissant's was a medita-tion on the *impossibility* of such strivings, using for his reference the island of Martinique. In the sections of *Caribbean Critique* that focus on Glissant's place in Antillean theory, Nick Nesbitt draws our attention to this.[3] In particular, Nesbitt raises the important question of how, precisely, readers of Glissant should understand the political nature of his work. By contrast, Fanon bears witness to the emergence of conditions in Algeria, which make possible the kind of anticolonial Algerian subject for whom a project of political liberation is possible. Nesbitt reminds us that, despite the "*poetics* of revolt" conveyed through Glissant's cultural critique, a more Fanonian project of political liberation is given over (in the Antillean context) as a tragic impossibility and unrealizable loss.[4] Glissant's analysis of the situation in Martinique is one of "dispossession," whereby "systematic resistance becomes impossible."[5]

But despite this important departure, both Fanon and Glissant understand the significance of emergence and alternative productions at the level of the cultural, for imagining an alternative future. In his writings on the Algerian Revolution, Fanon includes numerous accounts of such *cultural* transformation in the everyday lives of the Algerian people, which made possible the kind of anticolonial revolutionary struggle needed for *political* transformation. Indeed, he often identified "deculturization" as one of the negative consequences of the economic and political arms of colonialism across the continent of Africa and the broader diaspora, and he urged his readers to "look for the consequences of this racism on the cultural level . . . to tirelessly look for the repercussions of racism at all levels of sociability."[6] The colonial violence at the level of culture not only mattered to Fanon but also deeply informed his claim that an anticolonial and decolonizing political agenda would need to be foregrounded at the level of culture and would require fundamental transformations at the level of culture in order to be successful. In other words, though politically oriented, Fanon's critical project is attentive to the ways in which cultural violence underwrites (or supports) the economic and political work of colonial violence. Hence, the Fanonian project points to cultural generativity as a necessary part of a political program of bringing into being a new (postcolonial) future.

Similarly, Glissant's analysis of Antillean culture and poetics situates creative cultural production as the source of resistance, newness, and anticolonial relationality. His analysis identifies such productions to be most vital to the history of the Caribbean and to the ways in which Caribbean history has always been one of sabotaging (and sometimes overcoming) the spatial and temporal metrics of the plantation. Indeed, as Wendy Knepper points out, practices of creolization at the cultural level ought to be understood in terms of practicing freedom in a world where that freedom is made out to be structurally impossible.[7] The "bricoleur," on Knepper's account, adapts and improvises in response to a loss of power (social, political, cultural), not in an explicit attempt to reverse power relations but, rather, in an attempt to create alternative conditions within that experience of powerlessness.[8] Unlike these adaptive modes at the cultural level, the revolutionary and politically salient transformations that Fanon describes in Algeria (concerning the use of the radio, the practices surrounding the veil, the gradual openness of Algerian communities to European healthcare, and changes in traditional family structures) are all geared toward reversing relations of power, taking power away from colonial forces and putting it back into the hands of Algerians. Nonetheless, my goal in this chapter is to read both critical projects—Fanon's anticolonial revolutionary politics and Glissant's anticolonial resistant poetics—in terms of processes of creolization. I will show that, despite the differences that Nesbitt names, both Fanon and Glissant can be read as articulating how new and anticolonial ground might emerge from colonialism's totalizing historical legacy.

As Fanon reminds us in *A Dying Colonialism*, "Colonialism wants everything to come from it."[9] The cultural transformations accounted for in practices of creolization are similar to the subjective and "everyday" transformations that Fanon describes of a revolutionary Algeria in that both mark as possible emergences for which colonialism cannot account.[10] They both bear witness to the possibility that not everything comes from colonialism and that it is possible to generate, out of a colonial totality, new ground on which a politics of anticolonial resistance might come to fruition. Such possibilities of creative emergence are central to creolization, even though creolization often does not lead to an overt politics of resistance. More importantly, creolization is apt to account for how Fanon understands the living will of a people (the agency of this will) to be located at the level of the everyday, or at the level of the quotidian. So although the adaptations of creole processes are not overtly political, my goal here is to locate at the foundation of a Fanonian politics of decolonization the necessary transformative processes that are not unlike creolizing adaptations. In other words, readers of Fanon's politics would be remiss to ignore that, for him, a politics that gestures toward a decolonial mode of the nation finds its condition of possibility in living otherwise, at the level of the everyday. Hence, my interest in anchoring this conversation—between Fanon's politics and Glissant's poetics—in the process of creolization is to ultimately foreground for both thinkers this question of how to imagine the human (and human community) otherwise.

What Glissant offers in his "poetics of revolt" is in conjunction with his conception of Relation, and it is out of this conception that I find the potential for fruitful engagement with Fanon's more overtly political treatise. In a later section, I return in more detail to the limitations involved in using Glissant's program toward political ends. However, in the spirit of these introductory remarks, suffice it to say that, in his conception of Relation, we find a radical reimagination of the theoretical frameworks through which we engage with questions of ontological totality, difference, and the differentiations that give rise to relationships between "same" and "other." Indeed, this comes to the fore through the engagements offered in chapter 5, between Glissant's creolizing conceptions and Lugones's account of curdling and social heterogeneity. In this regard, though Glissant's notion of Relation facilitates a reimagining at the discursive level, I argue that it positions us to reimagine, at the political level, the meaning of totalities of which human communities (and the nation more specifically) are constituted.[11] For this reason, I limit most of my engagement with Glissant to his later work in *Poetics of Relation* (1997), drawing attention to the ways in which the conception of Relation resonates with his earlier collection of essays, *Caribbean Discourse* (1989).[12]

Against Ultranationalism

In the sections that follow, I discuss how Fanon understands the relationship between the national and the transnational, as well as the role of his conception of national culture in this relationship. I show that, on his account, a national culture is something other than the closed-off, reified nationalism on which chapter 1 of this book focused. In other words, the kind of national culture that Fanon has in mind, which would foreground the emergence of the decolonial nation in the *post*colonial stage, is markedly different from what scholars like George Mosse and Eric Hobsbawm critique in their expositions of Western nationalism. In his account of the trend in national anthems during the late eighteenth and nineteenth centuries, Mosse notes that the emphasis in national anthems was not so much "[an appeal] to a better world, a world in peace, [but rather a looking] backward, not forward: history, and not a utopian vision, gave [the nation] the immutability it needed in order to tame the accelerating speed of time."[13] This turn to a mythic and untainted past saw its peak in Germany when, beginning in the first half of the twentieth century, the most salient political rhetoric appealed to an authentic German *Volk*. In this appeal, "[nature], the soil, villages, and farms—all preindustrial symbols—spoke of rootedness and made the time stand still."[14]

We might hear, in this narrative of rootedness in a past life (either real or imagined), echoes of the work of the Negritude writers and poets of the early to mid-twentieth century. Both can be located in the nation's call for renewal, or rebirth: Germany in its World War I defeat; the African nation in the formal defeat of colonial rule. Mosse finds, in such "identification with a usable and stable past," a call to homogenize the life of the nation. And as I will show in the second section, this captures a large part of Fanon's reading of Negritude as well, as least in the movement's relationship to nation building. To be clear, this is not to minimize the differences between the historical context of (on the one hand) a European nation like Germany in 1933, and (on the other) the African ex-colony in 1957, faced with the insurmountable task of affirming its independence in the catastrophic wake of colonial rule. However, it is to show that, despite his call for national culture and national self-representation, Fanon was very much against the kind of nationalism of which scholars like Mosse are critical—the backward-looking, homogenizing version that characterized much of Europe's political rhetoric in the late 1800s.[15]

This brand of right-wing nationalism sought to re-create the "community of old": a creation of a nostalgic and atavistic imaginary, to be sure, but injected with enough reality to fuel what, for Hobsbawm, is nothing other than a patriotic program of xenophobia. He locates the traction for such programs in the so-called middle strata of European communities, "traders, independent craftsmen and some farmers threatened by the progress of the industrial economy."[16] But Hobsbawm does note that, for this threatened middle strata, "[the] foreigner came to symbolize the disruption of old ways and the capitalist system which disrupted [those old ways]."[17] We hear, in this, the kind of Manichean metaphysics that Fanon will both confirm as inevitable during the early stages of anticolonial revolutionary struggle and explicitly oppose once those early stages have passed. In its beginning, the anticolonial struggle is absolute and immediate in its violence, knowing only the urgency of "now." Fanon writes, "The natives' challenge to the colonial world [in these beginning stages of decolonization] is not a rational confrontation of points of view. It is not a treatise on the universal, but the untidy affirmation of an original idea propounded as an absolute. The colonial world is a Manichean world."[18] And as such, my violent resistance to this world must also be Manichean, total, and complete, "us" (natives, reclaiming our rights to our bread and our land) against "them" (agents of colonialism, charged with the crime of crushing the humanity of my black world). In the early stages of the struggle, the native's motivation is singular and immediate: "Replace the foreigner."[19]

But to read *all* of Fanon's exposition on anticolonial struggle is to understand his caution against "ending with the beginning"—against implementing, as a postindependence program for nation building, the antiforeigner Manichean violence that, to be sure, the colony must begin with, given the historical specificity of colonial violence.[20] On their way to independence from colonial rule, he describes a "people that has lost its birthright . . . [and that] will now proceed in an atmosphere of solemnity to cleanse and purify the face of the nation."[21] Mosse's critical reading of the Berlin book burnings of May 10, 1933, cautions against such nationalist tendencies toward purging and cleansing for the sake of some authentic and bygone Volk.[22] In other words, it is precisely in the face of this (right-wing) nationalism, with its call to "purge and cleanse," that one finds the "antiforeigner" labeling of the nonbelonging "other," who becomes the target of a defensive and warmongering xenophobia, too insecure to come to terms with the challenging work of forging a more positive national identity. And it is with a clear view of this nationalism that Fanon calls for a more intelligent "thoughtful" politics in the later stages of anticolonial struggle. We read this call for a more thoughtful revolutionary politics right alongside his legitimization of the "purging and cleansing" of the nation of a people who have lost their birthright to colonial domination.

And certainly, in the early stages of independence that often follows anticolonial struggle, when the task at hand involves implementing programs that will influence the direction of the nation, Fanon truly sees no place for a

Manichean (and homogenizing) worldview. In the section titled "The Pitfalls of National Consciousness," he writes a scathing critique of that class of nationalists who rise to positions of political power in those moments just after independence from colonial rule. "The bourgeois caste, that section of the nation which annexes for its own profit all the wealth of the country . . . will pass disparaging judgments upon the other Negroes and the other Arabs [persons deemed "other" within the context of national life] that more often than not are reminiscent of the racist doctrines of the former representatives of colonial power."[23] As Anthony Alessandrini points out, the nuance of the "postviolence" stages of decolonization is also the stage that calls for the difficult and sustained work of social and economic decolonization—stages that are important to attend to, so as to resist the implementation of neocolonial relationships with former colonial powers.[24] To effectively oppose such neocolonial arrangements, a Manichean and violent program spearheaded by "Replace the foreigner" must be replaced with a more nuanced and perhaps also postracial "Stop, thief."[25] Hence, the shared ethical project of building a nation after the end of formal colonial rule involves efforts geared toward *dismantling* the colonial apparatus of power and thus will no longer be able to rely on colonial (Manichean) divisions of morality and human relationality.[26] Failing to take heed of this produces the kind of "narrow nationalism" that Fanon finds empty of "even a minimum humanist content."[27] Fanon's objection to the kind of political leadership that grounds itself on this narrow nationalism is not only on economic terms, though, to be sure, this accounts for a large portion of his condemnation. He is also wary of the moral bankruptcy of this kind of "narrow nationalism," insofar as "Replace the foreigner" emerges out of reified and metaphysical conceptions of identity formation and belonging, the same formations that Hobsbawm identifies (and critiques) in the middle strata of late nineteenth-century European right-wing nationalism.[28]

It is with such rigid essentialisms in mind that Fanon warns, "[Racialism] and hatred and resentment . . . cannot sustain a war of liberation. . . . Hatred alone cannot draw up a program."[29] The absolute violence that is unavoidable and needed during the native's initial revolt against the colonizer works *against* the needs of the nation as it attempts to configure itself in terms of a new (indeed, *decolonial*) community, shaped in terms of free possibilities for all. Hence, temporality matters, in Fanon's account of anticolonial violence: the native's encounter with time (her experience of time) will determine not only the meaning of her anticolonial violence but also the legitimacy or illegitimacy of that violence. At the beginning of the struggle, what orients the native's revolt is solely the quest for her humanity. She lives in the urgency of a "now," a "now" that has been arrested in time, denied entrance into human history.[30] And in that arrested present, the choice is between life and death. This is because the very logic of colonial domination has foreclosed all possibility, for the native, to encounter time in terms of a future. She does not, *cannot*, organize her lifeworld in terms of possibilities (if, by "possibilities," one means more than the options of life or death). All there is, is the intensity of the now. All that matters is "now," so everything is invested in the urgency of the present, and all is risked for the urgency of the present. This is the conception of temporality that seems to ground Fanon's account of the FLN's absolute demands for Algerian independence from colonial France: "The revolution is by essence an enemy of half-measures, compromises, and backward steps. . . . Set in motion, they break with the structures that had kept them riveted to their immobility and passivity."[31]

But as the struggle continues, Fanon draws our attention to a shift in temporality. It is a shift that testifies to a reclaiming (and proclaiming) of the humanity of the native—indeed, made possible *only* through violent revolt. This shift will usher in a more *human* encounter with time, such that life becomes oriented in terms of a future, in terms of possibility, perhaps no longer foreclosed by the subjugating psychology of the colonizer. It is out of this more human encounter with time that Fanon identifies the question of the *future* of the struggle toward decolonization. He writes, "The fact is that in guerilla warfare [marking the second period of the struggle, a period in need of a more thoughtful, less spontaneous violence] the struggle no longer concerns the place where you are, but the place where you are going."[32] Hence, any legitimacy that Fanon grants to that "purging and cleansing" version of nationalism is in light of these nuances of temporality. In order to humanize her experience of time (to encounter time in terms of future possibilities, instead of an arrested "now" that forecloses all possibility of possibility), the native must engage in an initial period of spontaneous (nonthinking and immediate) violence. She must engage in purging and cleansing the nation of all that forecloses such possibilities of a more humanized encounter with time. But, to reiterate, Fanon warns of the dangers of ending at this beginning. His deliberation on a national culture shows us that what *he* has in mind by nationalism is not the xenophobic, closed-off, mummified nationalism of the modern colonial nation-states (the kind out of which could emerge something like the Berlin book burnings of May 1933). This is abundantly clear in his proposal for the cultural consciousness of the nation.

As I will show in the following section, Fanon holds that in order for culture to be connected to "the everyday," it cannot be frozen in an atavistic, backward-looking past. The nation and its culture must remain open and responsive to the creative forces and everyday struggle of the people. And this is why he warns against the poet and the native intellectual, who resort to a bygone set of customs and traditions and name this their national culture. For Fanon, tradition is to culture what the dead body might be to the living body. The former is but a shadowed harking back of what the latter would be if not for its creative and ever-moving force. Of this native intellectual, Fanon writes, "He wishes to attach himself to the people, but instead he only catches a glimpse of their outer garments. And these outer garments are

merely the reflection of a dynamic life, *teeming and perpetually in motion*."[33]
By describing it as "perpetually in motion," Fanon shows that this national
culture—that spirit and creative energy of which the nation is comprised—is
not static, can never be simplified ("abhors all signification"), and always
averts the easy grasp of "symbols of negation and outworn contrivances."[34]
To this end, Fanon claims that though the nation stands upon an essence, that
essence should by no means be in the business of essentializing the nation. He
warns against "mummified fragments" and "immobile pasts" that, in standing in the place of an actual living culture, are "evocative not of life but of
death."[35]

So Fanon likens an actual national culture (what comes out of the
everyday), "teeming with life and perpetual motion," to a "zone of occult
instability"—alive, unpredictable, without telos.[36] To this end, he is perfectly
willing to conceive of a nationalism that is active (and not a "throwback to
the laws of inertia"), full of life and dynamism, and open-ended toward a
perpetual reimagining of itself.[37] This is not the nationalism of Nazi Germany, which Mosse critiques—"the most elementary, most savage, and most
undifferentiated nationalism."[38] Fanon's nationalism is meant to be the kind
whose culture of "life and creative power" is "open to other cultures and . . .
[influences and permeates] other cultures."[39] Here Fanon's call for framing a
national culture as a culture that is "perpetually in motion" should be heard
as a call for an open-endedness and dialogic relationality, one that is resistant
to stagnation in its always being open to reimagination and renegotiation with
the diversity within the collective of its people. To be sure, this is rarely what
comes to mind when one thinks of nationalism.

Fanon on a National Culture of Emergence

In the "On National Culture" section of *The Wretched of the Earth*, Fanon
articulates a level of empathy for the one he names "the native intellectual."
In his return to an African past, this native intellectual rehabilitates an African
culture and aesthetic from the subhuman valuation ascribed to these through
colonization. Fanon identifies this program of cultural subhumanization as
essential to colonial domination, a program that "turns to the past of an
oppressed people, and distorts, disfigures and destroys it."[40] Colonialism's
cultural racism works toward "the destruction of cultural values, of ways of
life. Language, dress, techniques are devalorized [insofar as the] enslavement,
in the strictest sense, of the native population is [colonialism's] prime necessity."[41] Agents of colonialism then offer themselves as the saviors who bring
the only kind of enlightenment capable of redeeming the native from a dark,
barbaric past. In this regard, the native intellectual's dedication to reclaiming
Africa's cultural history is a dedication with which Fanon can empathize. In
other words, Negritude's revalorization of what colonialism has devalued

makes sense for Fanon—"the oppressed goes into ecstasies over each redis-
covery [of an African past culture, so that the] wonder is permanent. Having
formerly emigrated from his culture, the native today [via Negritude] explores
it with ardor."[42]

But in this turning back to a nostalgic past, Fanon sees not only a divorce
from the real (material) needs of the newly independent African nation but
also a curious estrangement from the everyday immanent life of that nation's
cultural sensibilities.[43] On the one hand, and by way of analogy, he notes that
"the past existence of an Aztec civilization does not change anything very
much in the diet of the Mexican peasant of today"; and so lauding a glorious
African past would be a similarly ineffective program of economic sovereignty.[44] But more relevant to my current purpose is Fanon's concern about
the implications—for the postcolonial *mode* of nation-ness—of using this
backward-looking approach to remedy the cultural racism of colonial rule.
Fanon's exposition on national culture is clearly motivated by his concern
for what the postcolonial nation might come to represent (or how it comes
to signify) subsequent to the end of formal colonialism. For those African
nations either fighting against or coming out from under colonial domination,
he reads, in the cultural implications of turning toward a previously devalued
past, certain dangers for the very tapestry of the community of the nation as
such.

With these dangers in mind, he notes that "[the] characteristic of a culture
is to be open, permeated by spontaneous, generous fertile lines of force."[45] Key
here are the traits of openness, spontaneity, and fertility, which Fanon uses to
describe a national culture that is produced by the people and for the people.[46]
These traits mean that such a national culture is diametrically opposed not
only to the *content* of colonialism's cultural racism but also, more importantly, to the *form* of that cultural racism. It is in this vein that Fanon notes
Negritude's failure to animate a national culture that is best suited for the
decolonized nation, or the nation in the process of determining how it will
be otherwise than what colonialism made it. It is not that Negritude fails to
revalue what has been devalued through the colonial metric; to be sure, it *does*
do this. However, because it reinstates this value in an absolute and closed-
off way, it reproduces the colonial *form* of cultural mummification. Recall
Fanon's account of the "*permanent* wonder" of the oppressed on her discovery of Negritude, which has already decided what cultural commitments will
express the people's humanity. Culture, here, does not come from the living
spontaneity of the people. Rather, it is the other way around (and hence
similar to colonialism's mummified approach to culture)—their humanity is
called to be in the service of an independent and detached cultural program. "Returning to one's roots," Fanon tells us, "is thus meaningless unless
it turned toward the future," a future that is determined by and for the
people themselves. Negritude, in its backward-looking orientation, positions a reified past in the driver's seat of cultural production.[47] So though

the content of Negritude's cultural reorientation might be different from the content of colonialism's cultural racism, its form—reified, removed from the "fertility" of a moving national culture, divorced from the spontaneity that such a national culture ought to remain sufficiently open to express—is not. Instead, Negritude's response to colonial cultural racism places culture "into capsules. . . . It is not reconceived, grasped anew, dynamized from within."[48] It is only through this dynamism from within that a postcolonial national culture allows for the kind of social and political generativity that genuinely undercuts the alienation and estrangement of colonial stagnation and devaluation.

For these reasons, in *A Dying Colonialism*, Fanon calls for a "modern Algeria" that moves beyond the shackles of traditional customs that are ultimately antidemocratic and unaccountable to the emerging needs of a (hopefully, soon-to-be-)decolonial nation.[49] In other words, for Fanon, the cultural orientation of a democratic nationalism is forward looking, grounded in the living will of the people, and not a culture steeped in archaic customs, the sedimentation of which means that they are divorced from the living needs of the people in question. This is not to say that Fanon's position is like that of the colonialist, who reads the tradition and custom of a colonized society as backward and primitive. Rather, on his account a society engaged in anticolonial struggle must have, as its first premise, the priority of an agential national will, a collective will that is generative and not narrowly restricted to a predetermined set of cultural codes. In other words, in order for such postcolonial societies to imagine themselves as decolonial, they must belong to individuals who "free themselves of everything that proves unnecessary and detrimental to the revolutionary situation. The person is born, assumes his autonomy, and becomes the creator of his own values."[50]

Hence, the cultural productions of a society (how they are shaped by an actively participating collective will) is vital for what has come to be understood as Fanon's revolutionary anticolonial politics. It is in this spirit that we should read some of Fanon's concrete descriptions from life on the ground during Algeria's anticolonial war, which, for him, operate as living examples of such cultural autonomy and spontaneity. Furthermore, the argument throughout *A Dying Colonialism* is that this spontaneous cultural negotiation at the level of the *subjective* (the level of the everyday) is what ultimately facilitated the emergence of an independent Algeria. This chapter is anchored in the claim that creolization gives an account of this transformative cultural spontaneity. On these grounds I argue that Fanon's conception of the postcolonial nation—a nation that gestures toward something other than the narrow nationalism of colonialism and imperialism—offers us a space in which Glissant's composite community (a community grounded in practices of creolization) might find political traction.

Fanon's description of the central role of the radio during the thick of the FLN's war against French colonial forces in Algeria is perhaps the most salient example of how creolization might be used to think about the ground-level cultural transformations that created conditions for the possibility of Algeria's political revolution.[51] Once an instrument of colonialism and its oppressive force, the radio was regarded as a sign of having succumbed to the cultural imperialism of the French and of losing one's sense of Algerian-ness in the face of such imperial domination. After 1954, however, having a transistor radio in one's household was not only a mark of resistance *against* colonial domination but also, more importantly, evidence of one's active solidarity with the newly emerging nation as it fought for its liberation. Fanon writes, "[The] technical instrument of the radio receiver lost its identity as an enemy object. The radio set was no longer a part of the occupier's arsenal of cultural oppression." Before 1954, "[having] a radio meant accepting being besieged from within [one's home] by the colonizer. . . . [After 1954,] having a radio seriously meant going to war."[52] This transformation in meaning—from the radio being a sign of one's proximity to dehumanization, to being a sign of one's proximity to revolution—captures much of what characterizes the adaptive practices of creolization. The Algerian people's intercepting and reworking of an artifact of French domination cleared ground (at the level of their everyday lives) for this artifact to be a symbol of hope (of a promise, even) for liberation from that domination. Like the bricolage constitutive of creole societies, a transformation such as this comes directly from the "people's will to survive" in the face of structures that code for a pervasive, all-encompassing social death.[53] It is in this vein that I read Fanon's account of this emergence as an instance of creolization—"What we have witnessed is a radical transformation of the means of perception, of the very world of perception . . . the technique [of deploying radio transmissions for the sake of the revolution] had virtually to be invented. The Voice of Algeria created out of nothing."[54] To be sure, Fanon's concern with the possibility of inserting invention into existence persists throughout his writings on colonial violence.[55] His assertion is clear—that we begin to approach something truly *post*colonial only through the possibility of generating a radically new mode of being, and of being human.[56] What I offer here, in reading these everyday inventions into everyday existence in terms of creolization, locates Fanon's aspiration of inserting a new way into an old (and supposedly totalizing) paradigm as integral to creolizing practices. This is why I argue that Fanon's conception of nation-ness should be brought to bear on creolizing practices of culture and community.

As I showed in chapter 2, creolization concerns everyday practices of resistance against structural domination, not to replace those dominating structures but to determine certain "cracks" in them, through which subjects engaged in adaptive creole practices might live more freely. To that end, Fanon's descriptions of the transformed meaning of the radio (and of the veil, as well as modern medicine) in Algeria find much resonance with the outcome of creolization, outcomes that point to "new content . . . creating cracks in the old forms which are trying to stifle it."[57] In this Fanonian formulation, what is at the heart of creole processes—of the "new" somehow finding a way to emerge from "old," of invention finding its way into existence—comes to the fore. Fanon's reference to such "cracks" also brings to mind my analysis in chapter 5, which offers María Lugones's conception of plural sociality to underscore what, through creolizing practices, emerges as a never-completely-closed system of cultural dominance. The transformations around the use of the radio attest to a new Algerian subject, to which French colonialism is forced to bear witness and, consequently, forced to see itself as a never-completely-closed system. Certain everyday mutations (creole mutations, I would argue) offer to French colonialism a "new content" in the cultural lives of Algerians, for which it could not account.

What this means is that the colonial machine in Algeria (much like the Antillean plantation machine out of which creole adaptations emerge) encountered new relations in Algerian society ("new links," as Fanon puts it) of which it was not the author.[58] Hence, the reworked signification of the radio is not merely about changes in the technological arch of the Algerian world. Rather, and more importantly, we ought to see the radio's new meaning as a cultural sabotage that undermines the apparent totality of colonial violence, since that new meaning emerges and operates (makes itself felt) despite the totality of that violence.[59] The cumulative effect of such acts of cultural sabotage is that "Algeria has become a country able to elude French mastery."[60] Creole adaptations insert such moments into everyday life as well; they insert into everyday culture evidence that not "everything comes from colonialism" after all.[61]

Eventually, the broadcasts that brought in news of the revolution through these radio transistors were in French, the colonizer's language, which prior to 1954 was collectively refused by Algerians. However, as the FLN's war unfolded and Algerian society transformed into something that eluded the grasp of French colonial forces, the "new relations" made it possible to take up the French language for new (and liberatory) means. "The broadcasting in French of the programs of Fighting-Algeria was to liberate the enemy language from its historic meanings" and thus offered the option of adopting the colonizer's language against the colonizer's program of domination.[62] Similar to how European medicine and medical practices were implemented into Algerian communities of resistance (particularly in dealing with the injuries incurred during revolutionary battle), the deployment of the French language for the sake of Algerian resistance evidenced the will of a people jostling the meaning of a cultural artifact that grounded their oppression, to give it a purpose for the sake of their liberation. Creolizing practices are marked with this sort of transformative meaning-making, against a script that codes for the most totalizing of violence. As Fanon tells us, "The colonial situation standardizes relations, for it dichotomizes the colonial society in a marked way."[63] Across those reified colonial divisions, we might find artifacts like the radio and the French language on the side of colonizer—the master's tools, if you will, totally void of any revolutionary purpose to the Algerian. However, what Fanon's descriptions—and my reading of them through a creolizing frame—illustrate are disruptions of those rigid "standardized relations," such that the vitality of a culture freely transforms and creates alternative significations that do not adhere to colonialism's Manichean organization of the world.[64] This is particularly creolizing, given how creole adaptations are precisely those that work against dichotomies as they animate fluid movements across and between "old" and "new."[65]

The Nation and the Transnational

Given this conception of an emergent national culture, Fanon's nationalism is in a significant sense quite antinationalist in nature. As Fanon continues to work within the frame of the nation, he is also acutely attentive to a vital transnational solidarity when it comes to effectively working toward a new and decolonial conception of the human. Hence, we can expect the content of his postindependence "nation-ness" to look markedly different from the account of nationalism treated in chapter 1 of this book. To look at the ways in which Fanon's national culture of emergence shapes his antinationalist nationalism, I'd like to begin with a recent set of events surrounding the decision of the Birmingham Civil Rights Institute Board of Directors to rescind the Fred Shuttlework Human Rights Award they had granted to Angela Y. Davis.[66] In her public response to this decision, Davis writes that "[the] rescinding of this invitation was . . . not primarily an attack against [her] but rather against the spirit of the indivisibility of justice."[67] In her statement, Davis references her support of Palestine as the ultimate reason for the board's decision. I cite this here not to invite discussion of the complex and important Palestinian-Israeli conflict, and the implications of this conflict for justice in Palestine, but to note that it recalls what was also (in 1954) Fanon's sensibility concerning this "indivisibility for justice." On the one hand are Fanon's fears that beginning with the idea of a diasporic "Negro" culture flattens the significant differences (and needs) of individual African nations, as well as the differences between those Negros on the African continent and those on the North American mainland. The "dangers of [such] indifferentiation," he tells us, are that those "fundamentally heterogeneous problems" encompassed by the African diaspora get masked in order to facilitate the somewhat defensive (though understandable) impetus to counter the fables spun by the project of Western colonialism concerning the African continent.[68] But on the other hand (and quite at the same time), Fanon acknowledges the sense in which anticolonial struggles across the globe (African, Asian, and Caribbean, in particular) must be in solidarity as they fight against colonial violence in the name of their respective national liberations. "The [colonizing]

wolves," Fanon urges, "must no longer find isolated lambs to prey upon."[69]
In other words, like Angela Davis's commitment to a global, transnational
solidarity in the name of justice, Fanon's insistence on the heterogeneity of
individual anticolonial struggles ultimately stands alongside his acknowledgment of a necessary global solidarity against colonialism's totalizing reach.

As I showed in the first section of this chapter, Fanon identifies this transnational struggle as particularly important in the early stages of anticolonial
resistance, when a somewhat Manichean divide must remain between "the
colonized" and "the colonizer" (irrespective of nationality). For instance,
across this divide, French Antilleans find community with Algerians in Africa
fighting against French domination. Despite the vast economic, sociopolitical,
and cultural differences between a place like Martinique and a place like Algeria, Fanon notes the ways in which the Algerian war against French colonialism reinvigorated, for the French departments in the Antilles, the question of a
Caribbean, transnational solidarity in the name of anticolonialism. "We know
now," Fanon writes in 1960, "that there are links between the Algerian war
and the recent events that have caused blood to be shed in Martinique. . . .
The West Indian question, the question of the Caribbean federation, can no
longer be disregarded."[70] But even after those early stages of anticolonial
struggle, Fanon finds it vital for that struggle at the national level to be attuned
to a broader planetary fight against colonial domination. In other words,
despite his insistence on the heterogeneity of the needs of individual colonized nations, he understands that for decolonization in the national context
to reverberate beyond the borders of that context, a successful program of
decolonization must take this global piece into account. How does one read
this relationship between the local and the global (between the national and
the transnational) in Fanon's nationalism? More importantly, how does this
relationship prime his nationalism for conversations with processes of creolization, as they shape Glissant's idea of the composite community?

Fanon's readers get a fuller sense of this national/transnational relationship
in much of his writings in *Toward an African Revolution*. On the one hand,
he is clear about how liberation from colonial violence must be about "the
total destruction of the colonial system."[71] As a total system, colonial violence
spills across national borders, which means that one's anticolonial struggle
must include an openness to being in solidarity with resistance movements
everywhere. On the other hand, he is also careful to point out that "[every]
former colony has a *particular* way of achieving independence" and, by extension, a particular way of fighting against neocolonialism for the sake of its
individual economic sovereignty.[72] From this, we can see Fanon keeping the
particularities of a national anticolonialism at the center of what it might
mean to rid the globe of colonial violence and to establish conditions for the
possibility of a new (decolonial) humanism. Hence, in 1964, his involvement
with the global fight to end colonial rule alongside his deep immersion in the

uniqueness of the Algerian war against the French shows Fanon that colonialism everywhere (in Asia, Africa, and the Caribbean) is both identical *and* territory-specific, and that to lose sight of either of these truths is to ultimately lose the fight against colonialism. Again, from *Toward an African Revolution*: "It is essential that the oppressed peoples join up with the peoples who are already sovereign [who have already won their political freedom from their former colonizers] if a humanism that can be considered valid is to be built to the dimensions of the universe."[73] Then he emphasizes the need for such oppressed peoples to demand "recognition of . . . *national* existence . . . existence as members of an independent, free, and sovereign state."[74]

My earlier discussion of Fanon's descriptions of the transformations in Algerian culture (post-1954) showed the integral relationship between the everyday, living culture of a society and the capacities of that society to resist external (colonial) domination. The cultural reworkings of the roles of the radio and European medicine in Algeria emerged from the ground of the Algerian people; the Algerians themselves authored the sabotage of the totality of the colonial machine. This sabotage—at the level of everyday culture—needed to be unique to Algeria so as to condition a political revolution unique to its colonial relationship with France. Speaking more broadly, this shows that, for Fanon, in order for transformations at the level of culture to produce the kind of anticolonial resistance necessary for anticolonial sabotage (sabotage that *may* lead to political revolution, as in Algeria, or may not), the workings of culture must concretely reflect the society to which that culture belongs. In other words, "every culture is first and foremost national," and national culture must come from the people themselves and respond to the living needs of the people themselves.[75] To be sure, Fanon was a black nationalist, but he was also, in an important sense, a black existentialist, attentive to the level of the everyday. Hence, his black nationalism complicated the meaning of a diasporic black culture insofar as it advocated for the singular autonomy of nations, with singular economic, sociocultural, and political needs. When a diasporic notion of black culture (like Negritude) took the place of a truly nation-specific culture, Fanon's worry was that "[culture becomes] more and more cut off from the events of today," or from what, in real time, marks the pulse of the national struggle.[76]

Nonetheless, time and time again Fanon cites the importance of the Algerian Revolution not only for Algeria but for all of colonized African peoples, and those beyond the continent who were fighting to rid themselves of colonial rule. Anthony Alessandrini's treatment of this complex relationship between the local and the global is helpful, particularly because it is grounded in how culture, at the level of the everyday, facilitates concrete imaginative capacities toward thinking the national and the transnational at the same time.[77] His analysis also moves from Paul Gilroy's notion of a planetary humanism, a notion with which my account of creolization in chapter 2 engages. Because

Alessandrini brings to the fore Gilroy's indebtedness to Fanon, I use his analysis here to further my current aim of bringing Fanon's work into conversation with those aspects of creolization that pertain to alternative formations
of relationality, community, and, ultimately, the nation.

Alessandrini reminds us that "Gilroy's model of solidarity not only opposes
nationalism, but refuses to even countenance the nation-state as a possible site
from which the strategy of solidarity might be operated."[78] Concerned with
the ways in which associations between identity and place lead to identity
productions that are reified and, moreover, are hostile to the other's alterity,
Gilroy calls for the use of "diaspora" instead of "nation" when it comes to
determining a better, more ethical conception of cultural politics. "Diaspora,"
he writes, "is an especially valuable idea because it points toward a more
refined and more wieldy sense of culture than . . . notions of rootedness
[allow]. It makes the spatialization of identity problematic and interrupts the
ontologization of place."[79] However, to my mind, the "nation" that Gilroy
wants to bypass in order to fashion global decolonial solidarity is already no
longer the "nation" in Fanon's sense of a "decolonial nation." As Alessandrini
puts it, Fanon's new humanism is "a position that must be seen as ultimately
nonnationalist without simply falling into a more traditional internationalism [that would undo the meaning of national sovereignty altogether]."[80] I
would go even further and say that if, by "nationalism" one has in mind the
metaphysically reified identity to which Gilroy points, or the rigidly bordered
cultural conceptions of the nation outlined in chapter 1 of this book, then
Fanon's decolonial nationalism is rather *anti*nationalist, insofar as his idea of
a decolonial nation already includes (or aligns significantly with) what Gilroy has in mind by the translocal. As Alessandrini notes, Fanon's "is hardly
the expression of a spontaneous anti-colonial nationalist fervor; rather, [his
nationalism] represents a conscious act of translocal solidarity."[81] In the first
section of this chapter, I discuss the place of this anticolonial nationalist fervor
in Fanon's revolutionary program. Here I will reiterate that when the time
comes for the newly independent nation to build toward what it will be (as
opposed to determining its being in terms of the colonized society it *no longer*
is), even conceptions of foreignness and belonging are in need of reformulation. Fanon addresses this in sharp detail as it plays out in the case of Algeria's struggle for independence. In the chapter of *A Dying Colonialism* that
focuses on Algeria's European minority, he writes, "For the F.L.N., in the new
society that is being built, there are only Algerians. From the outset, therefore,
every individual living in Algeria is an Algerian. . . . [The] Jewish doctors and
lawyers . . . share the fate of millions of Algerians [and therefore] attest to
the multi-racial reality of the Algerian Nation."[82] These concrete accounts
of a nation in the midst of the difficult negotiations around how to ground
its national sovereignty on something other than colonialism's Manichean
algorithm demonstrate that, for Fanon, national being and national health at
the postcolonial moment ought to be pursued independently of atavistic con-

ceptions of national identity. To be sure, this postcolonial moment continues to be squarely located within the operational frame of the nation, but Fanon's hope is for "nation" to signify more ethically, and more decolonially. My claim is that his more ethical, decolonial way of imagining the nation takes us to a creolizing conception of nation building in the moments after national liberation, and to that end, a Fanonian approach would have it that, in creolizing the nation, we are not creolizing *past* or *post-* the nation.[83]

On my reading of Fanon's critique of an ultranationalism, his proposal for a conception of the nation that is truly postcolonial would be one whose commitments are grounded in an anticolonial struggle, but whose community formations and modes of relationality are not closed off by the early stages of that struggle's identity productions. In other words, it is possible to enter into the ethical project of a "new humanity" in ways that transcend the old colonial/Manichean divisions of the colony (divisions that tend to ground the struggle's early stages). It is in this vein that I offer Glissant's model of Relation (and the conception of the composite community that this model supports) as what performs the decolonial work to which Fanon's project aspires. Both thinkers offer support for the claim that "[open] and strong identity is also a strong solidarity."[84] Like Fanon's writing on the implications of Algerian independence for Algeria's European minority, Glissant's use of creolization to structure his idea of the composite community tells a story about solidarity in the name of a more humane, postcolonial world no longer conditioned by atavistic conceptions of belonging. Rather, this more humane world would be structured by a fundamental commitment to a decolonial mode of being in the world, a mode of being that *must* be open to those who share in this ethical and decolonial project. One's nationalism is not decolonial unless it is open in this way.[85]

Though I address this in the previous chapters, it is worth reemphasizing here that despite the openness of this ethical project of bringing about a decolonial conception of the human, it is imperative that such an endeavor explicitly attend to the historicity of colonial violence. Neither Fanon's antinationalist nationalism nor Glissant's creolizing community advocates for an ahistorical approach to working toward a decolonial world. Indeed, bringing these two conceptions into conversation makes this especially clear.[86] As Alessandrini points out, Fanon's transnational anticolonial solidarity is not a reiteration of liberal (Enlightenment) humanism, insofar as the former demands certain conditions of possibility for the shared ethical project of decolonial resistance. Central to these conditions is an attention to the material reality of historical location, so that the unfolding of anticolonial resistance—and the building of a decolonial world—orients itself around the specific urgencies of the multiple historical positions involved. What this means is that "[this] new form of humanist strategy does not rest . . . on the prior assumption that 'we' all share a common humanity that transcends specific contexts."[87] Much like Maria Lugones's work on the complexity of building coalitions in the liminal spaces of structural domination, the "we" of Fanon's transnational solidarity is precisely what needs to be built (it is not pregiven, independent of the work of a shared decolonial project). More importantly, it needs to be built from an·acknowledgment of multiply different manifestations of colonial violence alongside the totality of colonial history.[88] Like the account of Fanon's transnational nationalism that emerges out of Alessandrini's reading, the syncretism of creolizing community formations jostle the clarity of identity divisions and therefore negotiate with identity positions in a nonessentializing way. But this is not to say that such positions are without historical signification when it comes to creolizing processes. On the contrary, the historical materialities of these positions make themselves quite present in the relational structures of creolizing communities; they are included without being assimilated· or eliminated.[89] I read the relationship between the national and the transnational in Fanon in a similar way—as offering a model of solidarity that neither squashes the urgencies of the local nor uses them to foreclose the possibility of a shared decolonial project. I identify Glissant's formulation of Relation as what might condition this kind of solidarity. Through the relationality of his composite community, we find conditions that support, in the words of Paul Gilroy, "how an understanding of one's own particularity or identity might be transformed as a result of a principled exposure to the claims of otherness."[90]

Glissant, Relation, and the Composite Community

It is on this alternative understanding of identity's relation to otherness that the poetics grounding Glissant's creolizing conception of community appears in the subtext of a Fanonian account of the nation. More specifically, the notions of opacity and Relation, which Glissant uses to center such modes of community, curiously resound in Fanon's use of descriptions like "zones of occult instability" (a description he uses to capture the creative life of a national culture). Hence, bringing Glissant into dialogue with Fanon's sense of nationalism opens up the possibility of articulating a version of the nation that is no longer centered in the "settler exploitation" concept of the colonial matrix of power.[91] Though Fanon seems to come from a place in history, whereby the need for collective agency and economic autonomy undeniably calls for a national identity, he is attuned to the dangers of that narrow nationalism through which productive programs of economic, political, and cultural autonomy are sidestepped in favor of the ineffective vitriol of xenophobia, purity obsession, and insecurity in the face of change. Though Glissant's work on the composite community can be read as diametrically opposing the ontology of the nation, I want to propose that, alongside Fanon, we are urged to think otherwise. And this is because Fanon himself urges us to think through the idea of the nation otherwise.

In chapter 3, I provide a detailed account of Glissant's use of creolization to develop his idea of a composite community. For the purposes of grounding my current claims, I add that in *Poetics of Relation*, he presents an analysis of Caribbean history anew, understanding its particular geography as a compulsion toward a radically different ontology (toward a thinking of "being" otherwise). Through this alternative ontology, we are called to think critically (and differently) about identity and difference (about how we wrestle with that pre-Socratic problem of the One versus the Many). To recall, Glissant names thought that reduces uncertainty for the sake of a (totalizing) understanding "onto-thinking," and thought that acknowledges the irreducible difference that emerges through the dynamic complexity of becoming, "errant thinking" (or errantry). H. Adlai Murdoch's description of errantry as "the turning away from stability and homogeneity toward an implicit heterogeneity" is helpful here. Murdoch also describes errantry as "[a thinking] that revels in the . . . rootlessness which Glissant claims [as characteristic of Antillean experience] in order to explore the creative possibilities of change and exchange."[92] When faced with this task of thinking such possibilities (of "change and exchange"), onto-thinking fails, insofar as it is equipped only with unifying principles that are unable to encounter difference on its own terms (particularly on the politico-cultural stage of the "everyday"). Errant thinking, on the other hand, includes the discursive tools that might guard against those unifying principles—principles that, in the political sphere, produce a narrow nationalism. To recall from *Poetics of Relation*, the errant thinker is likened to the poet in Plato's *Republic*, since both "[challenge] and [discard] the universal" for the "fathomless word" of the other's irreducible difference.[93] This "fathomless word" that Glissant references brings to mind Fanon's "zones of occult instability," to the degree that they both stand against essentializing, and against the grasp of an onto-understanding for the sake of control.[94]

Nick Nesbitt points to Glissant's commitment to a poetics of errantry as evidence of what one might call an impasse, when one attempts to make Glissant's project do political work. To think errantly is to resist all totalizing truth, lest the principles that establish such truth reduce the diversity of which the composite community will consist.[95] For scholars of Glissant like Clevis Headley, this commitment to errantry generates an "existential ontology of difference" out of which the question of being becomes oriented in terms of the dynamism and emergence of immanence, instead of a transcendence that is static and identity-obsessed. However, on Nesbitt's reading, this ontology of immanence sacrifices the very normativity on which any political program might seek liberation, justice, and equality for all. Of Glissant's poetics of errantry, he asks, "What are the normative criteria, explicit or not, that allow [him] to affirm the *rightful* development of the [composite community] as a fully articulated set of singular multiplicities?"[96] If all there is are unreducible singularities in relation, does Glissant give up the ethical standards needed for those singularities to be held accountable to principles that protect against injustice, antidemocracy, and oppression? To recall from chapter 3, Headley is sure to point out that the political work implicit in Glissant's existential ontology of difference is one of resistance. It calls for us to "[think] being as existence, as resistance, [and] from the perspective of 'the underside of modernity.'"[97] Even as Nesbitt outlines his critique concerning the apolitical nature of Glissant's exposition, he acknowledges the need for this kind of ontological resistance. In other words, Nesbitt recognizes the political problem that Glissant's project aims to address, which is that without such ontological resistance, "a politics of universalist prescription leads not to justice but to the guillotine and the Gulag."[98]

By way of resolution, we might take the route proposed by Nesbitt himself and understand Glissant's conception of errantry as nothing more (and nothing less) than a *poetics* of resistance whose absolute commitment to absolute immanence perpetually forecloses the possibility of an ensuing politics. Or we can understand the ontological resistance of errantry (a resistance out of which we get Glissant's conception of opacity) as the cultural and discursive spirit of the political work of a community committed to its compositeness. This spirit of errantry would not make *impossible* the articulation of what would do the work of normative principles. Instead, this errant spirit would serve as a foundational and cautionary "mechanism" against the normative becoming reductive or repressive (against principles of justice turning into "the guillotine and the Gulag"). In other words, as Glissant establishes the injustice of onto-thinking, I take him to urge us to attend to the irreducible vitality of human multiplicity, as that multiplicity lives together in Relation. Perhaps this is to say that an explicit *politics* of errantry would make actual politics impossible. But it is also to say that an anticolonial politics—one founded on dynamic and living cultures, and nonstatic (anti-Manichean) conceptions of the human—ought to unfold out of an errant spirit.[99]

We see this illustrated in the notion of opacity at the center of Glissant's conception of errant thinking. For Glissant, the opaqueness of the other—that singularity with whom I am in relation—stands as the source of resistance against this ontologizing of being. Of this resistant opacity, Headley writes, "Without the ontological armor of opacity, one is left vulnerable to the oppressive gaze of transparency that demands the right to assimilate the Other within the Same."[100] Opacity is the frame through which errant thinking thinks errantly (i.e., thinks without reducing the diversity of the content of its thought). Thinking errantly, I encounter the other in her opaqueness—gather in community with her—without freezing her in a frame of epistemological transparency, for the sake of epistemological possession.[101] Instead, it is as epistemologically *unstable* (occult, to recall Fanon) that she is in relation with me.

Of the nature of this relation—between the errant thinker and the opaque other—Nesbitt writes (somewhat bleakly), "In the opacity of his time and of his place . . . surrounded by injustice and suffering at every turn, the Glissantian subject [irreducible in her opacity] can be happy to know that she need not look any further than her own self-same identity."[102] For Nesbitt, the subject's opacity is precedent for a somewhat monadic conception of human relationships, whereby all we have is an incommensurability among selves who are essentially locked in (and with) themselves, as a consequence of opacity. However, this reading seems to emphasize the opacity that protects against totalization at the expense of the *relationality* in which such opacity resides. Nesbitt is correct to remind us that, for Glissant, "it is impossible to [legitimately] reduce anyone to a truth that he will not have generated himself."[103] But on Glissant's existential ontology of Relation, we must not forget to take into account what is included in the "himself" to which Nesbitt refers.

In my and your opacity, we both exist in a totality of Relation, a totality that Glissant understands to be dynamic and differentiating (and, therefore, a totality that is not totalizing). The immanent nature of Glissant's existential ontology emphasizes the dynamic nature of the multiple singularities in question. Later in this section, I discuss the notion of Relation in more detail. But suffice it to say here that this nonstasis implies two things. First, it means that that which is "other" is already implicated in who I am, therefore the process of coming to my own truth, on Glissant's conception of Relation, is by definition a dialogic process. And second, the identity of the subject is not self-same (locked in a monadic stasis of being identical onto itself). Hence, in generating my truth, I am already a self-differentiating process that comes out of my being in relation with you, as well as with other singularities. It is with these points in mind that Headley offers his reading of opacity, duly noting that "opacity is not a form of communal [or individual] self-enclosure, an attempt to preserve or protect various types of purities (cultural, identity, historical, racial or ethnic)."[104] That is to say, a subject does not get to obnoxiously close herself off to variation and dialogue, in the name of opacity, and neither does a culture. This is because Glissant's account of opacity is already relational, resistant to the homogeny of a singular One as it is resistant to the homogeny of a universal One. To be sure, this is to engage with the somewhat aporetic conception of an opaque singularity that is not only "othering" onto itself in a self-differentiating process, but is also always already in relation to what is other. Murdoch recognizes this aporia as a "paradoxical perspective [that] acknowledges the limits of the knowability of the other even as it presents the twin subjective tensions on which it is formulated as an opportunity to extend and enrich the functional framework for interpersonal and intercultural subjectivity."[105] This seems to be the novelty of Glissant's ontological shift, or the ontological novelty of what Headley names "a creolizing of being."[106]

In this vein, I propose that we consider opacity and errantry as the dual undergirding spirits working to safeguard against the homogenizing frame of a narrow nationalism, which too hastily claims to be the voice of the diverse multiplicities of a composite community. This invariably gets us to the question of what it might mean for the composite community to signify in the political realm, as a political entity charged with accomplishing the specifically anticolonial (and therefore political) tasks of promoting justice, protecting equality, and fostering the kind of democratic participation out of which the people of a nation are self-governed. On Nesbitt's account, this is precisely where we cannot take Glissant's notion of opacity, given that he says Glissant is laying out "a defense of local specificities."[107] As local (or, perhaps, anticommunal), such groups would be antagonistic to the common concerns of a collective (like a national community), and (to return to the case of Algeria, post-1954) to the urgencies pertaining to building the nation anew in the aftermath of colonial rule. However, in order for these local interests to undermine, at the level of the political, those commonly felt national concerns, we have to understand these Glissantian singularities to be *themselves* political, located in such a way that it becomes possible to do such politically destructive work. If this is what Glissant gives us in his account of opacity, then yes, his would be "a defense of local specificities" that would make impossible the collective voice for which Fanon calls (in his rejection of a narrow nationalism). This seems to be Nesbitt's understanding when he writes, "Once all of the singularities in a Glissantian Totality have developed in their fullest singularity[,] Blacks will be fully determined as Black, Gays as Gay, Women as Women, Jews as Jews."[108] In other words, opacity would give us a radical and unproductive identity politics, the kind that the "national-transnational" modality of Fanon's antinationalist nationalism will ultimately not allow.

But if opacity is not this defense of *identity* but, instead, an orientation toward *singularity*, then it doesn't do this sort of counterpolitical work. As an orientation toward singularity, opacity *cannot* do such counterpolitical work because (as singularity) it signifies on a plane that is not the plane of the political. The categories of "Black," "Gay," "Woman," and "Jew" (cited in Nesbitt's critique) reside on this plane of politics insofar as they are meaningful in (socio)political terms. In other words, the existence of such identity markers evidence an identification process (political in nature) that has already occurred.[109] Here we should recall Headley's reading of Glissant, in which he cites opacity as what *resists* such identification. To be opaque is to signify as an absence of signification, and to be a singularity that is encountered as beyond identification.[110] Headley understands this to be the heart of Glissant's ontology—an "[ontology that] in this new setting, engages the world not as a constitution of individual essences [Black, Jew, Gay, etc.] but as a multiplicity, as creative becoming [that] does not generate antagonistic and contradictory differences, but pure and positive differences."[111] However, though opacity is not on the plane of the political, it can orient the plane of the political in two ways. First, as an ontological resistance, opacity would protect a community against the totalitarianism—the guillotine and the Gulag—of the One. Second, as an existential ontology of differences that are not antagonistic, opacity also protects against the tyranny of the Many. As Murdoch writes, mediated by opacity, an encounter with the other "avoids absolutes even as it recognizes and accepts the thickness of difference."[112]

If one's political program entails moving beyond both totalitarianism and radical identity politics, then opacity can serve as the undergirding spirit of that program. That is to say, opacity can serve as the grounding spirit of a national consciousness, working to safeguard against the homogenizing frame of a narrow nationalism. More significantly, the creative emergence of that national culture happens on a foundation of difference. To understand this foundation of difference in Glissantian terms—as a foundation of a relational opacity—is to conceive of a national culture that rejects principles that fail to articulate the living culture of the people themselves. To reiterate, opaque singularities are already relational; they are something other than the closed-off monads that, on Headley's account, "preserve or protect various types of purities [only to produce] a form of an obnoxious obscurantism."[113] Hence, in its rejection of totalitarian principles, the composite community grounded in opacity will also be one that honors the infinite variability of what it means to be a subject who differs to herself, as a consequence of being in relation with others. In other words, this opacity-grounded community rejects "the obsession with the One [or] non-relation." Hence, we can think of this community as aligning with a national culture whose more political articulations avoid the dangers that Fanon identifies in a narrow nationalism.[114] To be sure, this says much about the structure of the composite community, and about how we are called to radically reimagine the idea of community.[115] In a similar vein, Fanon asks us to reimagine a national culture (indeed, to reimagine the idea of the nation) as an emerging organism, not static and dead but, rather, "occult and unstable" in its opaque resistance to the transparency of a knowing language. Like Glissant, who wants to begin by "acknowledging the implicit density of all that is embodied in otherness," Fanon also urges us toward a transformative version of both collective and individual identity.

If onto-thinking moves toward universality, then errant thinking moves toward what Glissant names "le chaos-monde."[116] "Le chaos-monde" underscores the fluidity endemic to real diversity and provides a model for understanding how that diversity can be gathered without being universalized, or come together in what Glissant names "Relation" without resulting in a genocide (metaphorical or otherwise) of difference. The composite community is hospitable to difference, since, coded in the logic of Relation, the products of contact among cultures are themselves dynamically producing singular iterations of themselves. In this regard, "community" refers to a perpetual emerging of newness, and the kind of community produced in the relationality of Relation is unstable ("occultly" unstable, perhaps), is ever changing, and is itself "a product that in turn produces." Grounded in the logic of becoming and movement, composite communities do not close in on themselves (despite their internal coherence). Rather, they remain open to the uncertainty of emergent (creolizing) processes that produce, quite genuinely, what is new (or perhaps unprecedented). To be a community in Relation is to be amenable to change, since it is the dynamism of becoming.

How might the relationality of Relation provide an alternative (*the* alternative, perhaps) to the narrow nationalism of which Fanon is so critical? In returning to our earlier discussion (see above in this chapter) of the relationship between the national and the transnational in Fanon, we can see how Glissant's Relation provides conceptual support for some of Fanon's more concrete descriptions of the postcolonial nation as open, dynamic, and directed toward a not-yet-determined future sense of itself. In other words, the kind of antiessentialist, living national culture for which Fanon calls finds, in Glissant's notion of Relation, a promising response.

In *A Dying Colonialism*, Fanon stresses the need for a postindependence Algeria to engage in the collective work of determining how a new Algeria would accomplish its national identity in a decolonial way. Vital to this decolonial national identity is an openness to the other. In other words, to be decolonial is to resist the ultranationalist and chauvinist posture not only of an imperialist conception of the nation but also of the colony's early stages of anticolonial resistance.[117] With this hope for a newly independent Algeria, he writes, "[The] Algerian people is at once the most nationalist and the most open. . . . On November 1, 1954 . . . a creative dynamic synthesis took place between the aspirations of the national cultural ego and the modern spirit in its universality."[118] Hence, what Fanon has in mind regarding the self-assertion of a national culture and the political autonomy of the decolonial nation is not closed off to the other but instead, and much like the relationality of Glissant's composite community, is a nation with an orientation toward becoming-other-to-itself, toward fluid "experiments with itself" in an always ongoing practice of self-making. This orientation manifests in real time for Fanon, as he witnesses a self-asserting Algerian people reconstitute itself to include "the Jewish doctors and lawyers . . . [who] share the fate of millions of Algerians [and therefore] attest to the multi-racial reality of the [new] Algerian Nation."[119] Hence, just as we might read processes of creolization in Fanon's ground-level descriptions of the cultural transformations in Algerian everyday life (concerning the use of medicine and the use of the radio), we might also read a Glissantian relationality in his ground-level accounts of the dynamic and fluid negotiations concerning the meaning of national identity and belonging. To be sure, these negotiations are not at all divorced from the material urgencies of history (of what it meant to be in Algeria and to be *with* Algerians in their anticolonial struggle for independence). Again, Fanon's own life—as a citizen of Martinique whose full devotion to the Algerian cause ultimately gave him a home in Algeria—bears witness to this. The nonstasis of these identity negotiations (indeed, of the negotiations around the very meaning of the nation) points toward an engagement with history, without making history an essentializing force at the heart of one's nation-ness.

This captures the ways in which Glissant's conception of Relation grounds a coherent composite community in the midst of dynamic movement. By extension, Relation captures the ways in which, on Fanon's account, a national culture is "teeming with life" and open to being transformed through living relationships with others. Colonialism ultimately relies on stasis, on frozen locations, for identity within a Manichean world. Decolonization, then, would involve rupturing this stasis and replacing it with the fluid transformations that come out of concrete, everyday living.[120] For Fanon, a nation attentive to the task of decolonization would then make itself open to modes of relation deemed impossible by colonialism's stasis.[121] It is out of this openness that every individual "living in Algeria"—invested in the promise of a new and decolonial nation—"[gives]-on-and-with" (to use Glissant's terminology) a newly emerging Algerian nation.[122]

To this end, Glissant's sense of the totality constitutive of Relation gives us an alternative way of thinking community, which might fulfill Fanon's demands for a national culture that is not narrow. When we engage this idea of Relation with Fanon's political project of a truly decolonial nation, it is possible to envision what it would be to hold one's nationalism accountable to normative standards *and* simultaneously safeguard against a culture of walling off difference in the name of national health.[123] Alongside the incommensurability of identity politics, and the silencing oneness of xenophobic nationalism, Glissant's work invites us to think through the possibility of a community that remains in the process of making itself anew through the "ordered chaos" of being in Relation. In *le chaos-monde*, a community of diverse cultures and linguistic sensibilities can avoid both "ravenous integration" and "muddled nothingness."[124]

Fanon is clear about his caution against turning toward the past for the purpose of moving beyond colonialism. For him, this move beyond and toward something otherwise "requires . . . the liquidation of all the chains of the past."[125] The past that Fanon wants to liquidate is frozen, either reified in the terms offered by colonial decadence, or reified in a reactionary posture against that colonial decadence. Both options foreclose the possibility of what, for him, will be the most human in the age of the decolonial—the open-endedness of freedom. And in order to imagine a future in which freedom can truly unfold in this way, that future must not be beholden to colonialism's past. In what appears to be a contrasting approach, Glissant identifies the possibility of a new kind of human relationality (grounded in a compositeness of cultural imaginaries) through a creolized Caribbean *past*. In other words, it is in the historical legacies of colonial conquest, and the resulting transplantations of peoples, that the site of the Caribbean holds the promise (for Glissant) of something radically new, radically future. Given this turn to history in Glissant, what does Fanon's anti-past stance mean when it comes to my attempts to read his conception of the nation as a creolizing nation, or as a politicized version of Glissant's composite community?[126]

It is important to note that, shaped through processes of creolization, Glissant's composite community *is* quite future-oriented. This becomes clear when one attends to the nature of creolization's relationship to the past. In its syncretism, creolizing practices are already not beholden to the past qua reified. Instead, the past is taken up for the sake of refashioning, but that refashioning already accomplishes the kind of "liquidation" that Fanon's decolonial politics demands. In other words, like this liquidation of the past, creolization entails neither a return nor a commitment to atavistic endeavors that employ mummified conceptions of identity. To better understand what I am claiming as a *similarity* between Fanon's and Glissant's relationship with the past, I turn to John Drabinski's work on the role of memory in Glissant. He writes, "[For Glissant, colonialism] devastates the past. The moment of postcolony life is saturated with the question of the future precisely because an absolute gap is opened up."[127] In other words, for Drabinski, the question that Glissant poses to postcolonial critical discourse concerns the possibility of beginning after the catastrophe of colonial rule. But an acknowledgment of this catastrophe, along with an acknowledgment of the urgency of this question of how to begin in its aftermath, are present for both Glissant *and* Fanon. How does one embark on a political project of human liberation when all one faces upon turning toward the past is the absence of history, the absence of family lineage, the absence of all linkage to cultural identity?

It is on this rhetorical juncture that Fanon's rejection of the past turns and his demand for a future-oriented nationalism rests. However, Glissant's embracing of the past (as a past shaped through creolizing practices) rests here as well: the driving questions listed above are precisely the questions that inform Glissant's celebration of the Antillean history of creolization. This is because, for Glissant, this history is not *only* a history of pure abjection, or pure absence. He locates in this history, and among the wreckage of colonial conquest, the fragments whose being do not simply witness the destruction and the drowning of memory. More significantly, these fragments are what have been historically used in the emergent processes of creolization, to generate new and creative ways of being, and of beginning again. As Zimitri Erasmus writes, Antillean identity and culture for Glissant "are less about what was lost culturally along the Middle Passage and as a result of genocide, and more about the articulations of these diverse identities and fragments of cultural formations with colonial culture."[128] In other words, Glissant's "turn" toward a creolizing past is really, at its heart, just as future-oriented as Fanon's rejection of (colonial) history. Both understand that the postcolonial moment is ripe with an obligation to begin creatively, to generate emergent structures that have no precedents in the past of colonial domination. That is to say, both the Fanonian and Glissantian projects emerge in a spirit of creative antiteleology of a not-yet-known "new humanity" and a "new humanism." Glissant orients himself in a creolizing past because, for him, the existence of such creative productions of the new and the unprecedented (the future) simply *is* the meaning of Caribbean history. It is in this spirit that, in *Caribbean Discourse*, he asks us to understand "the transfer (by the slave trade) of a population to another place" as what results in that population "[changing] into something different, into a new set of possibilities. It is in this metamorphosis that we must try to detect one of the best kept secrets of creolization."[129] In this sense, his celebration of a colonial-yet-creolizing past rests on a rejection that is similar to Fanon's demand for the "post-" of the postcolonial to be grounded in a new humanism.[130]

Fanon's nationalism comes out of a struggle whose beginning happened as an abandoned present, unable to conceive of anything beyond "the urgency of the now," and immobile due to the crushing weight of colonial oppression. But it is also a nationalism of the future, of possibility, neither myopically grounded in "Replace the foreigner" nor chained to a frozen and mythic past. In turning to Glissant, we might describe this Fanonian nationalism as an *errant* nationalism, both autonomous *and* open to the "giving on and with" among differences in community. "The consciousness of self," Fanon tells us, "is not the closing of a door to communication. Philosophic thought teaches us, on the contrary, that it is its guarantee."[131] In the same vein, a national culture by no means implies the culture of a narrow nationalism. Thought of in terms of Glissant's composite community, we witness the contrary—a nationalism that is decolonial, no longer in the business of xenophobic mapping and control, and committed to "giving on and with" the intense diversity of free human life.

Conclusion

◆

Creolizing as an Imperative

It has been fascinating to develop this project during the latest resurgence of fascist nationalisms around the globe and to think about the meaning and implications of citizenship in the midst of the renewed traction of white nationalism in the era of Trump. Indeed, this book grew out of my own meditations on what it would mean to become a citizen of the United States, how it might change (or not change) my experience of being an immigrant—an experience out of which complex articulations of belonging and nonbelonging have grown over the twenty-two years since I left the place that continues—though in a complicated way—to be home. Writing this work in such a political climate has made its constituting argument feel both fundamentally impossible and necessary. Impossible, since there seems to be nothing to salvage in the idea of nation and nationalism. Why continue to work within this frame if at its heart is what Étienne Balibar identifies as a founding posture of defense that determines difference as a threat? Aren't the political orientations currently plaguing Europe, the United States, and Brazil (to name a few) already evidence of the impossibility of finding, within the nation-form, conditions that support human life for *all* humans? But the argument I make also feels necessary—the nation-form will more than likely continue to be the organizing frame for the political, economic, and sociocultural aspects of our lives. Thus, we're urgently called to determine conditions for some other possibility for the nation, some other relational living out of which there can be a plurality of futures, and open-ended self-formations with respect to the other.

My hope is to have offered creolization as a frame for thinking through such possibilities. As a set of practices that takes us to the level of intimate and everyday life, creolization not only names the emergence of new orientations toward time and place, world and others, but also locates that emergence within the orbit of the exigencies of subjects who *must* resist the totalizing effects of structural violence. For communities shaped by a history of creolization, subaltern agency in the face of colonial and neocolonial violence is the driving force of what ultimately emerges as the possibility of new world-relations and imaginaries. As these new ways of being in and relating to the world insert themselves into the liminal folds of the social, they jostle the mainstream codes of that social architecture, thus becoming, in a sense, sociality's constitutive "outside." My argument for creolizing the nation is an attempt to account for such constitutive "outsides" with respect to the nation. This effect of creolizing practices at the level of the everyday gestures toward what María Lugones conceptualizes as the heterogeneous socialities that are always already part of a social landscape. Plural world-orientations coexist, precisely because of the need (generated by dominant structures of violence) to resist life-as-unfreedom. As subjects encounter and respond to that need, they effectively insert traces of an otherwise into the totality of structures that are themselves unable to account for that otherwise. In so doing, the violence of these totalities do not have the last word when it comes to the contours of what it means to be human.

I've tried to show what it might mean to think creolization and nationalization together. I've argued for the feasibility of thinking about communities as national in structure and bureaucracy *and*, at the same time, as ever-dynamic and emerging constitutions of creolizing processes. These coconstitutive processes—nationalization and creolization—entangle at the level of everyday culture in ways that often make those everyday (creolizing) practices of sabotage invisible, or unrecognizable to more standard conceptions of resistance. Nevertheless, through that entanglement, new meaning is produced and discursive practices take shape in a way that makes the political *move* (as it were), instead of remaining a static and unchanging fait accompli. I've turned to Glissant's notion of rhizomatic errantry for the conceptual vocabulary to capture this movement, since Glissant's model of community would make the "All" of the nation-form accountable to the "Relation" among the multiple histories and social positionalities that negotiate together around questions of belonging, subject formation, and conditions of freedom. Thinking about the nation in terms of a rhizoming compositeness foregrounds the dynamic nature of a national culture, thus complementing the narrative of totalizing (and stable) national ontologies with formulations through which borders signify as ambiguously constituted (open to jostling and contestation), and through which subject formation is constituted in terms of difference. In this book I've proposed that in reorienting our understanding of the nation to include this dynamism, we not only utilize a sense of nation-ness as already open to different, better, and more liberatory constitutions of itself but also (and perhaps more significantly) make more visible what are, to my mind, radical agencies at the level of the mundane. To return again to Lugones, attention to the jostling effects *of* creolization *on* the nation's formation affords us a view of marginalized subjectivities as active and resisting subjects who, in making a way out of no way, change the course of the political.

To be sure, the actual course of such change remains open ended and not yet determined in its rewriting of the present. In other words, the possibilities toward which creolizing imaginaries lead are to be read as just that—in the register of possibility, the political effects of which are *not* in offering clear and delineated structures and codes. Rather, the political effect of alternative, creolizing imaginaries is in the rupturing of existing structures, in the ways those imaginaries contest the directionality and telos of existing power. What emerges, on the grounds of this undoing of power's claims to totality and legitimacy, is an "otherwise" that is (to borrow from David Marriott) opaquely so, seen as without telos precisely insofar as the ruptures in question are located radically outside the frame of the power being contested.[1] Anthony Alessandrini gives an account of the possibility of a decolonial conception of the human as a possibility that must emerge as "an orientation toward a future that has not yet come," insofar as the radical nature of this decolonial conception—its *newness*—means that it will remain unsignifiable within the coloniality from which we must break.[2] In this vein, any political program signifying as explicitly (and *visibly*) delineated in the present would be squarely *of* the present, and not yet an effect of its rupturing.

Hence, what I've offered as a properly creolizing account of the nation includes a set of everyday cultural and discursive practices that (in the words of Glissant) offers an imaginary sufficiently otherwise, so as to orient the nation in this way—"toward a future that has not yet come." This reframes the project of nation-ness as incomplete and dynamic as its self-formation moves in the to-and-fro of Glissant's rhizomatic and errant relationality. Out of this reframing, closure shows up as premature, already leaving out (in the form of silencing) histories and positionalities that are part of the "All is Relation." Stasis shows up as a failure to do what Amy Allen urges in her account of decolonizing critical theory—to enact "the project of decoupling progress as an imperative from progress as a 'fact.'"[3] In that vein, my subjection of the nation-form to creolization is also a caution against any "fact" of achieving, within nation-ness, conditions of freedom for plural conceptions of the human. It is a caution, in other words, against understanding a decolonizing of the nation as anything other than an *imperative* to decolonize, an imperative to remain with the process of orienting, and then reorienting again toward Alessandrini's future that has not yet come. Like Allen, I hold that any other narrative would ultimately signal the "end of progress" or, in language more pertinent to this book, would signal the end of a creolizing of the nation.

Hence, in this spirit I conclude this book by signaling its incompleteness, by orienting it toward the questions and problem spaces it generates, which—in the open-ended spirit of creolization—just might take us beyond the creolizing frame. In ending this way, my hope is to avoid framing a project of creolizing the nation as one *with an end*; rather, it is one through which we encounter decolonizing the nation-form as an imperative. Such an imperative calls for vigilance against narratives of the postcolonial that understands colonialism's past as a past that "[can be] easily left behind."[4] This is especially urgent given that much of the past practices of colonialism continue to directly inform its "post-" and can therefore be understood as past only through dangerous disavowals. Particular to these "post- but not past" practices is the occupation and settlement of lands stolen from indigenous nations in the Americas, which continue to support the neocolonial expansionism of settler states like the United States and Canada. Thus, the task of creolizing the nation is accountable to the stakes of those ongoing practices of settler colonialism, and to the indigenous anticolonial struggles that emerge in resistance to this ongoing colonial violence. Hence, I take a question like Jodi Byrd's to be part of the problem space generated by this book: What would it mean to give an account of creolization—as a frame out of which decolonial imaginaries might grow—that avoids the "syllogistic traps of participatory democracy born out of violent occupation of lands"?[5] Is such an account even possible?

Taking creolization to the nation-form allows us to think against the supposed finality of colonial violence (a violence that, more often than not, gets codified in the economic and bureaucratic performances of the nation). In that thinking-against, the frame of creolization allows us to theorize an anticolonial agency in subversive cultural productions, which work to undo colonialism's monopolies on subject formation, world-relation, and overall arrangements that enact community and belonging. I am drawn to Byrd's analysis of what it might mean to critically engage with the totality of colonial violence so as to determine paths that might move the world beyond that violence *without* deploying the logics circumscribed by it. In other words, what would it mean to move beyond coloniality via routes that are themselves illegible (or opaque) to coloniality? As a start (and only that) to responding to the question above, I offer Byrd's account of a decolonial option that begins in the horizontally oriented "cacophony" of the plural histories that emerge out of colonial violence, the cacophony of coloniality's plural violences (if you will). On my reading of her account, the possibility of decolonial futures rests squarely in the *horizontal* relationality among colonialism's resisting subjects, and squarely *outside* a colonial relationality of both the Manichean colonized-colonizer divide and the metrics of hierarchy among colonized histories. As Byrd aptly puts it, decolonial resistance grounded in cacophony "[decenters] the vertical interactions of colonizer and colonized and [recenters] the horizontal struggles among peoples with competing claims to historical oppressions."[6]

Like the characters in LeAnne Howe's short story, cacophonous negotiations of the implications of colonialism's past *and* present mean that we "bang [our] heads together in search of cross-cultural understanding."[7] The pain and intensity of Howe's imagery is meant to convey the difficulty involved in working toward these cross-cultural understandings, in bringing the histories of forced transplantation, coerced migratory labor, and diasporic placenessness into conversations—into Lugones's complex communication, quite frankly—with the "oppositional place-based" claims and experiences of First Peoples.[8] This is acutely pertinent to the process of creolization, which happens out of a history of radical rupture and absence. The "pre-" of colonial arrival and contact, according to these creolizing histories, remains only in fragments that will ultimately condition the reinventions and "beautiful inauthenticities" of those histories. Intact origins lie unrecoverable on the Atlantic Ocean's floor, which means that the generativity of creolization is grounded (ontologically) in the loss of a past, or, rather, in the present *absence* of the past. Byrd reminds us, however, that for indigeneity "there is a long line of continuity between the past and the present that has not been disrupted."[9] For First Peoples, the "pre-" of colonial conquest remains present—the continuity of the line connecting indigenous pasts to indigenous presents marks neocolonialism's *ongoing* occupation of native land. More significantly, the presence of colonialism's anti-indigenous past (genocide and dispossession) *conditions* the loss and rupture on which creolization becomes a constituting element of the colonized world. In other words, the clearing that makes possible the migrations and arrivals out of which creolization will grow is one of past and continuous projects of the "clearing away" of the native.

For Glen Coulthard, this means that indigenous justice needs to be grounded in a revitalization of the politics and culture of indigenous world-relations, so as to precisely resist the clearing away required by and for the continued expansion of neocolonial empires. Because of this, and in a vein similar to Jodi Byrd's critique of inclusion strategies of postcolonial platforms, Coulthard is avidly against grounding indigenous struggles in a need to be recognized by settler states. Against such aspirations for recognition, he offers what he calls a "resurgent indigenous politics," through which "the colonized must instead struggle/work through their alienation/subjection against the objectifying gaze and assimilative lure of colonial recognition."[10] In both positions (Coulthard's and Byrd's), one reads a commitment to keeping indigenous presence, along with its place-based memory and sovereign claims to land, both visible and audible.[11] Byrd's conception of horizontal cacophony is what, on her account, would ensue if such commitments were not erased by encounters with the resistance strategies of newly arriving multicultures of the Americas. By extension, we might read Coulthard's conception of resurgent indigenous politics as what would have to foreground any of the *political* negotiations coming out of such encounters.

When "heads bang together" in this way, in the aftermath and afterlives of Empire, it seems apt to say that we have arrived at a point in which "diaspora collides with settler colonialism," where any possibility of decolonizing imaginaries coming out of creolization calls for a kind of transformative accountability *to* this collision point.[12] On Byrd's analysis, postcolonial aspirations toward this kind of accountability often ultimately perpetuate the very settler colonial logics they aim to transgress and/or replace, insofar as the telos of inclusion, around which such aspirations are organized, only serves to make invisible the memory of indigenous genocide that renders the Americas a place into which the diasporas of colonial violence might be included to begin with. On certain readings, creolization might be interpreted as one such postcolonial aspiration (toward inclusion and assimilation into a multicultural settler state). However, as I have outlined and deployed it in this book, the relationality of creolizing processes are errant and rhizomatic and, perhaps most significantly, *keep opacity at the center*. Taking Glissant as my guide, I have shown that any relational process and practice conceptualized in a creolizing frame would be open ended in the messiness of the rhizome's routings, would gather singularities in a knowing that is *not* one of transparency and full access, and would be less about final resolutions and more about the complex communicative enactments of ongoing community formation. If, in its encounter with the "oppositional place-based" claims of indigenous peoples, a creolizing relation does *not* route differently in response, but instead retrenches into a "rationalizing [of] the originary historical traumas that birthed settler colonialism," then the relation is no longer shaped in a creolizing spirit.[13]

So there seem to be ways to bring Glissant's "All is Relation" into engagement— head-banging engagement, to be sure—with the antihierarchical and multi-directional implications of the cacophonous interventions for which Byrd calls. In that intervention, what is hoped for is "the possibility for [indigenous] memory and [migratory] resistance to forge alliances across historical and cultural experiences in opposition to the competitions upon which colonialism relies."[14] Indeed, this possibility might take us beyond creolization as a conceptual tool. But creolization, as I have tried to use it here, does not stand *in the way of* this possibility. Centered on relation-in-opacity, Glissant's composite community seems to be able to account for the kind of "radical alterity" that, on Byrd's analysis, is signaled by indigeneity in the Americas.[15] The errantry of Glissant's community seems to be able to account for the kind of indigestible nature of this indigenous alterity, since, on his formulations, errantry is not about digesting or consuming the singularities in relation. The "All" of the compositeness is never quite one of simple inclusion. Yet all are gathered into a composite (and perhaps cacophonous) totality.

To reiterate, what I offer here is only a beginning, in response to this question: What would it mean to give an account of creolization that avoids the "syllogistic traps of participatory democracy born out of violent occupation of lands"?[16] So I refrain from too quickly claiming that a theoretical frame of creolization alone can accomplish the kind of decolonial work called for by both Byrd and Coulthard. But it is important to note that the indigestibility of indigenous memory, to which Byrd alludes, does capture the work of opacity in Glissant's development of the rhizome. Indeed, this is the spirit of the distinction Glissant makes between thinking errantly and thinking onto-logically—the errant thinker enters into relationships of knowing and understanding without expecting (demanding) transparency. This nonexpectation of transparency also seems to position Glissant's creolization to address Coulthard's critique of the "recognition" approach to indigenous anticolonial activism. Though Coulthard's critique is directed toward what, on Byrd's analysis, would be the *vertical* relation between the settler state and the indigenous communities within the borders of that state, we can also read the opacity that resists the transparency of recognition as pertaining to the horizontal relationships between First Peoples and diasporic communities. In other words, if indigenous self-affirmation enacts a kind of indigenous illegibility, then Coulthard's decolonial approach would find resonance with Glissant's composite community—a community into which inclusion is *not* at the expense of the kind of recognition Coulthard critiques.

To note, Coulthard will point out that, though the revitalization at the foundation of his resurgent decolonial politics involves a return to indigenous pasts, this "turning back" must be *critical*. It must be a return that is neither nostalgic nor atavistic but is instead attuned to what those past practices mean for indigenous communities living *in* the present, and having to engage in the kinds of cacophonous encounters with other colonial histories. So though the goal of a resurgent decolonial politics is indigenous self-affirmation (an affirmation in resistance to colonial othering), Coulthard points out that resurgence must be mindful of "the pitfalls associated with retreating into an uncritical essentialism in . . . practices of cultural revitalization" (pitfalls that, as I show in chapter 6, Fanon similarly warns against in *Wretched of the Earth*).[17] Against this kind of essentialism, Coulthard cites Leanne Simpson's understanding of revitalizing indigenous traditions as a mandate to "[reclaim] the fluidity of [those] traditions, not the rigidity of colonialism."[18] We might read in this revitalization a turning-back to the place-based memory of native peoples that is also, at the same time, actively colliding with other colonized peoples "existing in the same geographical space [and time]" of contemporary indigenous resistance.[19] Through those collisions, indigenous revitalizations might be called to the kinds of fluid and "contaminated" world-relations not unlike what Glissant demonstrates in creolizing community formations. And likewise, those migratory communities, whose history is one of translocation and arrival, might be called to understand their own creole indigeneity alongside the particular colonial violence made visible by the revitalization of indigenous resurgence.

Hence, ending with creolizing the nation as an imperative and not as a "fact" (and perhaps opening up the possibility of having to move beyond creolization's conceptual frame) seems quite in line with the implications of creolization. These are implications that center cacophony, critical vigilance, and suspicions toward resolution, as they center those everyday practices of resisting subjects who "inhabit the power grid in great resistance."[20] Creolizing the nation takes our attention to those subaltern agencies—migratory, translocated, and indigenous alike—that are always already authoring new ways of relating to the world and enacting new imaginaries in the face of colonial and neocolonial violence. To think about the constituting totality of the nation in this way—creolizing, errant, and rhizomatically gathering through the irreducible gaps of plural histories and struggles—is to conceive the possibility of its decolonial future. Never easy, always cacophonous, but the opaque horizon toward which a properly creolizing conception of the nation-totality moves.

NOTES

Introduction

1. Michael J. Monahan, *The Creolizing Subject: Race, Reason, and the Politics of Purity* (New York: Fordham University Press, 2011).

2. Kris Sealey, "Dirty Consciousnesses and Runaway Selves: A Levinasian Response to Monahan," *Critical Philosophy of Race* 1, no. 2 (2013): 220; emphasis in original.

3. Sealey, "Dirty Consciousnesses and Runaway Selves," 227.

4. Though I bring it to bear on my current proposal to creolize the nation in the concluding sections of this book, I want to note Jodi Byrd's analysis here. Byrd aptly details the dangers of too easily conflating the violence of racialization and colonialism, or of reducing indigenous peoples to one of several minority racialized groups in neocolonial societies. Jodi Byrd, *The Transit of Empire: Indigenous Critiques of Colonialism* (Minneapolis: University of Minnesota Press, 2011).

5. Michaeline A. Crichlow, *Globalization and the Post-Creole Imagination: Notes on Fleeing the Plantation* (Durham, N.C.: Duke University Press, 2009).

6. Frantz Fanon, *Black Skin, White Masks*, trans. Charles Lam Markmann (London: Pluto Press, 1967), 229.

7. Though this book offers what would be a properly creolizing conception of the politics and poetics of the national community, my hope is that it also invites engagement with plurinationalist projects, particularly in the cases of Bolivia and Ecuador. In these two Latin American contexts, indigenous resistance against the neoliberal nationalist-developmental politics of the state has taken the form of a demand for multiple political and economic sovereignties determining policies/practices that have to do with statehood and self-determination. Under plurinationalism, there would be an internal recognition of "the right of indigenous peoples to self-governance." Roger Merino, "Reimagining the Nation-State: Indigenous Peoples and the Making of Plurinationalism in Latin America," *Leiden Journal of International Law* 31 (2018): 782. Such self-governance pertains not only to questions of cultural autonomy but also, more significantly, to the use of land and natural resources. As such, a plurinationalist orientation toward statehood contains at least the potential for "[indigenous] vision[s] and practice[s] of humanity, life, and living" to offer anticapitalist and antiextractionist articulations of the material and social well-being of the state. Catherine Walsh, "Afro and Indigenous Life—Visions in/and Politics: (De)Colonial Perspectives in Bolivia and Ecuador," *Bolivian Studies Journal/Revista de Estudios Bolivianos* 18 (2011): 51. Like my reading of creolization here, a plurinationalist position is fully grounded in history (namely, how colonial violence determines the neoliberal nationalism of previously colonized states as a nationalism that excludes the well-being of indigenous peoples) and is thus more than a multiculturalism. Hence, even

though plurinationalism's *frontal* interactions with the state are largely absent in creolizing comportments, one might find, in a properly creolizing conception of the nation, some symbolic ground for the more bureaucratic enactments of plurinationalism.

8. The human rights violations currently unfolding at the U.S.-Mexico border are, to my mind, such questions coming to a head.

9. Chandra Talpade Mohanty, *Feminism without Borders: Decolonizing Theory, Practicing Solidarity* (Durham, N.C.: Duke University Press, 2003), 87.

Introduction to part 1

1. Nelson Maldonado-Torres, "On the Coloniality of Being: Contributions to the Development of a Concept," *Cultural Studies* 21, nos. 2–3 (March/May 2007).

Chapter 1

1. Achille Mbembe, "The Idea of a Borderless World," Africa Is a Country, last modified November 18, 2017, https://africasacountry.com/2018/11/the-idea-of -a-borderless-world.

2. Étienne Balibar argues for the continued centrality of the nation-form by noting that "we are not only social beings but more significantly national beings." Étienne Balibar, *We, the People of Europe? Reflections on Transnational Citizenship* (Princeton, N.J.: Princeton University Press, 2004), 12.

3. Azar Gat is in this camp. See his account in *Nations: The Long History and Deep Roots of Political Ethnicity and Nationalism* (Cambridge: Cambridge University Press, 2013).

4. Balibar, *We, the People of Europe?*, 57.

5. Ricardo Sanín-Restrepo, *Decolonizing Democracy: Power in a Solid State* (Lanham, Md.: Rowman and Littlefield, 2016).

6. Sanín-Restrepo, *Decolonizing Democracy*, 53 (emphasis in the original).

7. Sanín-Restrepo, *Decolonizing Democracy*, 51.

8. To note, this "model to copy" is a developmental movement *in* time, as it sustains a certain timelessness of the model that reproduces itself. This will figure in my account of national destiny (below), through which I show that, on certain formulations of the nation-form, the timelessness of a destiny is set up (as it were) in advance of the contingencies of history.

9. Sanín-Restrepo, *Decolonizing Democracy*, 54 (emphasis in the original).

10. I say more about the temporality of the nation-form in the second section of this chapter.

11. Étienne Balibar, "The Nation Form: History and Ideology," in *Race, Nation, Class: Ambiguous Identities*, ed. Étienne Balibar and Immanuel Wallerstein (London: Verso, 1991), 90.

12. Balibar, "The Nation," 93.

13. Balibar, "The Nation," 96 (emphasis in the original).

14. George L. Mosse, *Confronting the Nation: Jewish and Western Nationalism* (Hanover, N.H.: Brandeis University Press, 1993), 28.

15. Mosse, *Confronting the Nation*, 23.

16. In the following section I discuss the role of a recourse to nature on the linear construction of the nation's temporality and spatiality.

17. This anticipates my analysis in part 2 of this book, of María Lugones's

conception of fragmentation in its relation to a politics of purity. I note that what I am currently naming a metaphysics of the One resonates with much of Lugones's critical account of a politics of purity.

18. Benedict Anderson, *Imagined Communities: Reflections on the Origin and Spread of Nationalism*, rev. ed. (London: Verso, 2006), 184.

19. Anderson, *Imagined Communities*, 184.

20. Sanín-Restrepo, *Decolonizing Democracy*, 53.

21. Balibar, "The Nation Form," 87.

22. Gat, *Nations*, 42.

23. Gat, *Nations*, 44.

24. Gat is somewhat critical (and indeed, dismissive) of attempts to understand nationalism that fail to ground themselves in these materially real ethnic affinities. He finds, in these attempts, the influence of liberalism and Marxism, and accuses them of "[lacking] the conceptual frameworks within which the deeper roots of ethnicity and nationalism can be comprehended"; Gat, *Nations*, 16.

25. Gat, *Nations*, 17.

26. Echoed here is Homi Bhabha's description of this relationship between the insiders and the outsiders, of national space in terms of "the *heimlich* pleasures of hearth, the *unheimlich* terror of the space or race of the Other." Homi K. Bhabha, ed., *Nation and Narration* (London: Routledge, 1990), 2.

27. I quote Gat's somewhat dismissive commentary of immigrant refugees below.

28. Gat, *Nations*, 16–17 (emphasis added).

29. Barnor Hesse, "Symptomatically Black: A Creolization of the Politics," in *The Creolization of Theory*, ed. Françoise Lionnet and Shu-mei Shih (Durham, N.C.: Duke University Press, 2011), 41.

30. Aijaz Ahmad, "The Politics of Literary Postcoloniality," in *Contemporary Postcolonial Theory: A Reader*, ed. Padmini Mongia (London: Arnold, 1996), 286.

31. Readers should anticipate the ways in which Édouard Glissant's taking up of the process of creolization frames this alternate sense of community. The details of this work will come later, in chapter 3.

32. Anderson, Imagined Communities, 36.

33. Balibar, "The Nation Form," 86. To reiterate, this points to the sense in which the nation's destiny, though situated as timeless, nonetheless unfolded (in a developmental way) in historical time.

34. Balibar, "The Nation Form," 86.

35. Balibar, "The Nation Form," 86.

36. Anderson, *Imagined Communities*, 181.

37. Anderson, *Imagined Communities*, 36.

38. Mosse, *Confronting the Nation*, 17.

39. Recall those sections of John Locke's *Two Treatises of Government* that establish the essential relationship between the fundamental laws of a state of nature, and those founding laws that would uphold the structure of a social contract. John Locke, *Two Treatises on Government*, accessed May 28, 2019, www .yorku.ca/comninel/courses/3025pdf/Locke.pdf.

40. Mosse, *Confronting the Nation*, 29.

41. "We are now so used to an ethnic-linguistic definition of nations that

we forget that this was, essentially, invented in the later nineteenth century." Eric Hobsbawm, *The Age of Empire: 1875–1914* (New York: Vintage Books, 1987), 146.

42. Hobsbawm goes on to name this the "non-territorialist" brand of nationalism (*The Age of Empire*, 148).

43. Hobsbawm, *The Age of Empire*, 158.

44. Hobsbawm, *The Age of Empire*, 146.

45. Balibar, "The Nation Form," 98.

46. Balibar, "The Nation Form," 99.

47. Balibar, "The Nation Form," 99.

48. Balibar, "The Nation Form," 96. This account of territorial nationalism has significant implications for how indigenous communities understand their relationship to land. I will address this in the concluding sections of this book.

49. Étienne Balibar, "Toward a Diasporic Citizenship? From Internationalism to Cosmopolitics," in Lionnet and Shih, *The Creolization of Theory*, 220–21 (emphasis in the original).

50. Balibar, "Toward a Diasporic Citizenship?," 221. Elsewhere Balibar also names the emergence of the nuclear family as a consequence of this limiting function of the state. In the phenomenon of the nuclear family, he notes "the dissolution of relations of 'extended' kinship and the penetration of family relations by the intervention of the nation-state"; Balibar, "The Nation Form," 101.

51. Balibar, "Toward a Diasporic Citizenship?," 224.

52. Balibar, "Toward a Diasporic Citizenship?," 221.

53. Balibar, "Toward a Diasporic Citizenship?," 224.

54. Balibar, "Toward a Diasporic Citizenship?," 224.

55. Hobsbawm, *The Age of Empire*, 59.

56. Hobsbawm, *The Age of Empire*, 148.

57. Mosse, *Confronting the Nation*, 40.

58. Mariana Ortega, "Hometactics: Self-Mapping, Belonging, and the Home Question," in *Living Alterities: Phenomenology, Embodiment, and Race*, ed. Emily Lee (Albany: State University of New York Press, 2014), 179. In another work, I engage with Ortega's conception of hometactics; see Kris Sealey, "Resisting the Logic of Ambivalence: Bad Faith as Subversive, Anti-colonial Practice," *Hypatia* 33, no. 2 (Spring 2018).

59. Judith Butler and Gayatri Chakravorty Spivak, *Who Sings the Nation-State?* (Calcutta: Seagull Books, 2010), 25.

60. I say more about the role of the general will in late nineteenth-century national life, later in this section. But I want to note here that, in her work on creolizing Rousseau through Fanon, Jane Anna Gordon provides a thorough analysis of how Rousseau's general will might be used to ground a radically democratic public; see Jane Anna Gordon, *Creolizing Politics Theory: Reading Rousseau through Fanon* (New York: Fordham University Press, 2014). I engage with Gordon's work in an article-length version of chapter 6 of this book; see Kris Sealey, "The Composite Community: Thinking Through Fanon's Critique of a Narrow Nationalism," *Critical Philosophy of Race* 6, no. 1 (2018).

61. Balibar, "The Nation Form," 100–105; and Hobsbawm, *The Age of Empire: 1875–1914*, 146.

62. Butler and Spivak, *Who Sings the Nation-State?*, 33. Michael Monahan also draws attention to such consequences of a politics of purity: Michael J. Monahan, *The Creolizing Subject: Race, Reason, and the Politics of Purity* (New York: Fordham University Press, 2011).

63. Balibar, *We, the People of Europe?*, 23.

64. Balibar, *We, the People of Europe?*, 23.

65. Balibar, *We, the People of Europe?*, 23.

66. Balibar, "The Nation Form," 94. Elsewhere Balibar also points to an important distinction between "foreigner" and "foreigner as enemy." It is through the latter construction that much of contemporary nationalist ideology figures the foreign, nonbelonging other. I discuss this in more detail later in this section.

67. Balibar, "Toward a Diasporic Citizenship?," 218 (emphasis in the original).

68. Mosse, *Confronting the Nation*, 27 (first quotation); Balibar, "The Nation Form," 93 (second quotation).

69. Balibar, *We, the People of Europe?*, 29.

70. Balibar, "Toward a Diasporic Citizenship?," 218.

71. Hobsbawm, *The Age of Empire*, 150.

72. Gat, *Nations*, 248.

73. Gat, *Nations*, 249–50.

74. Gat, *Nations*, 259.

75. I want to thank Michael Monahan for pointing this out, and, more generally, for his generosity in reading early drafts of this work.

76. Mosse, *Confronting the Nation*, 15.

77. Hobsbawm, *The Age of Empire*, 160.

78. Hobsbawm, *The Age of Empire*, 158.

79. Sylvia Wynter's critique of modern narratives of the human as "Man" serves as an excellent analysis of this; see Sylvia Wynter, "1492: A New World View," in *Race, Discourse and the Origin of the Americas: A New World View*, ed. Vera Lawrence Hyatt and Rex Nettleford (Washington, D.C.: Smithsonian Institute Press, 1995).

80. "The dreams of racism actually have their origin in ideologies of *class*, rather than in those of nation"; Anderson, *Imagined Communities*, 149.

81. Anderson, *Imagined Communities*, 149.

82. Anderson, *Imagined Communities*, 149.

83. Timothy Brennan, "The National Longing for Form," in Bhabha, *Nation and Narration*, 51 (emphasis in the original).

84. See George Mosse's 1995 essay, in which he makes the case that "racism was never an indispensable element of nationalism." George L. Mosse, "Racism and Nationalism," *Nation and Nationalism* 1, no. 2 (1995).

85. Gat, *Nations*, 280.

86. Gat, *Nations*, 280.

87. Gat, *Nations*, 271.

88. Gat's sweeping over of colonial conquest, the genocide of indigenous communities and the transplanting of African peoples as slaves, under the mantle of "immigration" is telling.

89. He speaks somewhat favorably about the dominance of the United States' "ideology and policy of a 'melting pot'"; Gat, *Nations*, 271.

Chapter 2

1. Ernest Renan, "What Is a Nation?," trans. Martin Thom, in *Nation and Narration*, ed. Homi K. Bhabha (London: Routledge, 1990), 20.

2. Aime Cesaire, *Discourse on Colonialism*, trans. Joan Pinkham (New York: Monthly Review Press), 37–38.

3. Sylvia Wynter, "The Ceremony·Must Be Found: After Humanism," *boundary 2* 12/13, nos. 3/1 (Spring–Autumn 1984): 31–32. Elsewhere I foreground the place of play, parody, and carnival practices in creolization processes; see Kris Sealey, "Creolization and Playful Sabotage at the Brink of Politics in Earl Lovelace's *The Dragon Can't Dance*," in *Decolonizing American Philosophy*, ed. Corey McCall and Phillip McReynolds (Albany: State University of New York Press, forthcoming).

4. Mimi Sheller, "Creolization in Discourses of Global Culture," in *Uprootings/Regroundings: Questions of Home and Migration*, ed. Sara Ahmed et al. (London: Berg, 2003), 282.

5. Robert Baron and Ana C. Cara, eds., *Creolization as Cultural Creativity* (Jackson: University Press of Mississippi, 2011), 3.

6. Timothy Brennan, "The National Longing for Form," in Bhabha, *Nation and Narration*, 57.

7. Chapter 6 gives an extensive account of Fanon's position on the nation, and brings this position into conversation with the work of Martinican scholar Édouard Glissant.

8. Michaeline A. Crichlow, *Globalization and the Post-Creole Imagination: Notes on Fleeing the Plantation* (Durham, N.C.: Duke University Press, 2009), xi.

9. Brennan, "The National Longing for Form," 51.

10. Eric Prieto, "Edouard Glissant, Littérature-monde, and Tout-monde," *small axe* 14, no. 3 (November 2010): 117.

11. Prieto, "Edouard Glissant, Littérature-monde, and Tout-monde," 117.

12. Rinaldo Walcott's reference to David Scott is helpful here. Scott describes the problem-space as "an ensemble of questions and answers around which a horizon of identifiable stakes . . . hangs . . . a problem-space is very much a context of dispute, a context of rival views, a context, if you like, of knowledge and power. But from within the terms of any given problem-space what is in dispute, what the argument is effectively about, is not itself being argued over." Rinaldo Walcott, "Genres of Human: Multiculturalism, Cosmo-politics, and the Caribbean Basin," in *Sylvia Wynter: On Being Human as Praxis*, ed. Katherine McKittrick (Durham, N.C.: Duke University Press, 2015), 189.

13. Baron and Cara, *Creolization as Cultural Creativity*, 3.

14. See my discussion of this in the first section of chapter 1 above.

15. Carolyn Allen, "Creole: The Problem of Definition," in *Questioning Creole: Creolization Discourses in Caribbean Culture*, ed. Verene A. Shepherd and Glen L. Richards (London: Ian Randle, 2002), 56–57 (first quotation); Sheller, "Creolization in Discourses of Global Culture," 276 (second quotation). See also chapter 2 of John E. Drabinski, *Glissant and the Middle Passage: Philosophy, Beginning, Abyss* (Minneapolis: University of Minnesota Press, 2019), 61–98.

16. Richard Price, "The Miracle of Creolization: A Retrospective," *New West Indian Guide* 75, nos. 1–2 (2001): 41 (emphasis added).

17. Sheller's genealogy of the history of creolization as a conceptual tool for understanding Caribbean identity in its relationship to the black diaspora is helpful here. She offers creolization in a Caribbean nationalist context as what, in the 1960s and 1970s, responded to a view of Caribbean societies as an identity-less place with "separate cultural strands . . . [no] indigenous culture, and only the broken remnants of African cultures." The strand of theory that Richard Price names "Africanist" resisted this characterization with claims of clearly surviving African histories in the Caribbean. The "creolists," on the other hand argued for "uniquely creole cultural formations that drew on both European and African elements, but was distinctive to New World plantation societies" of the Caribbean archipelago. Sheller, "Creolization in Discourses of Global Culture," 279.

18. Stuart Hall, "Créolité and the Process of Creolization," in *Creolizing Europe: Legacies and Transformations*, ed. Encarnación Gutiérrez Rodríguez and Shirley Anne Tate (Liverpool: Liverpool University Press, 2015), 31.

19. Price, "The Miracle of Creolization," 40.

20. John Drabinski reminds us of the logics of this "shore-line thinking" in the context of becoming Caribbean. *Glissant and the Middle Passage*, 51.

21. Jean Bernabé et al., "In Praise of Creoleness," *Callaloo* 13, no. 4 (Autumn 1990): 886–909.

22. Stuart Hall, "Introduction: Who Needs Identity?," in *Questions of Cultural Identity*, ed. Stuart Hall and Paul du Gay (London: Sage, 1996), 16.

23. Bernabé et al., "In Praise of Creoleness," 890.

24. Crichlow, *Globalization and the Post-Creole Imagination*, 77.

25. Chapter 3 is a detailed account of Glissant's conception of creolization, which is squarely grounded in his determination of being in Relation.

26. Crichlow, *Globalization and the Post-Creole Imagination*, 77.

27. Bernabé et al., "In Praise of Creoleness," 903. Sheller describes the "achieved indigeneity" of creolizing practices as "a belonging grounded in movement, difference and transformation rather than stasis or permanence"; Sheller, "Creolization in Discourses of Global Culture," 276.

28. Richard Price outlines the "African-centric" critique of this creolist reading of the Caribbean and the New World. He cites at length one such critique by Paul Lovejoy, as follows: "The focus from Africa [which the African-centric critique attempts to save from creolization's reading] implies that not all of the enslaved who went to the Americas were thoroughly deracinated, as the 'creolization' model assumes. . . . The creole model assumes that African history did not cross the Atlantic because the enslaved population was too diverse in origins to sustain the continuities of history. . . . The perspective of the Americas as conceived by the creolization school often misrepresents Africa and indeed is ahistorical"; Price, "The Miracle of Creolization," 39. I offer two things in response to Lovejoy's reading. First, creolization's syncretisms/translations of African histories and cultures is not a denial of African pasts as much as it is a nonlinear conceptualization of the very idea of "past." And second, creolization's conception of a relationship with the past that retains the possibility of being free in that relationship to the past is not quite the same as ahistoricity.

29. Heather Smyth, "The Black Atlantic Meets the Black Pacific: Multimodality in Kamau Brathwaite and Wayde Compton," *Callaloo* 37, no. 2 (Spring 2014): 399.

30. Juliana Snapper, "Scratching the Surface: Spinning Time and Identity in Hip Hop Turntablism, *European Journal of Cultural Studies* 7, no. 1 (2004): 13, cited in Smyth, "The Black Atlantic Meets the Black Pacific," 399.

31. Smyth, "The Black Atlantic Meets the Black Pacific," 393.

32. Crichlow, *Globalization and the Post-Creole Imagination*, x (emphasis added).

33. Smyth, "The Black Atlantic Meets the Black Pacific," 399.

34. Much of Gilroy's position on his planetary humanism can be found in *Against Race: Imagining Political Culture beyond the Color Line* (Cambridge, Mass.: Belknap Press of Harvard University Press, 2000). I return to this text in a later section, where I situate my reading of creolization alongside Gilroy's account of diasporic temporality. My account of Fanon's decolonial nationalism in chapter 6 also addresses the implications of Gilroy's planetary humanism.

35. Drabinski, *Glissant and the Middle Passage*, xviii.

36. Bernabé et al., "In Praise of Creoleness," 890.

37. Crichlow, *Globalization and the Post-Creole Imagination*, 21.

38. Crichlow, *Globalization and the Post-Creole Imagination*, 22.

39. Bernabé et al., "In Praise of Creoleness," 891.

40. "Glissant [as a theorist of creolization] calls us to *think* like an archipelago [whereby] Relation is . . . dynamic, productive, dangerous, and alive with fecund engagement and appropriation"; Drabinski, *Glissant and the Middle Passage*, xviii.

41. Hall and du Gay, *Questions of Cultural Identity*; Crichlow, *Globalization and the Post-Creole Imagination*, x.

42. Hall and du Gay, *Questions of Cultural Identity*, 2.

43. Hall and du Gay, *Questions of Cultural Identity*, 3.

44. Eric Prieto situates Glissant's work within this frame, showing how Glissant's use of creolization opens him up (somewhat paradoxically) to both universalist and essentialist critiques of his work. In chapter 3 (where I focus on Glissant's use of creolization), I engage with Prieto's analysis in more detail. But I want to quote his reading of Glissant here, since it offers a helpful synopsis of the logic of what I refer to as the simultaneous "plunge and outreach" of a creolizing sense of identity. Prieto writes, "This, then, may be Glissant's greatest contribution to postcolonial political theory: his apparently apolitical insistence on the big picture, his ability to keep our focus on the larger, strategic field [namely, the global as the object of the reaching-out] within which the local battles [characteristic of the plunge] are fought." Eric Prieto, "Édouard Glissant, Littérature-monde, and Tout-monde," *small axe* 14, no. 3 (November 2010): 120.

45. Smyth, "The Black Atlantic Meets the Black Pacific," 399.

46. Stuart Hall's language of suturing provides pertinent imagery for this way of reconstituting identity as an impossible end, as the relational play among differences. I also want to point out that this conception of suturing plays a key role in George Yancy's engagement with the possibility of white ally-ship and white antiracist criticality; see George Yancy, ed., *White Self-Criticality beyond Anti-racism: How Does It Feel to Be a White Problem?* (Lanham, Md.: Lexington Books, 2015). Also see Kris Sealey, review of *White Criticality beyond Anti-racism: How Does It Feel to Be a White Problem? Hypatia Reviews Online* (2016), https://www.hypatiareviews.org/reviews/content/23.

47. The role of opacity in Glissant's work will trouble this reading of creoliza-tion, somewhat. In chapter 3, I detail the ways in which opacity captures that aspect of identities (individual or community) that remains untranslatable in the terms offered by the relationship about those identities.

48. Hall, "Introduction: Who Needs Identity?," 4; Bernabé et al., "In Praise of Creolization," 903.

49. Crichlow, *Globalization and the Post-Creole Imagination*, xiv.

50. Robert D. Abrahams, "About Face: Rethinking Creolization," in Baron and Cara, *Creolization as Cultural Creativity*, 297.

51. Crichlow's work does a bit of both—situates creolization processes as grounded in histories of the plantation and Middle Passage and as open to being dynamized in contemporary postcolonial routings of modern subjects. I expand on this later in this section.

52. I develop the relationship between creolization and diaspora in a later section of this chapter.

53. Crichlow, *Globalization and the Post-Creole Imagination*, xiii.

54. Crichlow, *Globalization and the Post-Creole Imagination*, xiii.

55. Sheller, "Creolization in Discourses of Global Culture," 276.

56. L. Taylor, "Créolité Bites: A Conversation with Patrick Charmoiseau, Raphaël Confiant, and Jean Bernabé," *Transition* 74 (1989): 132.

57. Hall, "Créolité and the Process of Creolization," 29.

58. Hall, "Créolité and the Process of Creolization," 29.

59. Percy Hintzen, "The Caribbean: Race and Creole Ethnicity," in *Cultural Identity and Creolization in National Unity: The Multiethnic Caribbean*, ed. Prem Misir (Lanham, Md.: University Press of America, 2006), 9–31.

60. Hintzen, "The Caribbean," 14.

61. Hintzen, "The Caribbean," 12.

62. Recall, here, Richard Price's citation from Paul Lovejoy's work. Price, "The Miracle of Creolization," 38.

63. See also Aisha Khan, "Journey to the Center of the Earth: The Caribbean as Master Symbol," *Cultural Anthropology* 16, no. 3 (2001).

64. Crichlow, *Globalization and the Post-Creole Imagination*, 7.

65. For a thorough engagement with the politics of purity, as well as its impli-cations for racial justice, see Michael Monahan's *The Creolizing Subject: Race, Reason, and the Politics of Purity* (New York: Fordham University Press, 2011). See also my review of this work: Kris Sealey, "Dirty Consciousnesses and Run-away Selves: Anti-racism's Tragic Hero," *Critical Philosophy of Race* 1, no. 1 (January 2013).

66. Jane Anna Gordon, *Creolizing Political Theory: Reading Rousseau through Fanon* (New York: Fordham University Press, 2014).

67. Gordon, *Creolizing Political Theory*, 181.

68. Gordon, *Creolizing Political Theory*, 183; emphasis added.

69. Crichlow, *Globalization and the Post-Creole Imagination*, 36.

70. Crichlow, *Globalization and the Post-Creole Imagination*, 37.

71. Crichlow, *Globalization and the Post-Creole Imagination*, 37.

72. Sheller, "Creolization in Discourses of Global Culture," 278.

73. I engage with Gilroy's account in more detail in the third section of this chapter.

74. Hall, "Créolité and the Process of Creolization," 31.

75. Crichlow, *Globalization and the Post-Creole Imagination*, 48, quoting Homi K. Bhabha, *Location of Culture* (London: Routledge, 2004), 205.

76. John F. Szwed, "Metaphors of Incommensurability," in Baron and Cara, *Creolization as Cultural Creativity*, 28.

77. Edward Kamau Brathwaite, *Caribbean Man in Space and Time: A Bibliographical and Conceptual Approach* (Mona, Jamaica: Savacou, 1974), 1–14.

78. "The amount of time it takes for a substance to enter the ocean and then leave the ocean is called residence time. . . . Human blood is salty, and sodium . . . has a residence time of 260 million years." Christina Sharpe, *In the Wake: On Blackness and Being* (Durham, N.C.: Duke University Press, 2016), 41.

79. Szwed, "Metaphors of Incommensurability," 21.

80. Lisa Guenther, "Fecundity and Natal Alienation: Rethinking Kinship with Levinas and Orlando Patterson," *Levinas Studies* 7 (2012): 1–19.

81. Walter Mignolo, *The Darker Side of Western Modernity: Global Futures, Decolonial Options* (Durham, N.C.: Duke University Press, 2011), 152.

82. Gilroy, *Against Race*, 332.

83. Crichlow, *Globalization and the Post-Creole Imagination*, 48, quoting Bhabha, *Location of Culture*, 2. On the idea of these "innovative sites of collaboration," I ask readers to anticipate my account in chapters 4 and 5 of this book, in which I offer Lugones's notion of complex communication as a possible way of accounting for new articulations of community.

84. Crichlow, *Globalization and the Post-Creole Imagination*, 33.

85. Drabinski, *Glissant and the Middle Passage*, xiii–xiv.

86. Recall, here, Price's account of the tensions between these creolizing readings of New World cultures and the "Africanist" criticisms of such readings. Price, "The Miracle of Creolization."

87. Homi Bhabha, "Editor's Introduction: Minority Maneuvers and Unsettled Negotiations," *Critical Inquiry* 23, no. 3 (Spring 1997): 434.

88. I take up this notion of in-between-ness in part 2 of this book, using Mariana Ortega's work.

89. Bhabha, "Editor's Introduction," 434; Hall and du Gay, *Questions of Cultural Identity*, 4.

90. Bhabha, "Editor's Introduction," 436.

91. Gilroy, *Against Race*, 332.

92. Gilroy, *Against Race*, 124.

93. Sheller, "Creolization in Discourses of Global Culture," 282.

94. Gilroy identifies such "processes of cultural mutation and restless (dis)continuity" to hold the promise of "[exceeding] racial discourse and [avoiding] capture by its agents." Paul Gilroy, *The Black Atlantic: Modernity and Double Consciousness* (London: Verso, 1993), 2. As I will show in chapter 6, my project of creolizing the nation is somewhat sympathetic to this valuation of "exceeding racial discourse." But I also want to urge that, in the move toward what Gilroy will refer to as a planetary humanism, we not lose sight of the historical materiality of that racial discourse. Chapter 6 is significantly devoted to this argument.

95. Baron and Cara, *Creolization as Cultural Creativity*, 7.

96. Gilroy, *Against Race*, 123.

97. In his account, Gilroy describes the diasporic articulation of the borders between "same" and "different" in terms of a "sameness within differentiation and a differentiation within sameness"; Gilroy, *Against Race*, 124.

98. Gilroy, *Against Race*, 123.

99. Gilroy, *Against Race*, 123 (emphasis added).

100. Gilroy, *Against Race*, 128.

101. Gilroy, *Against Race*, 124.

102. To that end, creolizing practices really ought to be understood as the nation's "constitutive outside." This construction frames much of my analysis in part 3 of this book.

103. Bernabé et al., "In Praise of Creoleness," 891.

104. "[Creoleness] is intimate, it is home culture, the native culture of a people voicing alternative ways of being to those imposed hegemonically by colonial powers and elite cultural forces"; Baron and Cara, *Creolization as Cultural Creativity*, 6.

105. In chapter 3, I show that Glissant's conceptual metaphor of the rhizome has significant implications for how we are to understand the role of local place in the creolizing context.

106. Hall, "Créolité and the Process of Creolization," 30.

107. Drabinski, *Glissant and the Middle Passage*, xviii. In the concluding sections of this work, I will return to these implications of the question of place for the sake of engaging with the role of land in indigenous critiques of settler colonialism.

108. Szwed, "Metaphors of Incommensurability," 25.

109. In chapter 3, I turn to Glissant's work on creolization in order to set up the first premises of thinking through an ontology that might allow for this kind of spatial organization. I ask that readers anticipate his call for onto-logy to be replaced with an errant-ology out of which organizational modes of creolization might signify.

110. Edward Casey, "Walling Racialized Bodies Out: Border versus Boundary at La Frontera," in *Living Alterities: Phenomenology, Embodiment, and Race*, ed. Emily Lee (Albany: State University of New York Press, 2014), 189–212.

111. Casey, "Walling Racialized Bodies Out," 203.

112. Casey, "Walling Racialized Bodies Out," 196.

113. Casey, "Walling Racialized Bodies Out," 202 (emphasis in the original). To be sure, this creolizing conception of the border is a speculative (and perhaps also aspirational) project. It in no way purports that the real time and space of current geopolitics maps onto a world in which borders are, in fact, becoming more open/less restrictive. To borrow from Mimi Sheller, "If some borders are dissolving in the 'world of creolization,' it should not go without saying that others are being kept in place"; Sheller, "Creolization in Discourses of Global Culture," 287.

114. Crichlow, *Globalization and the Post-Creole Imagination*, 63.

115. Crichlow, *Globalization and the Post-Creole Imagination*, 67 (emphasis added).

116. Crichlow, *Globalization and the Post-Creole Imagination*, 68 (emphasis added).

117. Crichlow, *Globalization and the Post-Creole Imagination*, 252.

118. Nick Spitzer, "Monde Créole: The Cultural World of French Louisiana Creoles and the Creolization of World Cultures," in Baron and Cara, *Creolization as Cultural Creativity*, 34.

119. Robert Baron, "Amalgams and Mosaics, Syncretisms and Reinterpretations: Reading Herskovits and Contemporary Creolists for Metaphors of Creolization," in Baron and Cara, *Creolization as Cultural Creativity*, 249.

120. Baron and Cara, *Creolization as Cultural Creativity*, 249.

121. This recalls what Kamau Brathwaite names as the task of "[rounding] the sharp edges of . . . dichotomy"; Brathwaite, *Caribbean Man in Space and Time*, 7.

122. Baron, "Amalgams and Mosaics, Syncretisms and Reinterpretations," 252–53.

123. Baron, "Amalgams and Mosaics, Syncretisms and Reinterpretations," 256.

124. Gilroy, *Against Race*, 328.

125. Sheller, "Creolization in Discourses of Global Culture," 287.

126. Rex Nettleford, *Caribbean Cultural Identity: The Case of Jamaica, an Essay in Cultural Dynamics* (Kingston: Institute of Jamaica, 1978), 280.

127. Prieto, "Édouard Glissant, Littérature-monde, and Tout-monde," 117.

Introduction to part 2

1. Mariana Ortega, *In-Between: Latina Feminist Phenomenology and the Self* (Albany: State University of New York Press, 2016), 39.

2. In her essay "Radical Multiculturalism and Women of Color Feminisms," Lugones opens her exposition with a quotation from Glissant's *Caribbean Discourse*. Though anchored in this way (in Glissant's creolizing entry into multilingualism), the essay does not pursue much relation between Lugones's notion of a radical multiculturalism and Glissant's cultural creolization. My hope, in this chapter, is to pursue these possibilities; see María Lugones, "Radical Multiculturalism and Women of Color Feminisms," *Journal for Cultural and Religious Theory* 13, no. 1 (Winter 2014).

3. Gloria Anzaldúa, *Borderlands/La Frontera: The New Mestiza*, 4th ed. (San Francisco: Aunt Lute Books, 2007), 103.

Chapter 3

1. Édouard Glissant, *Caribbean Discourse: Selected Essays*, trans. J. Michael Dash (Charlottesville: University Press of Virginia, 1989), 14.

2. John E. Drabinski, "What Is Trauma to the Future? On Glissant's Poetics," *Qui Parle* 18, no. 2 (Spring/Summer 2010). In this essay, Drabinski sets up the difference between the trauma of the Holocaust, which retains the subject's relation to memory, and the *catastrophic* trauma of the Middle Passage—catastrophic insofar as there is an annihilation of the possibility of that relationship to memory. Drabinski writes, "Where is the wreckage of the Middle Passage? This question breaks the Caribbean question of trauma from that of the Holocaust, *for piles of wreckage are still history, even if an impossible history*. Where are the bodies of the Middle Passage—the memorial sites of loss, however ruined—in that wreckage?" (295–96; emphasis in the original).

3. Clevis Headley, "Glissant's Existential Ontology of Difference," in *Theorizing*

Glissant: Sites and Citations, ed. John E. Drabinski and Marisa Parham (Lanham, Md.: Rowman and Littlefield, 2015), 55.

4. Ricardo Sanín-Restrepo offers a critique of Deleuze's ontology of immanence, for the sake of decolonizing (or radicalizing) that ontology. Sanín-Restrepo writes, "Deleuze liberates the power of the simulacrum against the unity of the Platonic model, but this is done within parallel planes of reality that are incommensurable to each other" (49). He shows that, as a consequence of these "parallel planes," Deleuze's simulacrum cannot ground the kind of resistive power necessary for accomplishing political (decolonial) work. Sanín-Restrepo describes this failure in Deleuze as a failure to "lock horns" with the political machinations of Plato's metaphysics of the One: Ricardo Sanín-Restrepo, *Decolonizing Democracy: Power in a Solid State* (Lanham, Md.: Rowman and Littlefield, 2016). I address the political implications of Glissant's use of creolization (to support his theory of Relation) in chapter 6 of this book. But I note that, though Glissant's conceptions are Deleuzian, their operations do ultimately "lock horns" with workings of power and colonial domination. Hence, in avoiding the shortcomings cited by Sanín-Restrepo, Glissant's work is both indebted to Deleuze and does something more overtly political than Deleuze's ontology of immanence.

5. Headley, "Glissant's Existential Ontology of Difference," 54.

6. It is in this sense that Glissant's ontology of singular difference does ultimately "lock horns" with power.

7. Michael Wiedorn, *Think Like an Archipelago: Paradox in the Work of Edouard Glissant* (Albany: State University of New York Press, 2018), xv.

8. "For Glissant, the Caribbean *is* futuricity precisely because of the abyssal effect and affect of loss"; Drabinski, "What Is Trauma to the Future?," 296.

9. Drabinski, "What Is Trauma to the Future?," 295.

10. Like Glissant, I treat subjectivity as though it lives in, and is shaped by the political. So when Glissant talks about the spontaneous resistance of immanent life, readers are to understand that immanent life as already collective and shared. In other words, the immanence of subjectivity is not divorced from the political, but is rather shaped by it.

11. Omise'eke Natasha Tinsley, "Black Atlantic, Queer Atlantic: Queer Imaginings of the Middle Passage," *GLQ: A Journal of Lesbian and Gay Studies* 14, nos. 2–3 (2008): 199.

12. Headley, "Glissant's Existential Ontology of Difference," 54.

13. Glissant, *Caribbean Discourse,* 23.

14. I would be remiss not to cite Ortega's rich exposition of such complexities involved in questions of belonging, when it comes to migrating subjects in the postcolonial era; Mariana Ortega, *In-Between: Latina Feminist Phenomenology, Multiplicity, and the Self* (Albany: State University of New York Press, 2016). I engage with Ortega's work (with her account of "hometactics" elsewhere; see Kris Sealey, "Resisting the Logic of Ambivalence: Bad Faith as Subversive, Anticolonial Practice," *Hypatia* 33, no. 2 (Spring 2018), and also in chapters 4 and 5 of this book.

15. For an in-depth exposition on these complex negotiations of home and belonging in the postcolonial age, see Sara Ahmed et al., eds., *Uprootings/Regroundings: Questions of Home and Migration* (London: Berg, 2003).

16. Bill Clinton, "Decoding Science and Politics with Bill Clinton," interview by Neil deGrasse Tyson, *StarTalk Radio*, season 6, episode 43, November 6, 2015, https://www.startalkradio.net/show/decoding-science-and-politics-with -bill-clinton/.

17. Stuart Hall and Paul du Gay, eds., *Questions of Cultural Identity* (London: Sage, 1996), 4.

18. One can read Walter Mignolo's work as a critical engagement with the supposed advantages of deploying unifying principles. A decolonial option, Mignolo claims, exists, whereby one has access to an epistemology that decenters the center, and supports a "pluriversal" worldview in place of a universal one. Such epistemologies are concerned with ways of knowing that avoid the systematicity and totalization characteristic of what deGrasse Tyson valorizes as scientific advancement. Hence, Mignolo's decolonial options are built around organizational frames that, despite the production of knowledge, are not reductive. Decolonial options encounter difference as such; see Walter Mignolo, *The Darker Side of Modernity: Global Futures, Decolonial Options* (Durham, N.C.: Duke University Press, 2011).

19. Glissant develops a notion of opacity to account for this way of encountering the other. On this notion, Clevis Headley writes, "Without the ontological armor of opacity, one is left vulnerable to the oppressive gaze of transparency that demands the right to assimilate the Other within the Same"; Headley, "Glissant's Existential Ontology of Difference," 9.

20. Édouard Glissant, *Poetics of Relation*, trans. Betsy Wing (Ann Arbor: University of Michigan Press, 1997), 21.

21. Glissant, *Poetics of Relation*, 20–21.

22. Eric Prieto, "Edouard Glissant, Littérature-monde, and Tout-monde," *small axe* 14, no. 3 (November 2010): 117.

23. Édouard Glissant, *La cohée du Lamentin* (Paris: Gallimard, 1981), 87, cited and translated by Wiedorn, *Think Like an Archipelago*, 8.

24. Prieto, "Edouard Glissant, Littérature-monde, and Tout-Monde," 114.

25. Prieto, "Edouard Glissant, Littérature-monde, and Tout-Monde," 114.

26. Michael Wiedorn, *Think Like an Archipelago*, 8.

27. "We can sum up by positing the opposition between an archipelagic thinking and a continental thinking, with continental thinking being a system-thinking and archipelagic thinking being the thinking of the ambiguous." Édouard Glissant, *Introduction à une poetics du Divers* (Paris: Gallimard, 1981), 89, cited and translated by Wiedorn, *Think Like an Archipelago*, 8.

28. In a later section, I discuss the role of Glissant's metaphor of the rhizome (in particular, this metaphor's rejection of the root). In chapter 4, I also bring together the rhizome's capacity to think relationality and totality alongside the opacity of difference, with Lugones's account of complex communication (namely, its role in building effective decolonial coalitions against oppression).

29. Glissant, *Poetics of Relation*, 160.

30. What this means is that, when creolization is an imperative (as I frame it in the concluding sections of this book), any working conception of community coherence must always be ready to be contested.

31. The knowledge emerging out of errantry (and consequently, the knowledge one gains of Relation) is not scientific but, rather, poetic. Like the errant thinker,

the poet chooses to inhabit that undecidable place that knows not where, or how, thought will move. No one direction is legitimized over another, no (spontaneous) outcome of the immanent dynamism of the community in Relation is more justifiable than another. In chapter 6, I address the implications of this for the possibility of developing normative standards out of which the political workings of the nation operates.

32. Headley, "Glissant's Existential Ontology of Difference," 63.

33. Gilles Deleuze and Félix Guattari, *What Is Philosophy?* (New York: Columbia University Press, 1996), 118.

34. Glissant, *Poetics of Relation*, 34.

35. Eric Prieto cites Glissant's account in *Traité du Tout-monde* (Gallimard, Paris, 1997) when he writes, "Chaos-monde is, well, chaotic, whereas Tout-monde is the order that can be drawn out of this chaos, a unifying perspective, a totalizing vision"; Prieto, "Édouard Glissant, Littérature-monde, and Tout-monde," 117.

36. Glissant, *Poetics of Relation*, xv.

37. Glissant, *Poetics of Relation*, 94.

38. Headley, "Glissant's Existential Ontology of Difference," 70.

39. Drabinski, "What Is Trauma to the Future?," 300. Glissant often references the metal balls and chains, at the bottom of that part of the Atlantic Ocean spanning the coasts of West Africa and the Caribbean isles, as he describes the "drowned memory" on which the Caribbean imaginary rests. These objects that litter the sea floor of the Atlantic mark the practice of throwing West African captives (dead and living) overboard, in order to lighten the "cargo" of slaving ships as they made passage through the Triangle.

40. "Our [Caribbean] historical consciousness could not be deposited gradually and continuously like sediment . . . but came together in the context of shock, contraction, painful negation, and explosive forces. This dislocation of the continuum, and the inability of the collective consciousness to absorb it all, characterizes what I call nonhistory"; Glissant, *Caribbean Discourse*, 61–62.

41. Drabinski describes the Caribbean—that place full of the ocean's drowning and the ocean's salt—as a "tortured geography . . . absent rocks of departure and bitter sands of arrival"; Drabinski, "What Is Trauma to the Future?," 298.

42. Glissant, *Poetics of Relation*, 141.

43. Drabinski, "What Is Trauma to the Future?," 300–301.

44. Glissant, *Poetics of Relation*, 61.

45. This is no longer the community grounded in the nation-form discussed in chapter 1 of this book.

46. Glissant, *Poetics of Relation*, 11.

47. "Glissant calls this affirmation of opacity *Relation*"; Drabinski, "What Is Trauma to the Future?," 305.

48. In the concluding chapter of this book, I engage with Jodi Byrd's work on indigenous critiques of colonial violence, so as to bring such conceptions of place and groundedness under the critical lens of indigenous first principles of land and memory in resistance strategies against settler colonial violence.

49. Chapter 6 of this book explores this possibility in greater detail.

50. Drabinski, "What Is Trauma to the Future?," 303.

51. The value of this absence of the linearity of filiation is underscored by Gayatri Spivak's criticism of what she names the "reproductive heteronormativity"

of nationalism. Gayatri Chakravorty Spivak, "Nationalism and the Imagination," *Lectora* 15 (2009). Reproductive heteronormativity captures the sense in which the imaginary of the nation (at least, in the Western imperialist formulation sketched in chapter 1 of this book) deploys the privacy of mothering and birth as the deriving event of the being of the nation. In other words, the publicly venerated narrative of national unity rests on an unarticulated private space that is the woman's womb, "the most primitive instrument of nationalism" (80). We might be inclined to read Glissant's analysis of root-nationalism differently, insofar as he underscores the *filial* relation between father and son as the legitimizing narrative of that kind of national collectivity and belonging. But to be clear, though Spivak traces the literal act of birthing the nation to the woman, she also marks this act as signifying heteronormatively. That is to say, the future of the nation, emerging out of the mother's womb is legitimized (indeed, a particular womb space is marked as a legitimate *source* of legitimacy) only to the extent of its ties to patriarchal forms of domination. In other words, it is through its connection to the father that the womb can be a sacred originating place and time of the nation. Perhaps we might read, in Spivak's analysis of the reproductive heteronormativity of nationalism, an important feminist development of Glissant's account of linear filiation.

52. Glissant, *Poetics of Relation*, 47.

53. This formulation also captures Heather Smyth's description of the creolizing artifact as "creative misduplications" (see chapter 1 of this book). For Ahmed, see Sara Ahmed, *Queer Phenomenology: Orientations, Objects, Others* (Durham, N.C.: Duke University Press, 2006).

54. Ahmed, *Queer Phenomenology*, 61–62.

55. Ahmed, *Queer Phenomenology*, 117.

56. Ahmed, *Queer Phenomenology*, 116.

57. I want to thank Samir Haddad for suggesting this language of rhythm to theorize the detoured errantry of Caribbean social life.

58. It is on this account that Glissant is clear to distinguish between the process of creolization, and the process of *métissage*. "If we posit *métissage* as, generally speaking, the meeting and synthesis of two differences, creolization seems to be a limitless *métissage*, its elements diffracted and its consequences unforeseeable"; Glissant, *Poetics of Relation*, 34. I discuss Anzaldúa's formulation of *métissage* in chapter 5.

59. Glissant, *Poetics of Relation*, 62.

60. Glissant, *Poetics of Relation*, 52.

61. Glissant, *Poetics of Relation*, 82.

62. Glissant, *Poetics of Relation*, 52.

63. Glissant, *Poetics of Relation*, 32.

64. Glissant, *Caribbean Discourse*, 62, cited in H. Adlai Murdoch, "Glissant's *Opacité* and the Re-Conceptualization of Identity," in *Theorizing Glissant: Sites and Citations*, ed. John E. Drabinski and Marisa Parham (Lanham, Md.: Rowman & Littlefield, 2015), 15.

65. Grant Farred, "Wretchedness," in *Living Fanon: Global Perspectives*, ed. Nigel C. Gibson (New York: Palgrave Macmillan, 2011), 159–72. Elsewhere I bring Fanon's rejection of ultranationalism into dialogue with Emmanuel Levinas's understanding of the subject as openness onto the other; see Kris Sealey,

"Power as (or in) Vulnerability: Fanon and Levinas on an Ethical Politics," *Listening: Journal of Communication Ethics, Religion, and Culture* 51, no. 1 (Winter 2015).

66. Édouard Glissant, *Tout-monde* (Paris: Gallimard, 1993), 179.

Chapter 4

1. Nelson Maldonado-Torres, "On the Coloniality of Being: Contributions to the Development of a Concept," *Cultural Studies* 21, nos. 2–3 (March/May 2007).

2. Maldonado-Torres, "On the Coloniality of Being," 245.

3. Hence, there is a relationship between *how* the world is encountered, and the nature/structure of the self doing the encountering. To be sure, this relationship is hermeneutic. That is to say, how I encounter the world shapes who I must be in order to facilitate that encounter. To use Ortega's words, "[When] we think about worlds . . . we have to think about the ways in which such worlds are connected to the self and the ways in which the self *is* in them." Mariana Ortega, *In-Between: Latina Feminist Phenomenology and the Self* (Albany: State University of New York Press, 2016), 66.

4. On such reconceptualizations, identity is an identification-with, see Allison Weir, "Global Feminism and Transformative Identity Politics," *Hypatia* 23, no. 4 (October–December 2008). See also Ortega's account of Bernice Johnson Reagon's "barred room"; Ortega, *In-Between*, 194. In such reconceptions, the choice between insecurity and reification is troubled, and it is unclear whether we attain one by giving up the other. Must there be this correlation? Are there ways to surrender reification (replace with fluidity, relationality, transformation) in ways that are independent of the question of the security of a home-space? This is what this book tries to negotiate: If alterity no longer signifies in terms of a threat, then relationality would not have to come at the expense of security. In other words, the promise of security comes with "limits and pitfalls" when security is in terms of "alterity as threat," or in terms of "intersubjectivity as threat." Much of the opposition between "security" and "relationality" seems to be grounded in the equation between "otherness" and "fear" (in a formulation of otherness as a source of fear). Hence, for the task of creolizing the nation, the question is: Are there ways for alterity to signify *as alterity* without signifying as threatening?

5. Ortega, *In-Between*, 148.

6. By this, I do not mean to endorse the claim that identities are for strategic purposes only. That is to say, though a political conception of the subject foregrounds the "why" of subject constitutions, I do not want to say that the identity of the subject is reducible to its political telos (such that, in the doing-away of that telos, the identity of the subject becomes no longer). Rather, in thinking about the purposive nature of how we constitute ourselves as subjects (or perhaps how we are constituted as subjects by the political), we open ways to think differently about ourselves in community with others.

7. María Lugones, *Pilgrimages/Peregrinajes: Theorizing Coalition against Multiple Oppressions* (Lanham, Md.: Rowman and Littlefield, 2003), 8.

8. Lugones, *Pilgrimages/Peregrinajes*, 89.

9. Ortega is critical of this conception of antistructure in Lugones's account. I address this critique shortly.

10. In *Pilgrimages/Peregrinajes*, Lugones is critical of theories of oppression that fail to account for such possibilities of resistance. For her, there is always the possibility of resistance, and it is often actualized in ways that ought to be named in any theorizing about oppression.

11. Of this account of theorizing the possibility of resistance in the midst of a totalizing oppression, Ortega writes, "The self that is constructed as alien, as unwanted, as disposable in one world can travel to another world and find herself as resistant and as a constructor of new visions"; Ortega, *In-Between*, 92–93.

12. Ortega, *In-Between*, 96.

13. Lugones, *Pilgrimages/Peregrinajes*, 89.

14. Lugones, *Pilgrimages/Peregrinajes*, 89.

15. I flesh out Ortega's critique of Lugones's plurality of selves later in this section. But, as a snapshot of her position, she writes, "[In] my view, the key question that remains is why in Lugones's view *world*-traveling means *self*-traveling"; Ortega, *In-Between*, 97. See also Mariana Ortega, "'New Mestizas,' 'World-Travelers,' and 'Dasein': Phenomenology and the Multi-voiced, Multi-cultural Self," *Hypatia* 16, no. 3 (Summer 2001): 14.

16. I also explore this navigation in Kris Sealey, "Resisting the Logic of Ambivalence: Bad Faith as Subversive, Anti-colonial Practice," *Hypatia* 33, no. 2 (Spring 2018).

17. Ortega, *In-Between*, 28.

18. Paula Moya's work is in this vein, as she distances the liberatory and resistive politics coming out of third-world feminisms from postmodern conceptions of identity: see *Learning from Experience: Minority Identities, Multicultural Struggles* (Oakland: University of California Press, 2002). According to Moya, a postmodern reading of Latina and Chicana feminisms results in "a substitution of a politics of difference for a politics of liberation," since the postmodern endgame is about "the decentering of the subject, the jettisoning of 'grand theories,' a turn toward local and even nonrational [poetic] knowledges [and] a valorization of flux and mobility" (60). To that end, nothing remains to legitimize the identity claims that these third-world feminisms need to make in order to ground their epistemological and political resistance. According to Moya, the postmodernist would not allow for this, since "all truth claims are complicit with oppressive authoritarianism," and simply reproduce the violence of grand narratives (61).

19. Paula Moya (*Learning from Experience*, 7) references this position of Moraga's, on Chicano nationalism. It captures Moraga's recognition that communities like hers, under the domination of neocolonial structures, must enact their struggles in a nationalist register. Her call for a "broader and wiser revolution" desires a national struggle that can facilitate plural conceptions of liberation, and is a warning against what Fanon critiques as a not-yet-decolonial ultranationalism (see chapter 6 of this book). Cherrie Moraga, *The Last Generation* (Boston: South End Press, 1993), 150.

20. Ortega, *In-Between*, 97.

21. Lugones, *Pilgrimages/Peregrinajes*, 127.

22. "[Fragmentation] generates the fictional construction of a vantage point from which unified wholes, totalities, can be captured. . . . Both the vantage point and the [occupying] subject are outside historicity and concreteness"; Lugones, *Pilgrimages/Peregrinajes*, 128.

23. Lugones, *Pilgrimages/Peregrinajes*, 128.

24. A complete account of Lugones's reimagined sense of this "one vs. many" relation is found in her conception of curdling. I discuss this metaphor of curdling in the second section of this chapter, where I treat the question of difference.

25. Lugones, *Pilgrimages/Peregrinajes*, 132.

26. For a sustained analysis of such questions pertaining to intersectionality, fragmentation, and feminisms, see the following: Ann Gary, "Intersectionality, Metaphors, and the Multiplicity of Gender," *Hypatia* 26, no. 4 (Fall 2011); María Lugones, "Heterosexualism and the Colonial/Modern Gender System," *Hypatia* 22, no. 1 (2007); María Lugones, "Toward a Decolonial Feminism," *Hypatia* 25, no. 4 (2010).

27. Lugones, *Pilgrimages/Peregrinajes*, 133.

28. Lugones, *Pilgrimages/Peregrinajes*, 133.

29. In the third section of this chapter, I show resonances between this and the kind of social heterogeneity called for by Lugones's account of active subjectivity.

30. Ortega, *In-Between*, 90.

31. Lugones, *Pilgrimages/Peregrinajes*, 216–17.

32. Though I do not address this, I want to point to what I imagine would be significant differences in the affective dimensions of such constructions (creolizing and multiplicitous in-between-ness).

33. Ortega, *In-Between*, 74.

34. Ortega, *In-Between*, 60–61.

35. Ortega, *In-Between*, 62.

36. Ortega, *In-Between*, 70–71.

37. Ortega, *In-Between*, 71.

38. For a development of this claim, see Sealey, "Resisting the Logic of Ambivalence."

39. Ortega, *In-Between*, 61.

40. Ortega, *In-Between*, 61.

41. Ortega, *In-Between*, 70.

42. Paula Moya's critique is important here. She reads certain threads of postmodernism as reducing politically salient differences to "a kind of universalizing sameness" when postmodern theorists purport that all subjectivities are, in the end, marginal and liminally constructed. More significantly, Moya calls her readers' attention—in order to resist—a certain postmodern conception that identifies *any* use of identity as essentialist, exclusionary, and totalizing. Out of this conception, political platforms of resistance used by third-world feminisms, which begin their work of resistance with claims grounded in politically salient identity formations, are "tainted with exclusionary and totalizing forms of power"; Moya, *Learning from Experience*, 24. Like Moya, I also want to resist such conceptions in this project of creolizing the nation.

43. Ortega, *In-Between*, 155.

44. Cristina Beltrán, "Patrolling Borders: Hybrids, Hierarchies and the Challenge of Mestizaje," *Political Research Quarterly* 57, no. 4 (December 2004): 595.

45. Beltrán, "Patrolling Borders," 603.

46. In her critique of Anzaldúa on this point, Beltrán writes, "For Anzaldúa, writing in the borderlands requires a return to indigenous approaches to cultural production. . . . The radical and revolutionary potential of *mestiza* consciousness

can occur only if the border subject writes in [an] oppositional stance against 'Western' or 'Ethnocentric' practices"; Beltrán, "Patrolling Borders," 600.

47. Weir, "Global Feminism and Transformative Identity Politics," 110–33.

48. Weir acknowledges her indebtedness to Lugones here, noting that she borrows heavily from her accounts of deep coalition and world-traveling (which I detail in a later section of this chapter).

49. Weir, "Global Feminism and Transformative Identity Politics," 124–25.

50. Ortega, *In-Between*, 163.

51. In this sense, Ortega's conception of the multiplicitous self provides a ground for a politics that, in the words of Paula Moya, is not "tainted with exclusionary and totalizing forms of power," contrary to some postmodern accounts of political claims to identity. *Learning from Experience*, 24.

52. Ortega, "'New Mestizas,' 'World-Travelers,' and 'Dasein,'" 4.

53. Gloria Anzaldúa, *Borderlands/La Frontera: The New Mestiza*, 4th ed. (San Francisco: Aunt Lute Books, 1987), 60.

54. Anzaldúa, *Borderlands/La Frontera*, 61.

55. Anzaldúa, *Borderlands/La Frontera*, 120.

56. In a later section, I discuss Anzaldúa's accounts of her experiences of being caught in between the linguistic customs of American English, Mexican Spanish, and mainland Spanish. Her descriptions capture the kind of morphogenesis in the generativity of the mestiza.

57. "Western culture made 'objects' of things and people when it distanced itself from them, thereby losing 'touch' with them"; Anzaldúa, *Borderlands/La Frontera*, 59.

58. "We are taught that the body is an ignorant animal; intelligence dwells only in the head"; Anzaldúa, *Borderlands/La Frontera*, 59.

59. Anzaldúa, *Borderlands/La Frontera*, 68.

60. Anzaldúa, *Borderlands/La Frontera*, 68.

61. Anzaldúa, *Borderlands/La Frontera*, 72.

62. Recall, here Lugones's critique of the logic of purity/unity, which operates through the fragmentation of the world-traveling subject.

63. Shane Phelan's work on lesbian and mestiza identities grapples with the importance of attending to both the fluidity of identity categories and the need for identity markers in the work of political resistance. Shane Phelan, *Getting Specific: Postmodern Lesbian Politics* (Minneapolis: University of Minnesota Press, 1994).

64. Anzaldúa, *Borderlands/La Frontera*, 85.

65. Anzaldúa, *Borderlands/La Frontera*, 85.

66. Anzaldúa, *Borderlands/La Frontera*, 108.

67. See Kris Sealey, "Resisting the Logic of Ambivalence." This article traces the implications of the account of ambiguity found in Homi Bhabha's work, when it comes to questions of home-making and belonging for nonbelonging subjects.

68. Anzaldúa, *Borderlands/La Frontera*, 96.

69. Anzaldúa, *Borderlands/La Frontera*, 108.

70. Jean Bernabé et al., "In Praise of Creoleness," *Callaloo* 13, no. 4 (Autumn 1990): 903. I present a close reading of this essay in chapter 2.

71. Anzaldúa, *Borderlands/La Frontera*, 80.

72. "Ethnic identity is twin skin to linguistic identity—I am my language. Until

I can take pride in my language [in my accent], I cannot take pride in myself";
Anzaldúa, *Borderlands/La Frontera*, 81.

73. Recall, here, my discussion in chapter 3 of Sara Ahmed's work in *Queer Phenomenology*.

74. Anzaldúa, *Borderlands/La Frontera*, 103.

75. Elsewhere I pursue the relationship between home-making and resistance against structures that preclude the possibility of home; see Sealey, "Resisting the Logic of Ambivalence."

Chapter 5

1. Gloria Anzaldúa, *Borderlands/La Frontera: The New Mestiza* (San Francisco: Aunt Lute Books, 2007), 99.

2. Anzaldúa, *Borderlands/La Frontera*, 100.

3. By "decolonial" I mean a delegitimizing of the misanthropic skepticism noted in Nelson Maldonado-Torres's account of the ego conquiro, and thinking beyond the terms offered by colonial Manichaeism; see Nelson Maldonado-Torres, "On the Coloniality of Being: Contributions to the Development of a Concept," *Cultural Studies* 21, nos. 2–3 (March/May 2007).

4. Here my position is similar to Paul Gilroy's understanding of the possibility of the postracial (or what he often names a planetary humanism), which figures in the work of chapter 6 of this book. For now, I point to the significance, in Gilroy's proposal to move beyond colonial racialism, of precisely attending to the history of that racialism.

5. Linda Martín Alcoff, *Visible Identities: Race, Gender and the Self* (Oxford: Oxford University Press, 2005), 80.

6. Mariana Ortega, *In-Between: Latina Feminist Phenomenology, Multiplicity, and the Self* (Albany: State University of New York Press, 2016), 147.

7. Ortega, *In-Between*, 148. I discussed Allison Weir's conception of "transformative identity politics" in chapter 4. Through this, she aims to replace a postmodern politics oriented in terms of fear of the power of the other with a politics that is grounded in both "self-critique . . . and self-transformation." Allison Weir, "Global Feminism and Transformative Identity Politics," *Hypatia* 23, no. 4 (October–December 2008): 111–12.

8. Anzaldúa, *Borderlands/La Frontera*, 72.

9. Étienne Balibar, "The Nation Form: History and Ideology," in *Race, Nation, Class, Ambiguous Identities*, ed. Étienne Balibar and Immanuel Wallerstein (London: Verso, 1991), 86.

10. From Sylvia Wynter, on the kinds of persons that were sold to Europeans: "[These were] *lineageless men and women*. These were men and women who, because they had fallen out of the protection of their own lineages (in which metaphysically normal being was *alone* possible), had come to be represented . . . outside the limits of the real 'we.'" Sylvia Wynter, "1492: A New World View," in *Race, Discourse and the Origin of the Americas: A New World View*, ed. Vera Lawrence Hyatt and Rex Nettleford (Washington, D.C.: Smithsonian Institute Press, 1995), 33. Here Wynter describes grounding connections between legitimacy-through-lineage and those valuable enough to participate in the affective order of moral obligation/responsibility (the "we" for whom we must

care, with whom we must empathize, and toward whom we must act as though they are human). Also from Wynter: "[The] 'disobedient-by-nature' category of the *civil slave* (that is, the *negro* and the *negras*) were represented as the Other to both [Rational Man and savage Other]; and they [the negro and negra] were pictured as ambiguous on the chain of being of the new notion of order based on degrees of rationality . . . between the status of the human . . . and that of totally nonrational animal species" (36).

11. Édouard Glissant, *Poetics of Relation*, trans. Betsy Wing (Ann Arbor: University of Michigan Press, 1997), 20–21.

12. In chapter 6, where I bring his work into conversation with Fanon's critique of ultranationalism, I show the ways in which Glissant's poetics of resistance contains an urgency that allows us to take it to the political.

13. María Lugones, *Pilgrimages/Peregrinajes: Theorizing Coalition against Multiple Oppressions* (Lanham, Md.: Rowman and Littlefield, 2003), 20.

14. María Lugones, "Radical Multiculturalism and Women of Color Feminism," *Journal for Cultural and Religious Theory* 13, no. 1 (Winter 2014): 74.

15. Lugones, *Pilgrimages/Peregrinajes*, 20.

16. "Creolization is not a relation that reproduces the sum of its parts, but rather is a relation that produces what exceeds the expected." Clevis Headley, "Glissant's Existential Ontology," in *Theorizing Glissant: Sites and Citations*, ed. John E. Drabinski and Marisa Parham (Lanham, Md.: Rowman and Littlefield, 2015), 75.

17. In chapter 6, I address the charge that opacity might serve as a *shelter from* transformation, at the individual/subjective level. According to this reading, beginning from opacity produces a rigid and closed-off identity politics instead of a politics that is transformative, open-ended, and communicative. Chapter 6's reading of Glissant alongside the work of Fanon lays out a counterreading to this position.

18. Lugones, *Pilgrimages/Peregrinajes*, 18.

19. Marilyn Frye, *The Politics of Reality: Essays in Feminist Theory* (New York: Crossing Press, 1983), 75.

20. Lugones, *Pilgrimages/Peregrinajes*, 18.

21. María Lugones, "On Complex Communication," *Hypatia* 21, no. 3 (Summer 2006): 76.

22. Ortega discusses this possibility in her account of a coalitional politics, which is "not based on essentialist or categorical identity and that is mindful of both social location and relations with others . . . that we are both being and becoming, that we occupy certain social and material locations, and that we are relational"; Ortega, *In-Between*, 155.

23. Lugones, "On Complex Communication," 82.

24. Lugones, "On Complex Communication," 84.

25. Lugones, "On Complex Communication," 83.

26. The spirit of Ortega's account of a coalitional politics is captured here. Particularly in her development of the concept of hometactics, a politics of identity is replaced with a coalitional politics that strives to give an account of community without essentialism, belonging without homogenization, and solidarity without border policing.

27. Lugones, *Pilgrimages/Peregrinajes*, 18–19.

28. Lugones, *Pilgrimages/Peregrinajes*, 26.

29. Lugones, *Pilgrimages/Peregrinajes*, 96.

30. Lugones, *Pilgrimages/Peregrinajes*, 96.

31. Lugones, *Pilgrimages/Peregrinajes*, 18–19.

32. Ortega accounts for a similar movement, when she qualifies the fluidity included Anzaldúa's new mestiza. "[This fluidity] is not meant to be a call for the view that the new *mestiza* may choose any identity she wishes . . . as if the new *mestiza* could choose identities like articles of clothing"; *In-Between*, 45.

33. Ortega also notes her concern that a proposed everydayness of world-traveling might rob the practice of its vigilant eye to the degree that the plural subject grows accustomed to the dominant structures that produces her as a liminal subject; see Ortega, *In-Between*, 119–31. Ortega's Heideggerian interpretation of the everydayness of the practice of world-traveling is clear here, since, on Heidegger's account, the everydayness of my comportment in the world undermines the possibility of my being able to adopt a more authentic mode of being.

34. Ortega, *In-Between*, 131.

35. Ortega, *In-Between*, 137.

36. Elsewhere I use George Yancy's work on the role of unsuturing to offer a reading of Lugones's idea of playfulness that might address these criticisms by Ortega; see Kris Sealey, "Pain and Play: Building Coalitions toward Decolonizing Philosophy," *Southern Journal of Philosophy* 57, Spindel Supplement (2019).

37. Ortega makes a crucial distinction between the implications for the world-traveling of liminal/marginalized subjects, and the implications for the world-traveling of dominant subjects. I am in full agreement with her claim that, in the latter's case, it is imperative that vigilance take precedence over play, given how dominant structures empower/enable the dominant subject, and given how such dominant structures are naturalized from that dominant subject position.

38. For Lugones, world-traveling calls for "witnessing faithfully" as one travels. In this faithful witnessing, the self is no longer a collaborator witness—one that "witnesses on the side of power [instead of witnessing] against the grain of power, on the side of resistance"; Lugones, *Pilgrimages/Peregrinajes*, 7. The distinction that Lugones makes between collaborator witnessing and witnessing faithfully can give us ways to protect against an ahistorical spread of the rhizome, since it calls for both an anchoring in history and an understanding of oneself in terms of one's location in history. Though Lugones develops the idea of faithful witnessing as an alternative epistemic frame through which to engage in resistance and liberation, I wonder whether we might also understand these epistemic acts of faithful witnessing to have ontological implications. In other words, can the subject, through the practice of witnessing faithfully, come to *be* otherwise? Can we make the claim that, in faithfully witnessing against the complex interlocking of oppressions, this subject is *also* gathered in rhizoming, composite form, and therefore must *be* in a way that facilitates her participation in this composite formation? These are the questions the capture the stakes of the project of creolizing the nation.

39. Anzaldúa, *Borderlands/La Frontera*, 25.

40. In chapter 2's discussion of the time and place of creolization, I treat this question of borders in the context of creolizing processes, using Edward Casey's work as a point of entry.

41. Ortega (*In-Between*, 104) rightly notes that, for Lugones, curdling underscores the spirit of intersectional accounts of power and oppression. The concept of intersectionality (coined by Kimberlé Crenshaw) has been used to articulate the inseparability of oppressions; consequently, it provides a more holistic and liberatory assessment of the workings of dominant structures and of what it might mean to counter their effects (legally and existentially). In her 2014 article "Radical Multiculturalism and Women of Color Feminism," Lugones presents curdling as a way to account for the intermeshing of oppressions, or oppressions as they concretely signify at their fusion points. In this account, curdling further resists the temptations (that intersectionality works against) to abstract structures of oppression out of their lived (intermeshed) meaning.

42. Ortega, *In-Between*, 104.

43. See Weir, "Global Feminism and Transformative Identity Politics."

44. Lugones, *Pilgrimages/Peregrinajes*, 123.

45. Lugones, *Pilgrimages/Peregrinajes*, 122.

46. Lugones, *Pilgrimages/Peregrinajes*, 196 (emphasis added).

47. Lugones, *Pilgrimages/Peregrinajes*, 145. Elsewhere I develop this antitelos inherent in creolizing practices, with particular focus on how these practices shape the playful poetics of Carnival productions in the Caribbean; see Kris Sealey, "Creolization and Playful Sabotage at the Brink of Politics in Earl Lovelace's *The Dragon Can't Dance* in *Decolonizing American Philosophy*, ed. Corey McCall and Phillip McReynolds (Albany: State University of New York Press, forthcoming).

48. Lugones, *Pilgrimages/Peregrinajes*, 145.

49. The second section of chapter 4 gives an account of the distinction that Ortega makes between thick and thin senses of unease. Here I deploy this distinction to capture the various ways subjects constitute and experience their place in the communities to which they belong.

50. Lugones, *Pilgrimages/Peregrinajes*, 25.

51. This will be pivotal to my reading of Glissant alongside Fanon in chapter 6.

52. Lugones, *Pilgrimages/Peregrinajes*, 10.

53. Michaeline Crichlow's work (cited in chapter 2 of this book) details the ways in which rooting and routing within/across dominant maps of power is constitutive of creolizing enactments of resistance, freedom, and agency. Michaeline A. Crichlow, *Globalization and the Post-Creole Imagination: Notes on Fleeing the Plantation* (Durham, N.C.: Duke University Press, 2009).

54. Lugones, *Pilgrimages/Peregrinajes*, 24.

Chapter 6

1. Curdella Forbes discusses the ways in which Glissant's work meets Antonio Benitez-Rojo's account of the Caribbean. On her account, Glissant's arrow nomadism both articulates a sense of Caribbean uniqueness and avoids the essentialist orientations of imperialist/colonialist articulations of collective identity. Nonetheless, her exposition gives us a spectrum of sorts, which spans Benito-Rojo's insistent irreducibility of a Caribbean identity (on the one hand), and Glissant's openness to the ways in which Caribbean creolization (and the sense of Caribbean nation-ness that it might ground) bleeds into a global moment of migration and cultural meetings. Hence, on this spectrum, Glissant's concerns are much less with what it means to be a Caribbean *nation* than it is with how a

Caribbean sociality moves beyond itself in a global contemporary phenomenon. As Forbes writes, for Glissant "'creolization' may well be no longer a Caribbean phenomenon." Curdella Forbes, "The End of Nationalism? Performing the Question in Benitez-Rojo's *The Repeating Island* and Glissant's *Poetics of Relation*," *Journal of West Indian Literatures* 11, no. 1 (November 2002): 18. I address this—Glissant's composite community's relationship to "nation"—in a later section of this chapter.

2. Paul Gilroy, *Postcolonial Melancholia* (New York: Columbia University Press, 2005), 3. I treat Gilroy's work in chapter 2's overview of processes of creolization. Recall, here, the question that I pose there: Can the nation be creolized, if, like the diasporic, the outcomes of creolization must necessarily be something that the nation is not? To ask it differently—depending on how we understand the outcome of creolization with respect to a notion like diaspora, or to a notion like Gilroy's planetary humanism—is creolizing the nation a move that will take us beyond the nation? And if not, how so? Anthony Alessandrini's treatment of Gilroy's indebtedness to Fanon is relevant to this question, given the attention that Alessandrini brings to how Gilroy's position is (tensely) situated between identity politics and the need to move beyond the raciology of colonial modernity. I address this in further detail later in this chapter.

3. Nick Nesbitt, *Caribbean Critique: Antillean Critical Theory from Toussaint to Glissant* (Liverpool: Liverpool University Press, 2013).

4. The essays collected in Glissant's *Caribbean Discourse* articulate this loss. They account for "[diversion] as the ultimate resort of a population whose domination by an Other is concealed," and in that concealment lives the impossibility of generating collective political revolt (20). Such loss also grounds Glissant's account of the ways in which properly historical narratives of origins get replaced by myth and folktales as "[myth] coils meaning around the image itself" (71). As such, he speaks to the impossibility of articulating a linear narrative that reveals origins and thus legitimacy. Édouard Glissant, *Caribbean Discourse: Selected Essays*, trans. J. Michael Dash (Charlottesville: University Press of Virginia, 1989).

5. Nesbitt, *Caribbean Critique*, 151.

6. Frantz Fanon, *Toward an African Revolution*, trans. Haakon Chevalier (New York: Grove Press, 1965), 31, 33–36.

7. Wendy Knepper, "Colonization, Creolization, and Globalization: The Art and Ruses of Bricolage," *small axe* 10, no. 3 (October 2006).

8. In this regard, we can liken the bricoleur to the subject of streetwalker tactics, conceptualized by Lugones. Like the practitioner of creolization, the streetwalker enacts possibilities of resistance, and espouses an active (agential) subjectivity that refigures the time and space of dominant maps of power. This refiguring happens through the embodied transgressions of "hanging out"—intentional trespassing of the spatial mechanics of power that "permits [the streetwalker] to learn, to listen, to transmit information, to participate in communicative creations, to gauge possibilities." María Lugones, *Pilgrimages/Peregrinajes: Theorizing Coalition against Multiple Oppressions* (Lanham, Md.: Rowman and Littlefield, 2003), 209.

9. Frantz Fanon, *A Dying Colonialism*, trans. Haakon Chevalier (New York: Grove Press, 1965), 63.

10. Of the new cultural and symbolic relations that emerged post-1954 in a revolutionary Algeria, Fanon writes, "Algeria has become a country able to

elude French mastery." Jean Khalfa and Robert J. C. Young, eds., *Frantz Fanon: Alienation and Freedom*, trans. Steven Corcoran (London: Bloomsbury Academic, 2018), 555.

11. I offer such a reimagining as one that might join Wynter's call to think otherwise and differently about what it means to be human, and to move beyond the metrics of coloniality. For Wynter, such a move would be toward a certain "ceremonial production" (as she puts it in the essay, "The Ceremony Must Be Found: After Humanism") out of which colonialism's dyadic binaries of "self/ other," and "order/chaos" is ultimately transcended, so that "humanness [can be] newly conceptualized as a relational category." Katherine McKittrick, ed., *Sylvia Wynter: On Being Human as Praxis* (Durham, N.C.: Duke University Press, 2015), 8. See also Sylvia Wynter, "The Ceremony Must Be Found: After Humanism," *boundary 2* 12/13, nos. 3–1 (Spring–Autumn 1984).

12. Édouard Glissant, *Poetics of Relation*, trans. Betsy Wing (Ann Arbor: University of Michigan Press, 1997).

13. George L. Mosse, *Confronting the Nation: Jewish and Western Nationalism* (Hanover, N.H.: Brandeis University Press, 1993), 25.

14. Mosse, *Confronting the Nation* 29.

15. In the concluding section of this work, I bring Fanon's rejection of this sort of backward-looking orientation of national life into conversation with Glissant's celebration of a creolizing past of the Antilles. I show that these two positions are more temporally alike than they are different, given what Glissant wants to draw from the history of creolization. But for the moment it is important to note that Glissant's account of an Antillean imaginary rests on the impossibility of such atavistic returns to origins and roots. The essays included in the 1989 collection, *Caribbean Discourse*, speak of the "nonhistory" of the transplanted people in the Caribbean, referencing the impossible task of tracing some linear trajectory back to clear and pure origins. On this account, a returning to history does not lead to a place of pure origin. Instead, "origin" shows up as obscure and inaccessible. "There is no clear path, no *way forward*, in this density" (83). The subsequent notions of errantry, Relation, and opacity developed by Glissant come out of this encounter with this (non)history of permanently lost origins. As such, his account of the composite community is primed to resist the kind of atavism that scholars like Hobsbawm and Mosse warn against.

16. Eric Hobsbawm, *The Age of Empire: 1875–1914* (New York: Vintage Books, 1987), 158.

17. Hobsbawm, *The Age of Empire* 158.

18. Frantz Fanon, *The Wretched of the Earth*, trans. Constance Farrington (New York: Grove Press, 1963), 41. Fanon's writing on the Algerian Revolution places special emphasis on this absolute nature of the beginning stages of the war against French colonialism. Against pressures to negotiate with France, the FLN's demand for independence was never strategic, and always absolute. In other words, "the revolution [was] by essence an enemy of half-measures, compromises, and backward steps"; Khalfa and Young, *Frantz Fanon*, 853.

19. Fanon, *The Wretched of the Earth*, 158.

20. Jane Anna Gordon critiques this ineffective nation-building strategy in relation to what a genuine national consciousness must accomplish, namely a "[move] beyond an antagonism to foreigners which can quickly be redefined in

a xenophobic *reduction ad absurdum.*" Jane Anna Gordon, *Creolizing Political Theory: Reading Rousseau through Fanon* (New York: Fordham University Press, 2014), 132. Anthony Alessandrini also addresses Paul Gilroy's reading of this aspect of Fanon, a reading that accuses Fanon of offering a reactionary nationalism. "The insistent Manichean attitude that Gilroy attributes to [*The Wretched of the Earth*] as a whole is, in other words, just the first step in an ongoing (and not necessarily linear or dialectical) argument." Anthony Alessandrini, *Frantz Fanon and the Future of Cultural Politics: Finding Something Different* (London: Lexington Books, 2014), 146.

21. Fanon, *The Wretched of the Earth*, 132.

22. "The bookburnings were a spectacular act on the public stage, performed by a regime that relied on myths, symbols, representative art, and human stereotypes"; Mosse, *Confronting the Nation*, 106.

23. Fanon, *The Wretched of the Earth*, 167.

24. Anthony Alessandrini, *Frantz Fanon and the Future of Cultural Politics: Finding Something Different* (London: Lexington Books, 2014).

25. Alessandrini, *Frantz Fanon and the Future of Cultural Politics*, 145. Fanon also writes, "The people find out that the iniquitous fact of exploitation can wear a black face, or Arab one" (145).

26. I included a more detailed account of this in the third section.

27. Fanon, *The Wretched of the Earth*, 163.

28. Fanon, *The Wretched of the Earth*, 158.

29. Fanon, *The Wretched of the Earth*, 139.

30. Under colonial time, the native is always primitive/antimodern, construed metaphysically so as to never enter into the present. In the words of David Marriott, European/colonial history locates the prehuman in an "ultimate unlocalizability," as "out of time," as "in time but not yet in history." David Marriott, "Inventions of Existence: Sylvia Wynter, Frantz Fanon, Sociogeny and 'the Damned,'" *CR: The New Centennial Review* 11, no. 3 (Winter 2011): 51.

31. Khalfa and Young, *Frantz Fanon*, 852–53.

32. Fanon, *The Wretched of the Earth*, 134–35.

33. Fanon, *The Wretched of the Earth*, 224 (emphasis added).

34. Fanon, *The Wretched of the Earth*, 224.

35. Fanon, *The Wretched of the Earth*, 225.

36. Fanon, *The Wretched of the Earth*, 227.

37. Fanon, *The Wretched of the Earth*, 237.

38. Fanon, *The Wretched of the Earth*, 244.

39. Fanon, *The Wretched of the Earth*, 245.

40. Fanon, *The Wretched of the Earth*, 210.

41. Fanon, *Toward an African Revolution*, 33.

42. Fanon, *Toward an African Revolution*, 41.

43. Fanon, *The Wretched of the Earth*, 209.

44. Fanon, *The Wretched of the Earth*, 209. On the question of material need, it is important to note that, as Fanon develops his account of a postcolonial African nation, he is acutely sensitive to the economic demands to which that nation must respond. For this reason, he stresses the dangers of the opportunity hording that results when national infrastructure produces an "urban/rural" compartmentalization of national life. This organization produces opportunities for economic

growth and prosperity for the city dweller, while more rural regions continue to suffer under material conditions not much different from the days of colonial oppression. To carry this economic organization into the nation's independence from colonial rule is to make the newfound opportunity of independence available to some (the urban petit bourgeoisie) and retain de facto colonial subjugation for others (the peasant).

45. Fanon, *Toward an African Revolution*, 34.

46. For the article-length version of this chapter, see Kris Sealey, "The Composite Community: Thinking Through Fanon's Critique of a Narrow Nationalism," *Critical Philosophy of Race* 6, no. 1 (2018). In that article, I use Rousseau's conception of the general will in order to account for the ways in which this Fanonian national culture supports (and even generates) the diversity of the people to which that culture belongs, thus avoiding a homogenizing of the rich differences among the people themselves. My use of Rousseau for this is indebted to Jane Anna Gordon's *Creolizing Political Theory*.

47. Khalfa and Young, *Frantz Fanon*, 536.

48. Khalfa and Young, *Frantz Fanon*, 42.

49. "The 'Algerian revolution' expresses both a process of liberation from foreign yoke and the destruction of feudal relics from the middle ages, relics that must yield to democratic bases for a modern nation"; Khalfa and Young, *Frantz Fanon*, 570.

50. Fanon, *A Dying Colonialism*, 101.

51. I want to thank Jane Anna Gordon for helping me make this connection for the sake of my claims in this chapter. I owe her much gratitude for her intellectual support and mentorship.

52. Fanon, *A Dying Colonialism*, 84, 92–93.

53. Fanon, *A Dying Colonialism*, 47.

54. Fanon, *A Dying Colonialism*, 96.

55. "I should constantly remind myself that the real *leap* consists in introducing invention into existence." Frantz Fanon, *Black Skin, White Masks*, trans. Charles Lam Markmann (London: Pluto Press, 1967), 229.

56. To be sure, it is on these grounds that he will reject any turn to the past (to the history of colonialism). I address this in the last section of this chapter, particularly as it relates to my overall attempts to bring Fanon into the orbit of creolization.

57. Fanon, *A Dying Colonialism*, 19.

58. Fanon, *A Dying Colonialism*, 33.

59. As I noted above, there are no explicit political outcomes inherent to creole adaptive practices. On the other hand, the new meaning of the radio in Algeria, as well as the new Algerian subject who brings this invention into existence, carries explicit political valence. Despite this important difference, I hold that creolization points to a set of practices that rehearses comportments and subject formations for the sake of cultural vitality and social fertility. Hence, creolization captures what, for Fanon, would mark the national culture of a nation that might move beyond a colonial metrics into the truly postcolonial. Perhaps this means that creolization is what has always already occurred, by the time of armed struggle. Or perhaps this means that creolization is what we might look for after that

demand for independence, so that the antireifying spirit of an actual decolonial national culture can grow.

60. Khalfa and Young, *Frantz Fanon*, 555.

61. Fanon, *A Dying Colonialism*, 63.

62. Fanon, *A Dying Colonialism*, 89.

63. Fanon, *A Dying Colonialism*, 126.

64. As Anthony Alessandrini writes in his account of Fanon's cultural politics, "[What] we might call true decolonization involves precisely imploding these forms of identity that have become fixed and static"; Alessandrini, *Frantz Fanon and the Future of Cultural Politics*, 129. This implosion of the colonial divide will also come to bear in a later section, when I give an account of Glissant's conception of Relation in order to think Fanon's decolonial nationalism through it.

65. See my account in chapter 2.

66. "Birmingham Civil Rights Institute Rescinds Angela Davis Honor," NBC News, accessed June 7, 2019, https://www.nbcnews.com/news/nbcblk /birmingham-civil-rights-institute-rescinds-angela-davis-honor-n955886.

67. "Angela Davis's Statement on the Birmingham Civil Rights Institute + New Celebration Planned," last modified January 15, 2019, https://freepalestinemovement .org/2019/01/15/angela-davis-statement-on-the-birmingham-civil-rights-institute -new-celebration-planned/.

68. "The Negros of Chicago only resemble the Nigerians of the Tanganyikans in so far as they were all defined in relation to the whites"; Fanon, *The Wretched of the Earth*, 216.

69. Fanon, *Toward an African Revolution*, 126.

70. Fanon, *Toward an African Revolution*, 168–69.

71. Fanon, *Toward an African Revolution*, 105.

72. Fanon, *Toward an African Revolution*, 120 (emphasis added).

73. Fanon, *Toward an African Revolution*, 144.

74. Fanon, *Toward an African Revolution*, 114 (emphasis added).

75. Fanon, *The Wretched of the Earth*, 216.

76. Fanon, *The Wretched of the Earth*, 217.

77. Alessandrini, *Frantz Fanon and the Future of Cultural Politics*.

78. Alessandrini, *Frantz Fanon and the Future of Cultural Politics*, 152.

79. Paul Gilroy, *Against Race: Imagining Political Culture beyond the Color Line* (Cambridge, Mass.: Belknap Press of Harvard University Press, 2000), 122.

80. Alessandrini, *Franzt Fanon and the Future of Cultural Politics*, 154.

81. Alessandrini, *Franzt Fanon and the Future of Cultural Politics*, 154. Anthony Alessandrini's discussion of Fanon's personal experience—being a Martinican national who not only dedicates his life to the Algerian revolutionary war but is accepted by Algerians *as a fellow Algerian*—must be regarded as informing his more theoretical work on the meaning of nationalism in a global, anticolonial struggle.

82. Fanon, *A Dying Colonialism*, 152–57.

83. I want to acknowledge Jesús Luzardo for pushing me on this point. I am grateful for his intellectual comradery and (now PIKSI-strong) friendship.

84. Alessandrini, *Frantz Fanon and the Future of Cultural Politics*, 154.

85. Recall, here, "Angela Davis's Statement on the Birmingham Civil Rights Institute + New Celebration Planned."

86. Recall, here, chapter 5's discussion of Lugones's conception of complex communication, as well as its relationship to Allison Weir's notion of a transformative identity politics.

87. Alessandrini, *Frantz Fanon and the Future of Cultural Politics*, 162.

88. In the concluding section of this book, I bring Fanon's transnational nationalism, as well as its relationship to creolization to bear on notions like cosmopolitanism and internationalism.

89. I trace the details of such operations in chapter 2.

90. Gilroy, *Against Race*, 115.

91. As noted in the introductory sections of this chapter I am not claiming that Glissant's cultural exposition supplies the overt political impetus that shapes Fanon's pursuit of the possibility of postcolonial nationhood. On this point, Nick Nesbitt's caution is worth recalling—that "[Glissant's] turn from anticolonial political struggle to an autonomy of cultural production" (140) comes from a place (in this thinking) that acknowledges the possibility of true national sovereignty is foreclosed for a region like the Antilles (Martinique in particular), where there is only "extreme domination in the form of cultural alienation"; Nesbitt, *Caribbean Critique*, 137.

92. H. Adlai Murdoch, *Creolizing the Metropole: Migrant Caribbean Identities in Literature and Film* (Bloomington: Indiana University Press, 2012), 34.

93. Glissant, *Poetics of Relation*, 20–21.

94. In *Imagined Communities*, Benedict Anderson writes about the colonial practices of mapping and cartography that emerged at the end of the nineteenth century. "[European-style] maps worked on the basis of a totalizing classification . . . which squared off seas and unexplored regions into measured boxes." Benedict Anderson, *Imagined Communities* (London: Verso, 1983), 173.

95. "Diversity, which is neither chaos nor sterility, means the human spirit's striving for cross-cultural relationship, without universalist transcendence"; Glissant, *Caribbean Discourse*, 98.

96. Nesbitt, *Caribbean Critique*, 240.

97. Clevis Headley, "Glissant's Existential Ontology of Difference," in *Theorizing Glissant: Sites and Citations*, ed. John E. Drabinski and Marisa Parham (Lanham, Md.: Rowman and Littlefield, 2015), 54.

98. Nesbitt, *Caribbean Critique*, 243.

99. I make a similar argument in an article that brings Fanon into conversation with Emmanuel Levinas, which pursues the possibility of an ethical politics; see Kris Sealey, "Power as (or in) Vulnerability: Fanon and Levinas on an Ethical Politics," *Listening: Journal of Communication Ethics, Religion, and Culture* 51, no. 1 (Winter 2015).

100. Headley, "Glissant's Existential Ontology of Difference," 92.

101. In chapter 5, I bring this framing of ontological resistance into conversation with Lugones's account of the world-traveling subject, who is able to encounter the other despite an absence of transparency in her traveling to the other's world.

102. Nesbitt, *Caribbean Discourse*, 243.

103. Nesbitt, *Caribbean Discourse*, 243.

104. Headley, "Glissant's Existential Ontology of Difference," 78.

105. Murdoch, *Creolizing the Metropole*, 171.

106. Headley, "Glissant's Existential Ontology of Difference," 54.

107. Nesbitt, *Caribbean Critique*, 236.

108. Nesbitt, *Caribbean Critique*, 237.

109. In addition, this seems to pay insufficient attention to the ambiguity that Glissant identifies at the heart of the historical and cultural identities that emerge out of Antillean ways of being. In a section of *Caribbean Discourse*, titled "History, Time, Identity," Glissant outlines this experience of identity as uncertain and ambiguous, and makes sure to note that this "[ambiguity] is not always the sign of some shortcoming"; Glissant, *Caribbean Discourse*, 93.

110. Readers will hear, quite correctly, Levinasian undertones of my understanding of Glissant's conception of opacity. Similar to the ways in which Levinas asks us to be attuned to the trace of the Saying as a present absence alongside (or beneath) the Said, I understand the work of Glissant's notion of opacity to capture what must remain uncapturable by or through the work of political identification.

111. Headley, "Glissant's Existential Ontology of Difference," 56.

112. H. Adlai Murdoch, "Glissant's *Opacité* and the Re-conceptualization of Identity," in *Theorizing Glissant: Sites and Citations*, ed. John E. Drabinski and Marisa Parham (Lanham, Md.: Rowman and Littlefield, 2015), 23.

113. Headley, "Glissant's Existential Ontology of Difference," 78.

114. Murdoch, "Glissant's *Opacité* and the Re-conceptualization of Identity," 15.

115. See chapter 5, which treats such alternative conceptions of "community" using the work of thinkers such as Anzaldúa, Lugones, and Ortega.

116. Betsy Wing's translation of *Poetics of Relation* leaves the term untranslated, lest "the implications of ordered chaos implicit in chaos theory would slip away, leaving [only] the banality of world disorder"; Glissant, *Poetics of Relation*, xv.

117. See the first section of this chapter.

118. Khalfa and Young, *Frantz Fanon*, 571–72.

119. Fanon, *A Dying Colonialism*, 157.

120. To reiterate a point made in the third section of this chapter, this rupturing must pass through the historical materiality of colonial violence. Hence, a transcending of colonial stasis ought not produce an ahistorical, liberal universalism. The "we" toward which the rupturing moves is to be produced (it is not ready-made) through negotiations with histories of power relations.

121. It is on these grounds that Fanon imagines the possibility of a united Africa. "[Assemble] Africa, create the continent"; Khalfa and Young, *Frantz Fanon*, 169.

122. Fanon, *A Dying Colonialism*, 152 (first quotation); Glissant, *Poetics of Relation*, 203.

123. Here I do have in mind the contemporary global political landscape (of the United States and Europe specifically), where border reinforcement and travel bans seem to have acquired new or reinvigorated traction.

124. Glissant, *Poetics of Relation*, 94.

125. Khalfa and Young, *Frantz Fanon*, 569.

126. I am in gratitude to the anonymous review process, which my article in *Critical Philosophy of Race* went through, for pointing out the need to address this question for the sake of my claims in this chapter.

127. John E. Drabinski, *Levinas and the Postcolonial: Race, Nation, Other* (Edinburgh: Edinburgh University Press, 2011), 145.

128. Zimitri Erasmus, "Some Kind of White, Some Kind of Black: Living the Moments of Entanglement in South Africa and Its Academy," in *Un/settled Multiculturalism: Diasporas, Entanglements, Transruptions*, ed. Barnor Hesse (New York: Zed Books, 2000), 202.

129. Glissant, *Caribbean Discourse*, 14.

130. Barnor Hesse describes these two appropriations of the past in terms of "a temporal oscillation between what Glissant [in the 1989 collection, *Caribbean Discourse*] describes as 'reversion and diversion.' The former specifies the idea of a conceptual return to meanings associated with the historical revalorization of Africa, while the latter articulates a creolized engagement with contemporary complexities of racialized displacement in the West." This distinction (between "reversion and diversion") also provides a way to demonstrate more similarities than differences between Fanon and Glissant here; see Barnor Hesse, "Diasporicity: Black Britain's Post-colonial Formations," in *Un/settled Multiculturalism: Diasporas, Entanglements, Transruptions*, ed. Barnor Hesse (New York: Zed Books, 2000), 112.

131. Fanon, *The Wretched of the Earth*, 247.

Conclusion

1. David Marriott, "Inventions of Existence: Sylvia Wynter, Frantz Fanon, Sociogeny, and 'the Damned,'" *CR: The New Centennial Review* 11, no. 3 (Winter 2011).

2. Anthony Alessandrini, *Frantz Fanon and the Future of Cultural Politics: Finding Something Different* (Lexington: University Press of Kentucky, 2014), 139.

3. Amy Allen, *The End of Progress: Decolonizing the Normative Foundations of Critical Theory* (New York: Columbia University Press, 2016), 226.

4. Alessandrini, *Frantz Fanon and the Future of Cultural Politics*, 133.

5. Jodi Byrd, *The Transit of Empire: Indigenous Critiques of Colonialism* (Minneapolis: University of Minnesota Press, 2011), xii.

6. Byrd, *The Transit of Empire*, xxxiv.

7. LeAnne Howe, "The Chaos of Angels," in "Native American Literatures," special issue, *Callaloo* 17, no. 1 (Winter 1994): 108, cited in Byrd, *The Transit of Empire*, xxvii.

8. Byrd, *The Transit of Empire*, xxix.

9. Byrd, *The Transit of Empire*, xiv.

10. Glen Sean Coulthard, *Red Skin, White Masks: Rejecting the Colonial Politics of Recognition* (Minneapolis: University of Minnesota Press, 2014), 154, 43.

11. A key part of Byrd's development of the cacophonic approach to decolonial possibilities is her critique of easy conflations between the violence of colonialism and the violence of racialization. She shows how, in such conflations, there is a racializing of indigenous people that positions them as one of the many minority cultures that signify as a "'post-conquest' invasion that threatens white nativity"; Byrd, *The Transit of Empire*, 52. Further, this racialization of the indigenous subject includes her in a multiculture that works toward better and more complete inclusion into the settler state. Byrd rightly points out that, for native subjects,

such inclusion only furthers the project of the clearing away (or disappearing) of who they are as peoples, and of their claims to land.

12. Byrd, *The Transit of Empire*, xix.

13. Byrd, *The Transit of Empire*, xii.

14. Byrd, *The Transit of Empire*, 53.

15. Byrd, *The Transit of Empire*, xii.

16. Byrd, *The Transit of Empire*.

17. Coulthard, *Red Skin, White Masks*, 156.

18. Leanne Simpson, *Dancing on Our Turtle's Back: Stories of Nishnaabeg Recreation, Resurgence and a New Emergence* (Winnipeg: Arbeiter Ring Press, 2011), 51, cited in Coulthard, *Red Skin, White Masks*, 156.

19. Byrd, *The Transit of Empire*, 53.

20. María Lugones, *Pilgrimages/Peregrinajes: Theorizing Coalition against Multiple Oppressions* (Lanham, Md.: Rowman and Littlefield, 2003), 10.

SELECTED BIBLIOGRAPHY

Ahmad, Aijaz. "The Politics of Literary Postcoloniality." In *Contemporary Postcolonial Theory: A Reader*, edited by Padmini Mongia, 276–93. London: Arnold, 1996.

Ahmed, Sara. *Queer Phenomenology: Orientations, Objects, Others*. Durham, N.C.: Duke University Press, 2006.

Alcoff, Linda Martín. *Visible Identities: Race, Gender and the Self*. Oxford: Oxford University Press, 2005.

Alessandrini, Anthony C. *Frantz Fanon and the Future of Cultural Politics: Finding Something Different*. London: Lexington Books, 2014.

Allen, Amy. *The End of Progress: Decolonizing the Normative Foundations of Critical Theory*. New York: Columbia University Press, 2016.

Anderson, Benedict. *Imagined Communities: Reflections on the Origin and Spread of Nationalism*. Revised ed. London: Verso, 2006.

Anzaldúa, Gloria. *Borderlands/La Frontera: The New Mestiza*. 4th ed. San Francisco: Aunt Lute Books, 2007.

Balibar, Étienne. *We, the People of Europe? Reflections on Transnational Citizenship*. Princeton, N.J.: Princeton University Press, 2004.

Balibar, Étienne, and Emmanuel Wallerstein, eds. *Race, Nation, Class: Ambiguous Identities*. London: Verso, 1991.

Baron, Robert, and Ana C. Cara, eds. *Creolization as Cultural Creativity*. Jackson: University Press of Mississippi, 2011.

Beltrán, Cristina. "Patrolling Borders: Hybrids, Hierarchies and the Challenge of Mestizaje." *Political Research Quarterly* 57, no. 4 (December 2004): 595–607.

Bernabé, Jean, Patrick Chamoiseau, Raphaël Confiant, and Mohamed B. Taleb Kyhar. "In Praise of Creoleness." *Callaloo* 13, no. 4 (Autumn 1990): 886–909.

Bhabha, Homi K. *Location of Culture*. London: Routledge, 2004.

———, ed. *Nation and Narration*. London: Routledge, 1990.

Brathwaite, Kamau. *Caribbean Man in Space and Time: A Bibliographical and Conceptual Approach*. Mona, Jamaica: Savacou, 1974.

Butler, Judith, and Gayatri Chakravorty Spivak. *Who Sings the Nation-State?* Calcutta: Seagull Books, 2010.

Byrd, Jodi. *The Transit of Empire: Indigenous Critiques of Colonialism*. Minneapolis: University of Minnesota Press, 2011.

Childs, Peter, and R. J. Patrick Williams. *An Introduction to Postcolonial Theory*. New York: Routledge, 1997.

Ciccariello-Maher, George. *Decolonizing Dialectics*. Durham, N.C.: Duke University Press, 2017.

Clinton, Bill. "Decoding Science and Politics with Bill Clinton." Interview by Neil deGrasse Tyson. *StarTalk Radio*, season 6, episode 43, November 6, 2015. Audio, 50:00 min. https://www.startalkradio.net/show/decoding-science-and -politics-with-bill-clinton/.

Coulthard, Glen Sean. *Red Skin, White Masks: Rejecting the Colonial Politics of Recognition*. Minneapolis: University of Minnesota Press, 2014.

Crichlow, Michaeline A. *Globalization and the Post-Creole Imagination: Notes on Fleeing the Plantation*. Durham, N.C.: Duke University Press, 2009.

Crichlow, Michaeline A., and Patricia Northover. "Homing Modern Freedoms: Creolization and the Politics of Making Place." *Cultural Dynamics* 21, no. 3 (2009): 283–316.

Deleuze, Gilles. *Difference and Repetition*. Translated by Paul Patton. New York: Columbia University Press, 1994.

Deleuze, Gilles, and Félix Guattari. *What Is Philosophy?* New York: Columbia University Press, 1996.

Drabinski, John E. *Glissant and the Middle Passage: Philosophy, Beginning, Abyss*. Minneapolis: University of Minnesota Press, 2019.

——. *Levinas and the Postcolonial: Race, Nation, Other*. Edinburgh: Edinburgh University Press, 2011.

——. "What Is Trauma to the Future? On Glissant's Poetics." *Qui Parle* 18, no. 2 (Spring/Summer 2010): 291–307.

Drabinski, John E., and Marisa Parham, eds. *Theorizing Glissant: Sites and Citations*. Lanham, Md.: Rowman and Littlefield, 2015.

Fanon, Frantz. *Black Skin, White Masks*. Translated by Charles Lam Markmann. London: Pluto Press, 1967.

——. *A Dying Colonialism*. Translated by Haakon Chevalier. New York: Grove Press, 1965.

——. *Toward an African Revolution*. Translated by Haakon Chevalier. New York: Grove Press, 1964.

——. *The Wretched of the Earth*. Translated by Constance Farrington. New York: Grove Press, 1963.

Farred, Grant. "Wretchedness." In *Living Fanon: Global Perspectives*, edited by Nigel C. Gibson, 159–72. New York: Palgrave Macmillan, 2011.

Forbes, Curdella. "The End of Nationalism? Performing the Question in Benitez-Rojo's *The Repeating Island* and Glissant's *Poetics of Relation*." *Journal of West Indian Literatures* 11, no. 1 (November 2002): 4–23.

Frye, Marilyn. *The Politics of Reality: Essays in Feminist Theory*. New York: Crossing Press, 1983.

Gat, Azar. *Nations: The Long History and Deep Roots of Political Ethnicity and Nationalism*. New York: Cambridge University Press, 2013.

Gilroy, Paul. *Against Race: Imagining Political Culture beyond the Color Line*. Cambridge, Mass.: Belknap Press of Harvard University Press, 2000.

——. *The Black Atlantic: Modernity and Double Consciousness*. London: Verso, 1993.

——. *Postcolonial Melancholia*. New York: Columbia University Press, 2005.

Glissant, Édouard. *Caribbean Discourse: Selected Essays*. Translated by J. Michael Dash. Charlottesville: University Press of Virginia, 1989.

——. *La cohée du Lamentin*. Paris: Gallimard, 1981.

——. "Creolization in the Making of the Americas." In "60th Anniversary

Edition: Literature and Ideas." Special issue, *Caribbean Quarterly* 54, nos. 1–2 (March—June 2008): 81–89.

———. *Poetics of Relation*. Translated by Betsy Wing. Ann Arbor: University of Michigan Press, 1997.

———. *Tout-monde*. Paris: Gallimard, 1993.

———. *Le traité du Tout-monde*. Paris: Gallimard, 1997.

Gordon, Jane Anna. *Creolizing Political Theory: Reading Rousseau through Fanon*. New York: Fordham University Press, 2014.

Guenther, Lisa. "Fecundity and Natal Alienation: Rethinking Kinship with Levinas and Orlando Patterson." *Levinas Studies* 7 (2012): 1–19.

Hall, Stuart. "Créolité and the Process of Creolization." In *Creolizing Europe: Legacies and Transformations*, edited by Encarnación Gutiérrez Rodríguez and Shirley Anne Tate, 21–35. Liverpool: Liverpool University Press, 2015.

Hall, Stuart, and Paul du Gay, eds. *Questions of Cultural Identity*. London: Sage, 1996.

Hesse, Barnor, ed. *Un/settled Multiculturalism: Diasporas, Entanglements, Transruptions*. New York: Zed Books, 2000.

Hobsbawm, Eric. *The Age of Empire: 1875–1914*. New York: Vintage Books, 1987.

Howe, LeAnne. "The Chaos of Angels." In "Native American Literatures." Special issue, *Callaloo* 17, no. 1 (Winter 1994): 108–14.

Khalfa, Jean, and Robert J. C. Young, eds. *Frantz Fanon: Alienation and Freedom*. Translated by Steven Corcoran. London: Bloomsbury Academic, 2018.

Khan, Aisha. "Journey to the Center of the Earth: The Caribbean as Master Symbol." *Cultural Anthropology* 16, no. 3 (2001): 271–301.

Knepper, Wendy. "Colonization, Creolization, and Globalization: The Art and Ruses of Bricolage." *small axe* 10, no. 3 (October 2006): 70–86.

Lee, Emily, ed. *Living Alterities: Phenomenology, Embodiment, and Race*. Albany: State University of New York Press, 2014.

Lionnet, Françoise, and Shu-mei Shih, eds. *The Creolization of Theory*. Durham, N.C.: Duke University Press, 2011.

Lugones, María. "On Complex Communication." *Hypatia* 21, no. 3 (Summer 2006): 75–85.

———. *Pilgrimages/Peregrinajes: Theorizing Coalition against Multiple Oppressions*. Lanham, Md.: Rowman and Littlefield, 2003.

———. "Purity, Impurity, and Separation." *Signs* 19, no. 2 (Winter 1994): 458–79.

———. "Radical Multiculturalism and Women of Color Feminisms." *Journal for Cultural and Religious Theory* 13, no. 1 (Winter 2014): 68–80.

Maldonado-Torres, Nelson. "On the Coloniality of Being: Contributions to the Development of a Concept." *Cultural Studies* 21, nos. 2–3 (March/May 2007): 240–70.

Marriott, David. "Inventions of Existence: Sylvia Wynter, Frantz Fanon, Sociogeny, and 'the Damned.'" *CR: The New Centennial Review* 11, no. 3 (Winter 2011): 45–89.

McKittrick, Katherine, ed. *Sylvia Wynter: On Being Human as Praxis*. Durham, N.C.: Duke University Press, 2015.

Mignolo, Walter. *The Darker Side of Western Modernity: Global Futures, Decolonial Options*. Durham, N.C.: Duke University Press, 2011.

Misir, Prem, ed. *Cultural Identity and Creolization in National Unity: The Multi-ethnic Caribbean*. Lanham, Md.: University Press of America, 2006.

Mohanty, Chandra Talpade. *Feminism without Borders: Decolonizing Theory, Practicing Solidarity*. Durham, N.C.: Duke University Press, 2003.

Monahan, Michael J. *The Creolizing Subject: Race, Reason, and the Politics of Purity*. New York: Fordham University Press, 2011.

Mosse, George L. *Confronting the Nation: Jewish and Western Nationalism*. Hanover, N.H.: Brandeis University Press, 1993.

———. "Racism and Nationalism." *Nation and Nationalism* 1, no. 2 (1995): 163–73.

Moya, Paula. *Learning from Experience: Minority Identities, Multicultural Struggles*. Oakland: University of California Press, 2002.

Murdoch, H. Adlai. "Créolité, Creolization, and Contemporary Caribbean Culture." *small axe* 21, no. 1 (March 2017): 180–98.

———. *Creolizing the Metropole: Migrant Caribbean Identities in Literature and Film*. Bloomington: Indiana University Press, 2012.

———. "Glissant's *Opacité* and the Re-conceptualization of Identity." In *Theorizing Glissant: Sites and Citations*, edited by John E. Drabinski and Marisa Parham, 7–27. Lanham, Md.: Rowman and Littlefield, 2015.

Nesbitt, Nick. *Caribbean Critique: Antillean Critical Theory from Toussaint to Glissant*. Liverpool: Liverpool University Press, 2013.

Nettleford, Rex. *Caribbean Cultural Identity: The Case of Jamaica, an Essay in Cultural Dynamics*. Kingston: Institute of Jamaica, 1978.

Ortega, Mariana. *In-Between: Latina Feminist Phenomenology, Multiplicity, and the Self*. Albany: State University of New York Press, 2016.

———. "'New Mestizas,' 'World-Travelers,' and 'Dasein': Phenomenology and the Multi-voiced, Multi-cultural Self." *Hypatia* 16, no. 1 (Summer 2001): 1–29.

Ortega, Mariana, and Linda Alcoff, eds. *Constructing the Nation: A Race and Nationalism Reader*. Albany: State University of New York Press, 2009.

Phelan, Shane. *Getting Specific: Postmodern Lesbian Politics*. Minneapolis: University of Minnesota Press, 1994.

Price, Richard. "The Miracle of Creolization: A Retrospective." *New West Indian Guide* 75, nos. 1–2 (2001): 35–64.

Prieto, Eric. "Édouard Glissant, Littérature-monde, and Tout-monde." *small axe* 14, no. 3 (November 2010): 111–20.

Sanín-Restrepo, Ricardo. *Decolonizing Democracy: Power in a Solid State*. Lanham, Md.: Rowman and Littlefield, 2016.

Sealey, Kris. "The Composite Community: Thinking Through Fanon's Critique of a Narrow Nationalism." *Critical Philosophy of Race* 6, no. 1 (2018): 26–57.

———. "Dirty Consciences and Runaway Selves: A Levinasian Response to Monahan." *Critical Philosophy of Race* 1, no. 2 (2013): 219–28.

———. "Power as (or in) Vulnerability: Fanon and Levinas on an Ethical Politics." *Listening: Journal of Communication Ethics, Religion, and Culture* 51, no. 1 (Winter 2015): 38–45.

———. "Resisting the Logic of Ambivalence: Bad Faith as Subversive, Anti-colonial Practice." *Hypatia* 33, no. 2 (Spring 2018): 163–77.

———. Review of *White Criticality beyond Anti-racism: How Does It Feel to Be

a White Problem? Hypatia Reviews Online, 2016. https://www.hypatiareviews
.org/reviews/content/23.

Sharpe, Christina. *In the Wake: On Blackness and Being*. Durham, N.C.: Duke University Press, 2016.

Sheller, Mimi. "Creolization in Discourses of Global Culture." In *Uprootings/ Regroundings: Questions of Home and Migration*, edited by Sara Ahmed, Claudia Castada, Anne-Marie Fortier, and Mimi Sheller, 273–89. London: Berg, 2003.

Shepherd, Verene A., and Glen L. Richards, eds. *Questioning Creole: Creolization Discourses in Caribbean Culture*. London: Ian Randle, 2002.

Simpson, Leanne. *Dancing on Our Turtle's Back: Stories of Nishnaabeg Recreation, Resurgence and a New Emergence*. Winnipeg: Arbeiter Ring Press, 2011.

Smyth, Heather. "The Black Atlantic Meets the Black Pacific: Multimodality in Kamau Brathwaite and Wayde Compton." *Callaloo* 37, no. 2 (Spring 2014): 389–403.

Spivak, Gayatri Chakravorty. "Nationalism and the Imagination." *Lectora* 15 (2009): 75–98.

Taylor, L. "Créolité Bites: A Conversation with Patrick Chamoiseau, Raphaël Confiant, and Jean Bernabé." *Transition* 74 (1989): 124–61.

Tinsley, Omise'eke Natasha. "Black Atlantic, Queer Atlantic: Queer Imaginings of the Middle Passage." *GLQ: A Journal of Lesbian and Gay Studies* 14, nos. 2–3 (2008): 191–215.

Weir, Allison. "Global Feminism and Transformative Identity Politics." *Hypatia* 23, no. 4 (October–December 2008): 110–33.

Wynter, Sylvia. "1492: A New World View." In *Race, Discourse and the Origin of the Americas: A New World View*, edited by Vera Lawrence Hyatt and Rex Nettleford, 5–57. Washington, D.C.: Smithsonian Institute Press, 1995.

———. "The Ceremony Must Be Found: After Humanism." *boundary 2* 12/13, nos. 3/1 (Spring–Autumn 1984): 19–70.

———. "Unsettling the Coloniality of Being/Power/Truth/Freedom: Toward the Human, after Man, Its Overrepresentation—An Argument." *CR: The New Centennial Review* 3, no. 3 (Fall 2003): 257–337.

Yancy, George, ed. *White Self-Criticality beyond Anti-racism: How Does It Feel to Be a White Problem?* Lanham, Md.: Lexington Books, 2015.